W9-AYG-549

GREAT AMERICAN LIGHTHOUSES

UMPQUA LIGHTHOUSE, OREGON COAST HIGHWAY

SOUTHEAST LIGHT AND CLIFFS, BLOCK ISLAND, R.I.

THE OLD AND NEW LIGHTHOUSE, BY NIGHT, CAPE HENRY, VA.

A NATIONAL TRUST GUIDE

GREAT ☆ AMERICAN ☆ LIGHT-HOUSES

F. ROSS HOLLAND, JR.

Foreword by Sen. George J. Mitchell

GREAT AMERICAN PLACES SERIES
PRESERVATION PRESS

John Wiley & Sons, Inc.
New York • Chichester • Brisbane • Toronto • Singapore

Preservation Press
is an imprint of
John Wiley & Sons, Inc.

The National Trust for Historic Preservation is the only private, nonprofit organization chartered by Congress to encourage public participation in the preservation of sites, buildings and objects significant in American history and culture. Support is provided by membership dues, endowment funds, contributions and grants from federal agencies, including the U.S. Department of the Interior, under provisions of the National Historic Preservation Act of 1966. For information about membership, write to the Trust at

1785 Massachusetts Avenue, N.W.
Washington, D.C. 20036.

Copyright © 1994 F. Ross Holland, Jr. All rights reserved.
Reproduction or translation of any part of this work beyond that permitted by Section 107 or 108 of the 1976 United States Copyright Act without the permission of the copyright owner is unlawful. Requests for permission or further information should be addressed to the Permissions Department, John Wiley & Sons, Inc., 605 Third Avenue, New York, NY 10158-0012.

Printed in Hong Kong
5

Library of Congress Cataloging in Publication Data

Holland, F. Ross (Francis Ross), 1927-
    Great American lighthouses / F. Ross Holland, Jr. :
foreword by George J. Mitchell.
        p.   cm. — (Great American places series)
        Bibliography: p.
        Includes index.
        ISBN 0-471-14387-1
        1. Lighthouses — United States. I. Title. II. Series.
VK1023.H66 1989 89-8825
387.1'55—dc20

Edited by Diane Maddex with the assistance of Gretchen Smith. Produced by Janet Walker.

Designed by Meadows & Wiser, Washington, D.C.

Composed in Vladim by General Typographers, Washington, D.C.

Front cover: Portland Head light, Portland, Maine, at night. (Curt Teich Postcard Collection, Lake County Museum)
Back cover: Tillamook Rock lighthouse on the Oregon coast near Tillamook. (Curt Teich Postcard Collection, Lake County Museum)

CONTENTS

■ ■ ■ ■ ■ ■ THE LIGHTHOUSES ■ ■ ■ ■ ■ ■

POINT CONCORD LIGHTHOUSE BY NIGHT, HAVRE DE GRACE, MD.

A15885   PUBLISHED BY C. F. KUSTER, BOCA GRANDE, FLA.

Gasparilla Light Station, South Boca Grande, Fla.,
Deepest Natural Harbor in Florida.

EAGLE HARBOR LIGHTHOUSE, EAGLE HARBOR, MICH.

■ ■ ■ ■ ■ ■ ■ ■ ■ ■ ■ ■ ■ ■ ■ ■

FOREWORD

While no state, to my knowledge, has the official claim to be the Lighthouse State, Maine — which I'm privileged to represent in the U.S. Senate — could easily qualify and is often justifiably called this. A great many of the 60-plus traditional lighthouses that stand along Maine's magnificent coast from Kittery to Calais are listed in the National Register of Historic Places. Many are included in these pages. The people of Maine have a powerful emotional attachment to lighthouses generally and to specific lighthouses in particular. I'm no different.

But Mainers are not alone in having a love affair with lighthouses. The first lighthouse in the United States was built in Boston Harbor in 1716. In all, 1,200 to 1,300 lighthouses have been built in this country. There are lighthouses along the Atlantic and Pacific oceans, the Great Lakes and the Gulf of Mexico. For many people today these structures serve chiefly as romantic re-minders of a time past, a time before radar, sonar and on-ship electronics combined to diminish the need for sailors to use their light to navigate safely.

But there was a time when lighthouses served an important role, when the building and operating of lighthouses as aids for rendering safe and easy navigation of any bay, inlet, harbor or port in the United States was one of the principal activities of the federal government. In fact, one of the very first undertakings of the first Congress, organized on April 6, 1789, officially launched America's lighthouse system. In July, Rep. Eldridge Gerry of Massachusetts introduced legislation, H.R. 12, that called for the establishment and support of navigational aids. H.R. 12 was passed by the House on July 20, amended by the Senate on July 31 and signed into law by President Washington on August 7, 1789. This statute can be characterized as the first public works law of our nation. The act established a federal role in the support, maintenance and repair of all lighthouses, beacons, buoys and public piers necessary for safe navigation and also commissioned the first federal lighthouse.

For most people, the term "public works projects" has come to mean highways, bridges, dams and public buildings. Two hundred years ago, however, public works projects included — indeed, prominently included — lighthouses. As the first secretary of the Treasury, Alexander Hamilton was responsible for the care and superintendence of the lights. And he took this respon-sibility seriously. In fact, according to George Weiss in his book, *The Lighthouse Service: Its History, Activities and Organization*, many orders and contracts concerning the Lighthouse Service "of a comparatively insignificant nature bear the personal approval of Hamilton, George Washington and Thomas Jefferson."

The value of lighthouses to the development of maritime shipping and transportation in our country can

Opposite: Maine's Boon Island lighthouse (1855), one of the most isolated stations in a state noted for them. Keepers once hauled in soil from the mainland in order to plant a garden on the rocky site.

First Mount Desert lighthouse (1830), off Frenchboro, Maine, as shown in an 1839 engraving.

never be measured. Countless ships have made safe passage off our shores and on our lakes because of the beams of light from these stalwart structures, standing at land's end. How much easier it would be to measure the lost ships, the wreckage, the lost lives that might have occurred without lighthouses.

And while the contribution of lighthouses cannot be measured, the architectural beauty of these structures cannot be appreciated without recognizing the sacrifices and skills of the engineers and builders who built them in oftimes hazardous places and against almost insurmountable odds.

Nor can we today fully appreciate the sacrifices made by lighthouse keepers and their families who devoted — and, in some cases, jeopardized — their lives for the safety of others. Make no mistake about it: lighthouse duty was often an awful existence, lonely and boring for the great part and dangerous in times of crisis.

For two centuries, these impressive structures and the men and women who staffed them have come to symbolize stoicism, heroism, duty and faithfulness — characteristics that Americans exhibit, characteristics that Americans admire.

This book, the third in the National Trust's Great American Places Series, celebrates more than 300 of America's most historic lighthouses and lightships. Its publication coincides with two significant milestones for this nation's lighthouses. The first is that, in 1989, the Coast Guard planned to complete the automation of its lights, concluding a rich, colorful and significant chapter in American history. The second milestone is that August 7, 1989, marked the 200th anniversary of President Washington's signing of the first lighthouse act.

Unfortunately, many lighthouses are in danger. Without keepers, the tower, keepers' houses, catwalks and outbuildings are easy targets for vandalism and natural damage caused by storms or erosion. To lose them would be a tragic waste, because these structures have great potential as cultural, historic and recreational sites.

My expectation and hope are that this book will introduce more Americans to the stature and grace of the many beautiful lighthouses that dot this country's shorelines. When that happens, I think it will prompt renewed interest in preserving these structures. What a pleasure for me to be able to take part in that effort.

Sen. George J. Mitchell

PREFACE

A n old friend of mine says that there is no such thing as a bad beer; some beers are just better than others. That statement pretty well expresses my feelings about lighthouses. There is not a bad lighthouse because they come in such a variety of shapes and forms, and their settings — normally spectacular — increase their differences, their beauty and their charm. During the course of writing this book my feelings were reinforced as I explored the lighthouses of a region new to me — the Great Lakes.

This book permitted and forced me to become familiar with lighthouses of the Great Lakes. Previously I had known them only from writings and pictures. Now I could see them in person, and what a great joy that turned out to be, for I almost felt as though I were exploring a whole new set of lighthouses established and operated by an organization different from the one responsible for lighthouses on the East, Gulf and West coasts. I was continually surprised. The pierhead lighthouses of the Great Lakes are unlike lights on the other coasts and are more spectacular, perhaps because so many of them represent different styles. Paint schemes are varied, and the Italianate brackets on masonry towers receive special emphasis. One is struck not only by the variety of lighthouses, but also by their number. What a unique treasure trove of lighthouses the region has.

Other sections of the country are similarly blessed. One cannot travel the coast of New England without marveling at the serene beauty of its lighthouses or coming away saying, "Now I know why they call Maine the Lighthouse State." Nor can one explore the low coasts of the Mid-Atlantic and Southeast states and not be impressed by their tall masonry towers or the variety of lighthouses in their harbors and bays. A visit to the Gulf Coast, with its assortment of lighthouse sizes and styles, gives one a sense of the appropriateness of each design for the area's geographical and climatological conditions. And on the West Coast so many of the lighthouses are positioned on high and rugged settings that give them the spectacular, majestic quality of a Cecil B. de Mille production, the music supplied by the crashing sea. Many others in harbors, bays and sounds have the pacific charm of New England's lighthouses a continent away.

No, there is no such thing as a bad lighthouse. Hie thee to the coasts, Great Lakes, bays, sounds and rivers of this great country, and see that simple fact for yourself.

F. Ross Holland, Jr.

■ ■ ■ ■ ■ ■ ■ ■ ■ ■ ■ ■ ■ ■ ■ ■ ■

ACKNOWLEDGMENTS

First of all, I am grateful to the U.S. Coast Guard, whose staff over the past 30 years in which I have been doing research on lighthouses has always been friendly, cooperative and helpful with my endeavors. This time was no exception. Robert Scheina, chief historian of the Coast Guard, as usual, went well out of his way to assist me in locating information and photographs, as did his associate, Robert Browning. I am also grateful to Lt. Cmdr. Robert Garrett, recently of the Aids to Navigation Division, and his successor, Lt. John Brooks, for their assistance.

Wayne Wheeler of the U.S. Lighthouse Society, Richard Moehl of the Great Lakes Lighthouse Keepers Association and Valerie Nelson of the Lighthouse Preservation Society reviewed the initial list of lighthouses to be included and provided comments that were most helpful. Valerie Nelson also gave me access to the Lighthouse Preservation Society's files, which contained a great deal of information on the present condition of individual light stations.

James P. Delgado, chief maritime historian of the National Park Service, provided considerable information on lightships as well as lighthouses of the West Coast. His associate maritime historian, Kevin Foster, was also helpful in the area of lightships. Candace Clifford provided me with guides that speeded the search process for National Register nominations. Debbie Wade of Acadia National Park in Maine, Edmund Roberts of Cabrillo National Monument in San Diego, Carole Perrault and Walter Sedovic of the National Park Service's North Atlantic Historic Preservation Center in Boston, David Kayser of Salem Maritime National Historic Site in Massachusetts and Kirk Mohney of the Maine Historic Preservation Commission came to my rescue by obtaining some hard-to-find photographs, as did Tom Hartman of the Cape Hatteras National Seashore in North Carolina. Diane Chalfant and John "Butch" Celmer of Wisconsin's Apostle Islands National Lakeshore provided two enlightening and delightful days touring that park's marvelous collection of lighthouses.

I am also grateful to Mary Watkins of Seaway Trails, who helped me get acquainted with the lighthouses of Lake Ontario. My thanks go also to Bill Davis of the Genesee lighthouse, Jim Walker of the Selkirk lighthouse and Harold R. Lawson of the Dunkirk lighthouse, all in New York State, for their enthusiasm and aid. Special thanks are due to David Policansky, who provided several exhilarating days of touring Chesapeake Bay lighthouses sprinkled with intermittent periods of fishing.

I am profoundly grateful to the following state historic preservation offices and staff for providing helpful advice and, in some cases, photographs:

Alabama: Alabama Historical Commission. Alaska: Joan M. Antonson and Neil Johannsen. California: Joyce Law. Connecticut: Dave Poirier. Delaware: Stephen G. Del Sordo. Florida: Suzanne P. Walker and Bill Thurston. Georgia: Kenneth H. Thomas, Jr. Hawaii: Department of Land and Natural Resources. Illinois: Ann V. Swallow. Indiana: Department of Natural Resources. Louisiana: Office of Cultural Development. Maryland: Peter Kurtze. Massachusetts: Anne Tate. Michigan: Laura R. Ashlee. Minnesota: Dennis A. Gimmestad. Mississippi: Richard Cawthon and Elizabeth Bensey. New Hampshire: Division of Historical Resources and State Historic Preservation Office. New Jersey: Terry Karschner. New York: Julia S. Stokes. North Carolina: Michael T. Southern. Ohio: Alice M. Edwards. Oregon: Monte Turner. Pennsylvania: Brent Glass and Dan G. Deibler. Rhode Island: Pamela Kennedy. Virginia: H. Bryan Mitchell. Washington: David Hansen. Wisconsin: Paul R. Lusignan.

Others who provided assistance include Lynn Hickerson of the maritime office of the National Trust for Historic Preservation; W. Stephen Hart, legislative assistant to Sen. George J. Mitchell; Nancy Dubner, Marge McCleary and Debbie Krabill. The cooperation of the Island Institute, Rockland, Maine, in permitting use of its publication *Keeping the Light* is most appreciated.

I especially want to thank Peter Zabriskie, who was a constant source of assistance as I made the transition from manual typewriter to word processor.

Special recognition and thanks go also to the Preservation Press team of Diane Maddex, Janet Walker, Gretchen Smith and Joyce Miller, who worked so diligently and successfully, under constraints of a tight schedule, to edit and produce this book.

■ ■ ■ ■ ■ ■ ■ ■ ■ ■ ■ ■ ■ ■ ■ ■ ■ ■

LIGHTING AMERICA'S SHORES

Lighthouses have long had a strong appeal to Americans, an attraction that becomes more intense as time passes — fueled no doubt by the fact that our historic lights are being automated and in many cases replaced. Only someone with a closed mind or a cold heart will not be at least momentarily drawn to a lighthouse, for its attraction is at once visual, emotional and intellectual.

The appeal of lighthouses at first was romantic — based on the beautiful maritime setting of the structure, the loneliness of the job, the dutiful keepers who kept the lights burning to warn sailors of navigational hazards and, at times, risked their own lives to save the shipwrecked. Through the years lighthouses have retained all these attractions. But their appeal has taken on a more intellectual quality that has deepened interest in the subject. People now look for the design details that give distinctiveness to individual lighthouses and at the same time reflect different historical periods and sections of the country; for technological advancements in lighting and fog signals that increased mariners' safety; and for more insight into the people who chose the occupation of light keeper.

No matter what its current attraction, a light tower has one purpose: to get the light to a height where navigators can see it. For it is the light in a lighthouse that warns of the presence of navigational dangers, marks the entrance to harbors, guides vessels through shipping channels and lets mariners know their location. Mariners along a coast can take bearings off two or more lighthouses, which they can identify by the characteristics of their lights, and plot these bearings on a chart to determine location and whether they are on course or at the point where they need to make a course change. By the same method, navigators can supply course information to help bring ships safely into a harbor and to an anchorage.

The light served all who made their living on the sea — naval vessels, the merchant marine and those who harvested the products of the sea. Until fairly recently lighthouses were the principal aid navigators had as they approached or sailed along a coast, and the absence of an adequate light could cause the loss of a ship with its cargo and crew.

EARLY LIGHTS

Aids to navigation, from a lamp suspended on a tree limb to a fire on a hillside, have guided sailors to safe harbors since the earliest days of settlement in the New World. But these devices were casual and temporary lights, exhibited on an as-needed basis. The first permanent lighthouse in this country — and perhaps in the New World — was built in Boston Harbor, on Little Brewster Island, in 1716.

Opposite: Amelia Island light station (1839), at the mouth of the St. Marys River, Fernandina Beach, Fla. The light of the white conical tower shines 107 feet above the sea.

Original Boston Harbor lighthouse (1716), the first permanent American lighthouse. The current tower on the site dates from 1783.

As time went on other lighthouses were brought into existence by colonial governments or through private subscription, put up as the need arose and through the persistence of shipping interests in various ports. These lighthouses resulted solely from local concerns. No systematic effort was made to provide for safe navigation at all points along the coast.

Among the lighthouses constructed before the Revolution were those at Tybee Island, near Savannah, Ga. (1742); Brant Point, Nantucket, Mass. (1746); Jamestown (Beavertail), R.I. (1749); New London Harbor, Conn. (1760); Sandy Hook, N.J. (1764); Cape Henlopen, Del. (1767); Morris Island, Charleston, S.C. (1767); Plymouth, Mass. (1769); Portsmouth, N.H. (1771); and Thacher Island, Cape Ann, Mass. (1771). Only one survives today: the lighthouse at Sandy Hook in New Jersey. Most of the other colonial light station sites still exist, but none of them, with the possible exception of Tybee Island, has structures that were built during the colonial period.

The colonial lighthouses came into being at the time that European lighthouses were shifting to lamps as the source of light and developing other new lighting techniques. Although many European countries continued to use fires on their towers in the 18th century, by the end of the century lamps illuminated the majority of lighthouses. The Boston Harbor lighthouse of 1716 followed this lead and from the beginning used oil lamps, as did other colonial lighthouses. In the early part of the 18th century Europeans also began to experiment with parabolic and other light reflectors, multiple light towers at a single site, offshore lighthouses and techniques to obtain flashing lights. Americans did not begin to adopt these innovations until the 19th century and continued to remain behind Europe until the late 1800s.

After the Revolution, the individual states continued the responsibility for developing and administering

navigational aids started in the colonies. With the creation of the federal government in 1789, Congress viewed the establishment and maintenance of aids to navigation as the responsibility of the nation. In only its ninth official act, approved August 7, 1789, Congress stipulated that the government would assume control over them. Shortly afterward, those states with lighthouses turned them over to the Treasury Department, the agency Congress had specified to administer them.

Top: Point Conception light (1855) in California, based on a sketch by Maj. Hartman Bache. The light, along the "Graveyard of the Pacific," was one of the first 16 lights built on the West Coast. Above: Early midwestern lighthouse constructed near the fort at the entrance to the Chicago River.

LIGHTHOUSE TYPES

Lighthouses come in all shapes, sizes and materials. Sometimes they are conical, sometimes cylindrical, sometimes octagonal, sometimes square and sometimes they are skeleton-like. Some rise as well to a pyramidal point. Some are made of stone, some brick, some wood and some metal. They may be on land or in the water. Sometimes they are attached to the keeper's dwelling, sometimes they rise up through the middle of it, and

Top and above: Portland Head light station (1791), Portland, Maine. The complex includes the keeper's cottage attached by a covered walkway to the oil house and the conical stone and brick tower, plus a fog signal building at right.

sometimes they are detached completely from it. As well as holding the light, the tower itself had a secondary function: it served as a daymark, or landmark to aid navigators during daylight hours. Light towers were especially important to mariners sailing along an unfamiliar coast or entering a harbor for the first time.

The height of a tower depends on its purpose and the arc of the earth the light must overcome. A harbor light, for example, needs only a short tower because the light has to be seen only six or seven miles for the ship captain to maneuver into and about a harbor. The low coastal lands of the southern United States require that a lighthouse be tall, normally more than 160 feet, if its purpose is to guide shipping along that coast. On the other hand, a lighthouse that serves coastal traffic on the West Coast often can be relatively short, say 40 or 50 feet tall, because the land rises to great heights above the Pacific Ocean, so that a lighthouse on a bluff may be 200 feet or more above the sea.

In addition to the tower, light stations had a number of other structures, most of which were of plain and functional design. Such structures might include an oil house, usually small and made of brick or stone, although some were sheet iron; a fog signal building, a large square or rectangular structure often built of brick or a metronome-shaped enclosure; barns; workshops; storage sheds; privies; a tramway to move supplies and materials about the station; a boat house; cisterns and catch basins for water; occasionally a bridge; and, in more recent times, a garage. The most important structure was the living quarters for the keeper or keepers. Such houses could be single, double or triple dwellings, and they were the light station buildings that reflected most clearly prevailing architectural styles, adaptations to geographical conditions or regional design tastes. Sometimes a passageway connected the dwelling to the tower, to provide some protection from the often harsh environment.

In the early days of lighthouse construction in this country, light towers were usually made of stone or wood and typically were conical, such as the 1716 Boston Harbor lighthouse. A few were octagonal, among them the 1764 tower at Sandy Hook, N.J.

Until the mid-19th century the tendency was to build shorter towers than those built later, even though the site was low. For example, the original Cape Hatteras lighthouse (1803) was only 95 feet tall. In 1854 the tower was raised to 150 feet, a more realistic height for that section of the coast. Thereafter, at low sites light towers 150 to 170 feet tall were erected.

The government began to build lighthouses on iron pilings in the water in the mid-19th century. At Carysfort Reef, Fla., off Miami, Lt. George G. Meade in 1848 started work on a tall pile lighthouse whose skeleton framework offered little surface to resist the wind and

Cape Arago light station at the entrance to Coos Bay, Ore. This 1934 masonry tower, attached to the fog signal house, replaced the original 1866 iron lighthouse, the second on Oregon's coast. The fenced-in complex, reached by a bridge, originally included dwellings and other structures typical of light stations.

waves a hurricane might generate. Its light was 100 feet above sea level. This structure was the prototype for the string of lights that now dot the reefs off the coast of southern Florida, guarding vessels against this significant hazard. Two years later Maj. Hartman Bache initiated a screwpile lighthouse at Brandywine Shoal in the Delaware Bay. The design, from England, included legs with huge screws at each end that were twisted into the bottom. Eight of these legs, plus cross braces and tension rods, formed the skeleton foundation on which carpenters built a dwelling, topped by a lantern and lens. Its light was 46 feet above sea level.

A number of screwpile lighthouses soon dotted the Chesapeake Bay, but they were vulnerable to floating ice. At some, breakwaters were installed to divert ice floes. The Treasury Department's Lighthouse Board began using caisson structures in the bay and farther north, as well as in the Great Lakes. A huge round iron tube was fabricated in the depot shop and floated out to the site, where it was tipped into the water. Workers often had to use ingenuity to right and level it, and then they filled it with rocks and cement. This platform served as the foundation for the living quarters and a light tower and was sturdy enough to withstand ice.

In the 1850s with the building of the first eight lighthouses on the West Coast, a Cape Cod–style dwelling with a tower rising through its center came into use — a somewhat incongruous design reflecting its East Coast origins. The design was the work of Ammi B. Young, the first supervising architect of the Treasury Department, who was known for his classical structures. Built about the same time as the early West Coast lights, the St. Croix River lighthouse (1856) on Dochet Island, Maine, was strongly suggestive of this design. A metal skeleton tower with a cylinder containing the stairway became popular in the 1860s. Pyramidal in shape, this type of light tower was in use for a long period and can be found on the Great Lakes and East, Gulf and West coasts.

Range lights, consisting of paired towers, were developed to guide vessels into harbors and channels. The front light is low, while the rear light, some distance away, is much higher. When ship captains have these lights lined up — one on top of the other — they know that they are on a safe course.

Pierhead and breakwater lights are found in all sections of the country but are particularly common in the Great Lakes. Located on piers that normally mark harbor entrances, they are usually made of metal and vary in style. Cylindrical towers, painted white or red, have been popular, as has a square structure with a pyramidal roof and tower rising out of its center.

In addition to the body, the other two basic elements of a light tower are the foundation and the lantern. For some types of towers, such as skeleton and screwpile lighthouses, the foundation is quite simple; but for others, such as masonry and caisson lighthouses, the foundation can be substantial. Many masonry towers built on sandy soil first had piles driven into the ground. On the piles a

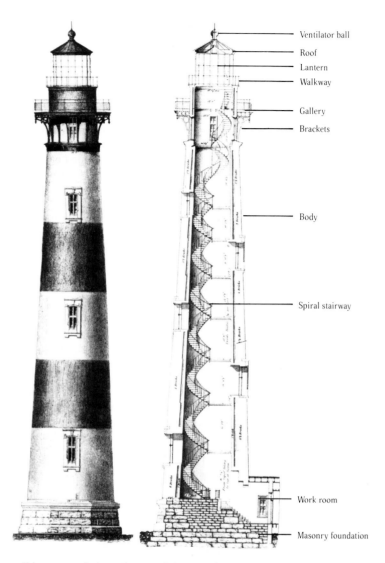

- Ventilator ball
- Roof
- Lantern
- Walkway
- Gallery
- Brackets
- Body
- Spiral stairway
- Work room
- Masonry foundation

cribbage consisting of several layers of 6-by-12-inch timbers would be laid, and on this was placed several courses of granite. The base of the tower would be erected on the granite. At some sites, such as Cape Hatteras and Bodie Island in North Carolina, the sand was so compact that piles were not needed; after scraping away the loose upper layer of sand, the builders laid only the wood grillage and granite foundation.

Lanterns varied in size, depending on the size of the lens they contained. The largest was topped by a shallow peaked metal roof. At the peak was a ventilator ball, on top of which was a short lightning rod, 18 to 24 inches high. A metal cable ran from the lantern to the ground to carry away the electricity. All lanterns had a walkway with a metal railing, called a gallery. Larger lanterns had a narrower walkway above the gallery that permitted the keepers to clean the outside of the glass; the level between the gallery and the work walkway would be the watch room. Inside the lantern was the lens, and inside the lens was the lamp, or illuminant. If the lens revolved, a clockwork mechanism would be placed below the lens.

Bodie Island light tower (1872), Oregon Inlet, N.C., shown in engineering drawings from the early 1870s. The vertical section at right illustrates the parts common to many towers. The black-and-white bands make this lighthouse a distinctive daymark.

Above left: Squat brick conical tower (1856) at Gay Head on Martha's Vineyard, Mass. Although the 47-foot tower is short, it is 160 feet above the sea. Behind it is a double keepers' dwelling. Above right: Another conical tower (1898), 65 feet tall and painted white, across the country at North Head, Ilwaco, Wash. Left: Conical cast-iron tower, one of the twin lights built at Cape Elizabeth, south of Portland, Maine, in 1874.

Top left: Short octagonal limestone tower of the Genesee light (1822), Rochester, N.Y. Top center: Tall octagonal masonry tower at the Tybee Island light (1867), Savannah, Ga., about 1885. The tower is now painted black and white. Top right: Square pyramidal tower (1886) framed in wood at Ship Island, Miss.

Top left to right: Tall conical towers typical of the Southeast coast, all painted to serve as daymarks distinguishable by mariners during daylight. The diamond-patterned Cape Lookout light (1859), near Beaufort, N.C., is 150 feet tall, the Loggerhead Key tower (1858) in Florida's Dry Tortugas is 157 feet, and the old Charleston, S.C., lighthouse (1876) on Morris Island, now threatened by erosion, is 161 feet. Left: Modern cylindrical tower placed in service on Oak Island, N.C., in 1958. Banded also, it is 155 feet high.

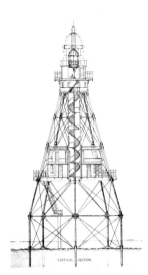

Above left: Pile reef light (1878) typical of the Florida coast at Fowey Rocks, Fla. Above right: Screwpile light (1855) at Point of Shoals, Va., a common Chesapeake Bay design. Right: Caisson light tower (1883) at Sandy Point Shoal, Md., a type used in the Chesapeake Bay and Northeast. Below: Skeleton tower at the Brazos River light station, Freeport, Tex., with a central cylinder housing the stairway.

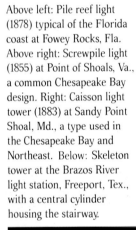

Left: Cape Cod–style light (1854) at Point Pinos, near Monterey, Calif., similar to many of the early West Coast lighthouses. The tower and dwelling are combined, with the tower rising through the roof of the house in this watercolor based on a sketch by Maj. Hartman Bache.

Above left: Victorian-era light at Fort Tompkins, N.Y., seen about 1900. Eclectic in style, the frame tower-house combination has a mansard roof. Above right: Pierhead light (1904) in Michigan City, Ind., at the end of the east pier. Other Great Lakes pierhead lights have a similar design. Left: Breakwater light station on Galveston Jetty, Galveston, Tex.

Above: Multiple-light station. The Three Sisters lights (1838) on Nauset Beach, North Eastham, Mass., were the only triple towers built in the United States but were considered "overlighting." They were replaced in 1892 by three more towers. Right: Range lights, designed as a pair to guide ships into harbors and channels. These Doubling Point lights (1898) are near Bath, Maine, on the Kennebec River. Bottom left: Modern metal post light (1957) on Raspberry Island in Wisconsin's Apostle Islands. Bottom right: Eight-day post light in Sand Shoal Inlet, Va., with four crosspieces to distinguish the light from others nearby.

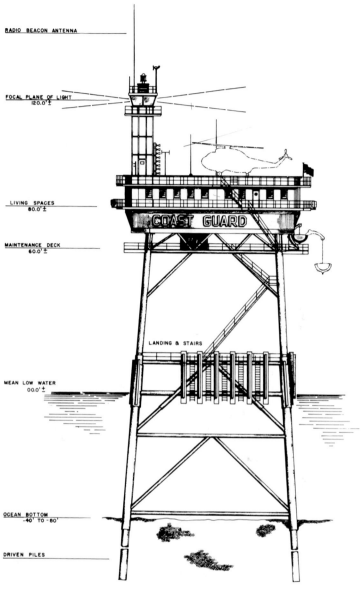

RADIO BEACON ANTENNA

FOCAL PLANE OF LIGHT
120.0' ±

LIVING SPACES
80.0' ±

MAINTENANCE DECK
60.0' ±

LANDING & STAIRS

MEAN LOW WATER
00.0' ±

OCEAN BOTTOM
-40' TO -80'

DRIVEN PILES

COAST GUARD

Above: "Texas tower," a massive pile structure built to replace some lightship stations such as Diamond Shoals, N.C., and Ambrose Channel, N.Y. Left: Ambrose Channel's "Texas tower," which replaced the station's lightship in 1967.

Until the advent of the Lighthouse Board in 1852, the building of lighthouses was done by contract. The builder who won the contract would be given minimal directions, usually little more than a sketch of the structure desired and specifications consisting of one page. It is not known who prepared these documents, but evidence exists that at least a few were done with the aid of Winslow Lewis, a retired ship captain who was active in the government's early lighthouse work. I. W. P. Lewis, an engineer and Lewis's nephew, designed the Carysfort Reef light in Florida, completed in 1852, and worked on several others. The Lighthouse Board prepared extensive and detailed drawings of lighthouses it built, leaving little to the imagination of the builders. Later, personnel from the U.S. Army Corps of Engineers designed lighthouses. The Bureau of Lighthouses, established in 1910, apparently had its own group of designers, as does the Coast Guard, the administrator of U.S. lighthouses since 1939.

Over the years some lighthouse plans became standardized. Screwpile lighthouses changed only in small details; the one in Alabama's Mobile Bay (1885) appears to be a duplicate of others in the Chesapeake Bay. The so-called sparkplug lights, such as Staten Island's Robbins Reef (1883) light and its match in North Tarrytown, N.Y. (1883), are duplicated in a number of places in the Northeast. The tall masonry towers built in the 1870s on the Southeast coast are all similar, with variations being mostly in height. Block Island's North lighthouse (1867) in Rhode Island is but one of several similar structures in the Long Island Sound area — the differences among them being only the color schemes. A number of steel skeleton towers with a cylinder enclosing the stairway are scattered about the country, differentiated mainly by the number of support legs.

Distinguishing one lighthouse from another to aid mariners was a problem the European lighthouse community wrestled with for a long time. In the 18th century England experimented with several techniques. At one lighthouse using a fire as its light, the keepers set off rockets every so often; at another lighthouse, they tried passing a screen back and forth in front of the light to simulate a flash; and one station tried multiple lights. Although the United States eventually used the screen technique in a few lighthouses in the 19th century as well as other devices to achieve a flashing light, the method that apparently appealed most was multiple lights, consisting of two or three towers at one site. Several of the colonial light stations, such as Thacher Island (1771), near Cape Ann, Mass., had twin lights, and during the 19th century the federal government erected several twin light towers, for example, at Matinicus Rock (1827), off Rockland, Maine, and Cape Elizabeth (1828) in Portland, Maine. The Three Sisters lights (1838) in North Eastham, Mass., were an attempt to make a site particularly distinctive. But the pressure to have multiple light towers lessened with the increased ease of making lights flash. Believing that an extra light was an unnecessary expense in personnel, materials and fuel, the government declared that by 1924 all multiple lights would be eliminated and each station would have only one light.

Many of the active lights today are not on traditional-style, or historic, towers but can be found on simple platforms or monopoles, because that is all that is required to support the modern plastic lens now being used. In Wisconsin's Apostle Islands in Lake Superior, the current Raspberry Island light is on a metal post. Advanced technology has reduced a light station that once had a double keepers' dwelling with attached tower, an oil house, storage and workshop structures and privies to a solar-powered light on a post that occupies a piece of land two feet square. Two keepers maintained the old light station and kept the light burning. The modern-day light tower at Raspberry Island requires attention just once a year.

LIGHTS IN THE LIGHTHOUSES

From the deep, dark past to the late 19th century, the flame, in one form or another, was the source of light for lighthouses. The first aid to navigation probably started with a fire on the beach as some early human waited for the return of an overdue fishing boat. As time went on, the flame moved to a tower. The tower at Pharos in the harbor of Alexandria, built about 300 B.C. and generally regarded as the world's first lighthouse, used an open flame as its light. Through the centuries wood, coal and bales of okum and pitch fueled the fire until keepers of light towers began to use candles and whale-oil lamps in the 18th century.

Little information exists on types of illuminants used during the colonial period. One knowledgeable European lighthouse historian says that oil lamps without reflectors were used. Around 1790 spider lamps were introduced into the United States. They were an improvement, although they gave off acrid fumes that periodically drove the keeper out of the lantern. The lamps were pans of oil in which four or more wicks were stuck. Apparently nothing better could be found, so these lamps continued in use until Winslow Lewis introduced his version of the French Argand lamp and parabolic reflector in 1810.

François-Pierre Ami Argand's lamp, designed about 1783, contained a hollow circular wick that permitted oxygen to pass evenly on both sides, thus permitting the flame to burn intensely, brightly and smokelessly. The flame of one lamp reportedly gave off more light than seven candles. England and France quickly adopted these lamps for their lighthouses. Shortly after installing them in 1789, England began fitting reflectors to them to achieve a better light. Europe had been experimenting with reflectors for some time and had settled on the parabolic reflector as the best type to use.

For several years Winslow Lewis, an unemployed ship captain, had been testing the lamp and reflector, and in 1810 he persuaded the federal government to adopt his Argand lamp and parabolic reflector system in all

Lucerne, used by 19th-century light keepers to light the concentric-wick lamps in Fresnel lenses.

Lamps for Fresnel lenses, including a two-wick lamp at left, five-wick lamp at center and three-wick lamp at right. The concentric wicks used in these lamps were a modification of the wick developed by Ami Argand in 1781.

lighthouses. Lewis had "borrowed" the idea from English lighthouses, whose well-made lights with true parabolic reflectors gave that country's lighthouses respectable lights. Lewis's reflectors were more spherical than parabolic, and the light came from an ersatz Argand lamp. Nonetheless, he sold his patent and agreed to install the lamps and reflectors in all existing lighthouses. The government paid him $60,000. He started installing the reflector system in 1812 but, because of the War of 1812, did not finish the task until 1815. A number of lamps and reflectors were placed in each lighthouse — the number, as well as the size of the reflectors, depended on the purpose the light served. The light could be made to flash by rotating the "tree" on which the lamps and reflectors hung.

Lewis's lighting system was never very good and by no means came close to equaling that of England and Scotland, whose lights had excellent reputations among the seafaring community. The main problem lay with the reflectors. One lighthouse historian in the 19th century said that the reflectors approached the paraboloid about as closely as did a barber's basin. The material of the reflectors was inferior also, with metal so thin that they bent out of shape easily and so thinly veneered with silver that the silver quickly wore off from cleaning, especially when the prescribed cleaning compound—an abrasive— was used.

Despite its drawbacks, Lewis's system lighted the lighthouses of this country for 40 years. One of the reasons his system remained so long was that Lewis had developed a close relationship with Stephen Pleasonton, the Treasury Department official responsible for lighthouses. Pleasonton more than dug in his heels when anyone tried to persuade him to adopt the better Fresnel lenses. As a result, the United States was slow to develop a good navigational system, even though the means to provide one had come on the scene just after Pleasonton took charge of lighthouses.

Augustin Fresnel, a French physicist, developed and perfected his lens in 1822. The lens looked like a glass beehive, and in its center was a single lamp. Prisms at the top and bottom refracted, or bent, the light into a narrow sheet, while glass at the center focus magnified the light. The bending and magnification produced a bright, narrow sheet of concentrated light. Fresnel's lenses came in six orders, or sizes, numbered one through six; a 3½-order lens was developed later. They ranged in diameter from six feet for the first order to 10 inches for the sixth order.

Pleasonton strongly resisted adopting the Fresnel lens, ostensibly because of the high initial cost. Several military engineers pointed out to him that the lenses would pay for themselves within a few years through the savings in oil, but Pleasonton maintained his opposition to change. In 1838 Congress sent Cmdr. Matthew C. Perry to Europe to look at lighthouses with Fresnel lenses and to purchase two lenses for experimentation — one of the first order with a fixed light and one of the second order that revolved. In 1840 these lenses were installed in the Twin Lights (1828) at Navesink, N.J. Before 1851 a special act of Congress equipped two other lighthouses — Sankaty Head (1850) on Nantucket, Mass., and Brandywine Shoal (1850) in Delaware — with Fresnel lenses. Everyone thought that these lights were vastly superior to the Lewis lamps and reflectors, but as late as 1851 Pleasonton asserted that more testing was needed and that the lamp was too complicated for most light keepers to operate. It mattered little at this point how he felt, because a Lighthouse Board had been authorized to investigate the state of the country's lighthouse system. The report of the board strongly urged the adoption of the Fresnel lens. Shortly after the Lighthouse Board took control of aids to navigation in 1852, it began installing Fresnel lenses in lighthouses.

The first three orders of lenses were considered seacoast lights; the fourth, fifth and sixth were considered harbor and bay lights. The 3½-order lens was used mostly in the Great Lakes in both coastal and harbor entrance lighthouses, although three were installed in Gulf Coast light towers; it was the size least used by the United States. Lamps in the Fresnel lenses varied in size. First- and second-order lenses had lamps with five concentric wicks, a third-order lens used a lamp with three wicks, and a sixth-order lens required a lamp with one concentric wick. To light these lamps, the keepers were supplied with lucernes, small metal devices with a protruding wick that was lighted and touched to the concentric wicks of the lamps.

At the time the United States adopted Fresnel lenses, lighthouse lamps were using whale oil, specifically spermacetti, the oil from the head of the sperm whale. The oil burned evenly and with a bright flame. Before the

Above: Fourth-order Fresnel lens with an incandescent oil vapor lamp, used at Fort Point, Calif., about 1912. The stand contains a clockwork system that rotated the bull's-eye lenses to achieve a flashing effect. Above right: Fresnel lens in place in the closed position.

introduction of sperm oil, lighthouses used two strains of whale oil: a thick oil for summer and a thinner oil for winter. Even the thin oil tended to congeal in colder areas in winter, with the result that keepers had to install warming stoves in the lantern to thin the oil before filling the lamps. Shortly after the Fresnel lenses came into use, sperm oil began to cost $2.25 a gallon, up sharply from an 1841 price of 55 cents a gallon. Two factors caused this increase: industrial use was growing, and whalers were taking fewer sperm whales.

The Lighthouse Board began to use colza or rapeseed oil, an oil the French were using. Unfortunately, farmers grew little rape in this country. The Lighthouse Board's Committee on Experiments tested lard oil, a product in plentiful supply in the United States. Earlier tests had been failures, but taking a different approach this time, the board found that lard oil burned well if heated to a high enough temperature. The board began to phase out the use of colza and started using lard oil in the larger lamps.

In the 1870s the committee conducted further fuel experiments, testing kerosene, or mineral oil as it was then more popularly known. These tests proved successful, so the board began using kerosene in fourth-order and lower lenses. A little later it began using this fuel in the larger lenses as well. Through the years the United States has experimented with a number of other fuel oils,

Hyper-radiant lens at the Makapuu Point light (1909), Oahu, Hawaii. Measuring 8½ feet in diameter and approximately 16 feet high, the lens was the largest used in an American lighthouse.

including fish, porpoise and olive oil, but each was eventually found to be wanting. Pleasonton before 1852 and the Lighthouse Board afterward experimented with the use of gas, which did not work out, primarily because water collected in the pipes. Pleasonton went so far as to experiment with manufacturing gas from coal at three light stations in Delaware, but the keepers apparently did not cooperate — they would let the furnaces and retorts burn through before notifying him. The next change in the illuminant of the lens was the introduction of the incandescent oil vapor lamp, one similar to the Coleman lantern that campers use today.

Although the Lighthouse Board had used electricity to illuminate the lens in the flame of the Statue of Liberty when it was erected in 1886, it did not really take electricity seriously until about 1900, when the board began converting lighthouses to electricity. The conversion went slowly, because many lighthouses were not near power lines and electric generators were expensive and difficult to use. But in the 1920s and 1930s the Bureau of Lighthouses, successor to the Lighthouse Board, converted the bulk of lighthouses to electricity. This change not only reduced personnel needs but also opened the door to eventual wholesale automation of lighthouses. By the late 1960s fewer than 60 lighthouses still had keepers, and they were to be all gone by 1989–90.

Above: District lens-repair shop in Buffalo, N.Y., in 1901. A fixed Fresnel lens is near the workbench at the back of the shop. Right: Electric arc bivalve lens installed in the south tower of the Navesink, N.J., twin lights in 1898. The first to use electricity for its primary light it was — at 25-million candlepower — also the most powerful.

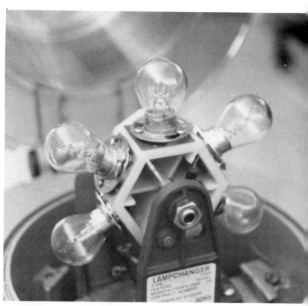

Above and left: Modern plastic lenses, including details of an automatic lamp changer. When one bulb burns out, the bulb holder moves a new one into place to keep a light shining.

During this middle period of automation, the fixed Fresnel lenses were sometimes left in place, and a timer switch turned the light on in the evening and off just after sunrise. The illuminant was still the 1,000-watt bulb, or lamp as it is officially known. A bulb holder inside the lens held several of these lamps, and if one went out, the holder automatically switched another lamp into position and turned it on. Sometimes the lenses were removed, in which case another type of light was installed in the lantern, such as an aerobeacon. Small, simple, weatherproof and easily automated, aerobeacons (which also guide planes at airports) are circular metal cylinders open on one end for the light and lens. Automated light stations were checked about every month to replace burned-out lamps and see that all else was going well.

Today, a number of Fresnel lenses still remain in lighthouses and a number of aerobeacons are still in place. But the Coast Guard is now installing the ATON

Coast Guardsman, before automation, inserting a new 1,000-watt bulb inside the lower mirrored compartment of a light tower.

system of automation. This system has several different sizes of optics, or plastic lenses, ranging from 155 to 300 millimeters. These lenses are molded in the Fresnel design, with little prisms that refract the light and clear plastic at the center for fixed lenses and bull's-eyes at the center for rotating lights. The smaller lenses are used on buoys and post lights, whereas the larger ones — 250 and 300 millimeters — are used in lighthouses. Inside these lenses are six or more small bulbs — roughly the size of Christmas tree lights — that illuminate the lens. They are installed on a belt, and when a bulb goes out, the belt is activated and moves another bulb into place. Electronic flasher units that turn the light off and on are used in some of the lenses to achieve a flashing effect. The Coast Guard is now installing solar panels to recharge batteries that power these lights. With this continual source of energy, Coast Guard personnel need inspect these lights only on a quarterly to annual basis. These men and women, known as ANTs — Aid to Navigation Teams — are the modern-day light keepers.

LIGHTSHIPS

England is usually given credit for establishing the first lightship, although there is some evidence that several centuries B.C. the Romans used a vessel displaying a lighted fire basket at night as a friendly sign to merchants and a warning to pirates. The first English lightship, which carried two lanterns on a cross arm tacked to the mast, was stationed at the Nore Sandbank in the Thames River estuary in 1731. It proved to be a popular navigational aid.

Nantucket New South Shoals lightship, rolling heavily on station in an 1891 view. The lanterns encircled the masts and were raised from their deck housings into position at nightfall.

Nearly 100 years passed before the United States introduced its first light vessel, in the Chesapeake Bay at Willoughby Spit, Va., in 1820. It was too small, some 70 tons, for this exposed position, and it had to be moved to more sheltered waters off Norfolk. The next year four more lightships were placed in the Chesapeake, and in 1823 the first "outside" (off a coast) light vessel went into service near Sandy Hook, N.J., at the entrance to New York Harbor. These lightships were usually more than 100 tons, but were called lightboats. The term "lightship" seems to have come into use about the time of the advent of the Lighthouse Board in the early 1850s.

By 1837 the United States had 26 lightboats; 15 years later the number had grown to 42. Until the Lighthouse Board took over aids to navigation only one relief, or extra, light vessel was available to fill in when an assigned lightboat had to leave its station for repairs or other reasons. This relief vessel was stationed at Norfolk, Va., in the Chesapeake Bay.

During this period there were two classes of lightboats: small and large. The distinction between the two is not clear, but small lightboats seemed to be about 100 to 120 tons and large ones were about 200 tons or more. These vessels were not designed specifically for the mission they served; rather, they were typical ships fitted with lanterns for lights. These lights usually came from compass lamps or common lamps, which were roughly equivalent to the light obtained when lighthouses used spider lamps.

When the Lighthouse Board came into being, it established an inventory of spare equipment for the light vessels, improved the light of the ships by substituting Argand lamps and parabolic reflectors for the lamps previously used and began replacing lightships with lighthouses. By 1860 the United States had three fewer lightships. During the Civil War, lightships became the targets of the Confederates, who sank every one they could capture. After the war the board raised some of these vessels and put them back into service.

The Lighthouse Board also began to number the lightships geographically starting at the northernmost lightship, so that for a number of years the numbering had little correspondence to the age of the vessels. In time, as new lightships were built and old ones were decommissioned, the number of a ship did reflect its age. The number is the real name of a lightship. The name shown on the side of each vessel is the name of the station to which it was assigned. For years a lightship's number was preceeded by the word "Lightship," for example, *Lightship No. 12*. In the 1940s the Navy, under whom the Coast Guard is assigned during wartime, insisted that the Coast Guard change its designation of vessels to conform more to the Navy's system. At that time the lightships received the WAL designation and a new number. Then in 1965 the Coast Guard changed the designation of lightships to WLV plus the number of the vessel.

Only in the second half of the 19th century did nations begin to consider that lightships had a special duty and thus should have a special design and construction. The United States joined England, France and Ireland in working to develop a better lightship, paying particular attention to design, construction, the lighting apparatus and living conditions. Marine architects began to flatten the bottoms of the hulls and install bilge keels to inhibit rolling.

One of the more difficult problems was changing to metal from wood hulls. Most marine architects did not believe that metal hulls could absorb the shock of the sea as well as wood hulls. Metal, they argued, would get fouled more quickly than wood hulls, would suffer more damage if driven ashore and would sweat on the interior, creating an unhealthful condition for the crew. It was not until 1881 that the United States began to ease into metal-hull construction. Its early vessels had hulls that were composite, part wood and part metal. But the United States moved slowly to metal hulls, and as late as 1902 the Lighthouse Board ordered a lightship whose hull was all wood.

The adaptation of propulsion machinery to lightships was equally slow in coming. The first light vessels to have engines were three the Lighthouse Board ordered in 1891.

The crew of early light vessels lived in quarters below the water line because these ships had only one deck. But during the last half of the 19th century, as naval architects developed better designs for lightships, the comfort of those who ran the vessels was taken into consideration. Increased space usually permitted officers to have individual staterooms, while the crew had two-person rooms.

The designers also increased the strength and weight

Above: Ambrose Channel, N.Y., lightship surrendering its station to a new "Texas tower" in 1967. A lightship had served the Ambrose station, off Sandy Hook, N.J., since 1908. The accessibility of the new tower, via helicopter and electronic communications, contrasts strongly with the isolation of most early lightships. Left: Last active American lightship, the *Nantucket (No. 112)*, which served one of the most exposed lightship stations in the world, 50 miles off Nantucket, Mass.

of the chain and anchor for each light vessel, so that they could stay on station better, aided eventually by more powerful engines. The Lighthouse Board and Bureau of Lighthouses set high standards for the operation of lightships and expected them to remain on station except for unusual circumstances. The bureau publicly reprimanded one lightship captain who, when his mooring lines parted, headed for port to obtain a new anchor and chain. The bureau said the captain should have used his engines to remain on station and called a tender to bring out new equipment.

In the late 19th century a writer visited one lightship and painted a picture of routine and dullness. But he was there in calm seas. He did not experience foul weather, but if he had, a different story would have flowed from his pen. A normal storm, on the ocean or in the Great Lakes, could test the metal of a ship and the mettle of a seaman. But in severe storms, such as a hurricane, the adrenalin could flow at a rapid rate. Often the crew came out of these storms with only a battered ship, but on several occasions lightships sank. In 1913 the lightship off Buffalo went down with all hands when water apparently smashed the lantern house and poured inside. In 1918 the Cross Rip lightship on Nantucket Sound mysteriously sank. The Five Fathom lightship off the Delaware Bay went under in an 1893 storm, and four men were lost, because someone failed to secure a hatch cover properly and a series of waves dumped water into the ship. In 1944 the Cuttyhunk lightship sank with all hands in a hurricane. Two bodies later washed ashore, but the ship was never found.

A lightship also faced the possibility of breaking its moorings and drifting ashore. When this happened, the vessel was usually hauled off the beach, repaired and returned to duty. In 1855 the one-year-old Nantucket Shoals lightship had this experience, and the Lighthouse Board spent 90 percent of the vessel's initial cost to repair it. Ten years later the same ship was blown off station at Brenton Reef and required extensive repairs before it could be placed back in service. The first lightship on the West Coast, *No. 50*, broke its moorings in 1899 near the mouth of the Columbia River between Oregon and Washington, and while being towed to port the tug's hawser snapped and the vessel drifted onto the beach. It eventually had to be pulled higher on the beach and then hauled by rail 700 yards overland to an adjacent bay. There it was repaired and towed back to its station.

On other occasions ships and barges, particularly in fog, collided with lightships. The colliding vessel, if it could be identified, paid for repairs to the lightship. In many instances the offending vessel just bounced off the lightship and disappeared into the mist. A Standard Oil barge in 1919 rammed the lightship assigned to Cornfield Point off Connecticut and sank it. The crew abandoned ship, and no lives were lost.

The most unusual catastrophe to sink a lightship occurred in North Carolina in 1918 when a German submarine, after letting the crew leave, fired shells into the Diamond Shoals, N.C., lightship until it went down. The Germans sank the vessel in retaliation for the lightship's sending out a signal warning shippers of the presence of the submarine. About 25 commercial vessels had received the signal and took refuge in the bight of Cape Lookout to the south.

Through the years lightships served well and effectively, operated by crews equal in competence and dedication to their counterparts ashore. But technology was to doom this form of navigational aid. The Lighthouse Board began replacing "inner" lightships (those assigned to bays and sounds) from the time it was established. Their replacement at first was the screwpile and later the caisson lighthouse. It was inevitable that "outside" lightships would in time be removed from the coasts. At first, buoys replaced a few of them. In the 1960s the Coast Guard built "Texas towers" to take the place of lightships at stations such as Diamond Shoals, N.C., but these four-legged towers that resemble oil rigs were expensive, so the Coast Guard turned to the large navigational buoy. Today, the United States has no active lightships. The last, the *Nantucket* serving the Nantucket South Shoals station in Massachusetts, was retired in 1984. Their history, however, is commemorated by a number of vessels that have been preserved by maritime museums and local historical societies.

THE LESSER AIDS

Over the years buoys, fog signals and river lights also have been the responsibility of the various lighthouse agencies. These are all important navigational aids, and they are designated as lesser only because they are smaller.

Buoys have always been important to navigation. In this country they date to the colonial period and were used at least by 1767 to mark hazards in the Delaware Bay. These early buoys were wood, some of them barrels made of wood staves, some of iron and others simply solid wood spars. They were used not only in the calmer waters of bays and rivers, but also in more rugged places such as Diamond Shoals and Cape Lookout Shoals, N.C. They were taken out of the water regularly so that seagrowth could be removed and the buoys could be painted. Buoys could be damaged easily by vessels, particularly by ship propellers.

The use of buoys grew rapidly over the years. In 1842 the country had 1,000 of them; by 1860 the number had grown to more than 1,700, by 1857 to 2,800, by 1900 to nearly 5,000 and by the mid-1930s to more than 14,000. In time buoys began to be made of boiler plate. These iron buoys, compartmentalized so that they would not sink easily, stood up better to vessels. A ship whose screw bit into an iron buoy might find itself limping away from the scene with an expensive repair bill to straighten out the propeller. Buoys also are sometimes damaged or dragged off position by tugs with tows. To combat this problem the Bureau of Lighthouses had sawteeth placed on the most susceptible buoys. The teeth could cut through a manila hemp towline, and because towlines were expensive, the tug operators learned to give the buoys a wide berth. The use of sawteeth was later stopped to reduce the government's liability for damage.

The United States began in the 1850s to systematize the coloring of buoys. For a long time red buoys marked the starboard side of the channel and black buoys the port side when inbound. White buoys designated anchorages, yellow buoys quarantine anchorages. Today, in conforming to international agreement, a system of buoys and daymarks is used, and colors have been changed. For instance, buoys on the port side of a channel are green.

Buoys now are held in place by concrete sinkers. Despite the use of chain or synthetic rope moorings, buoys break away on occasion. Adrift, they become a

Top: Buoys outside the carpenter shop at the Lighthouse Board's Staten Island, N.Y., depot in 1890. The large ones in the foreground are whistling buoys. Above: Can and nun buoys (foreground), whistling buoys (left rear) and lighted buoys (right rear) at the Little Diamond Island depot in Maine, 1930. Right: Large navigational buoy similar to others that replaced lightships. Located near the old Scotland lightship station off Sandy Hook, N.J., this 104-ton buoy was equipped with a 7,500-candlepower light and a fog signal.

hazard to navigation; consequently, the Coast Guard attempts to locate these buoys immediately. But in a few instances buoys have traveled a considerable distance before someone finds and reports them to the Coast Guard. The Frying Pan Shoals, N.C., buoy once was missing for a year, and in that time it had drifted 4,000 miles.

Buoys are sometimes equipped with fog signals — whistles, bells or gongs — that are activated by the action of the sea and thus do not sound very often in a calm sea.

Ashore, fog signals are found at light stations in certain sections of the country — in plentiful number on the East Coast from Delaware north, on the West Coast and in the Great Lakes. But on the Southeast and Gulf coasts, fog is rarely a problem; consequently, few fog signals are found there. Puerto Rico and Hawaii do not have fog, so they do not have fog signals. The Coast Guard, in any case, warns mariners of the unpredictability of sound as it travels over water, cautioning them about relying on fog signals to determine position.

The first fog signal in this country was a cannon used at the Boston Harbor light (1716). In the 1820s fog bells arrived at several New England lighthouses. At first they were operated by hand, but later, machinery powered by a clockwork system was introduced. C. L. Daboll developed a whistle fog signal in the 1850s that directed the sound through a large trumpet. The large trumpet does not appear to have been widely adopted, but the whistle remained. In the 1860s the Lighthouse Board's Committee on Experiments tested steam whistles but was not satisfied until it tested a steam locomotive whistle that Maj. Hartman Bache had used. This whistle proved satisfactory and was installed at a number of light stations and was used well into the 20th century.

Several types of fog signals are used at light stations today: sirens, foghorns, two-tone diaphone fog signals (invented by a Canadian and adopted by the United States in 1915), single-tone signals and chimes. The diaphone fog signal was the basis for a famous commercial for Lifebuoy soap that translated the sound as "beeeooooooo." As the light towers themselves are shrinking with advanced technology, the fog signal has also been reduced in size. The FA-232, which can be heard one-half mile, or one mile if two are put together, is quite small. Although it cannot be heard as far as the older fog signals, the distance it can reach, the Coast Guard believes, is adequate for today's navigational needs.

Rivers such as the Mississippi, Missouri and Ohio have always been important routes of transportation and commerce. But the twists and turns of these waterways once permitted travel only in daylight hours. A congressionally authorized study in the 1870s resulted in the Lighthouse Board's establishing two districts embracing these rivers. District officials then went about designating sites and placing post lights, which were lens lanterns hung from posts that held an eight-day supply of oil. A local farmer often tended three or four of these lights. Over the years the districts added more and more lights,

Right: Boston Harbor fog cannon, installed in 1719 as the first U.S. fog signal. Below: Foghorn with trumpet extension in Boston about 1890. Bottom left: Fog signals on the Los Angeles Harbor light (1913) in 1945. Bottom right: Typical metronome-shaped enclosure for a fog bell.

Frederick Meissner tending a Mississippi River post light near St. Louis, carrying on a family custom that began in the 1890s.

and by 1890, 1,500 post lights illuminated nearly 4,500 miles of 18 rivers and Puget Sound in Washington. The people who tended these lights were conscientious about their work, and tales about their attention to duty rival the stories told of the keepers at the larger light stations.

THE KEEPERS

Before the advent of the Lighthouse Board in 1852, politics often played an important part in the selection of lighthouse keepers, and as a result the quality of light keepers was mixed. There were those who worked diligently and kept a good light. And there were those who were less conscientious in the performance of their duties and kept a light mariners could barely see.

The average light keeper before the mid-19th century received minimal training and had little direction. This lack of instruction and training appalled the Lighthouse Board, so it went about issuing directions for all keepers in the most minute detail. The board began to require that light keepers be not only at least 18 years old — but also able to read the ample new written instructions.

Instructions spelled out daily duties and how the keepers were to perform them, all very specific and covering just about every topic or condition the keepers might encounter. For example, if keepers dropped oil on the lens, the instructions told them to clean it off with spirits of wine. If they did not know how to trim a wick or adjust a lamp, they could find a detailed step-by-step description, including a picture of what the flame should look like. And keepers were clearly told that they were to have the light ready by 10 a.m. for evening lighting. These instructions left little to the discretion or imagination of the keeper.

Once the keepers had finished their work in the lantern, their attention was turned to maintenance and repairs at the light station. Painting, including the tower, was an important chore. Repairs done by the keepers were minor; major repairs and construction were the responsibility of the district office.

The Lighthouse Board set high standards and instituted a system of supervision to see that the keepers carried out these standards. The board did not tolerate mistakes or dereliction of duty. Once it determined guilt, it meted out stern justice. In 1891 a 21-year veteran lighthouse keeper on the West Coast was found to have an untidy station on two quarterly inspections in a row. The inspector warned him the first time. He dismissed him after the second inspection. The keeper of the Cape Hatteras lighthouse once reported that he caught his assistant keeper asleep on duty. Without investigation, the board ordered the keeper to discharge the assistant.

Stern discipline, adequate instructions, capable people, an opportunity for a career and a good lighting system drew the Lighthouse Service out of the doldrums of mediocrity and established the United States's navigational aid system as being among the best in the world. At the same time employee morale was improved and keepers began to feel proud of their work.

One factor in building pride was the program of awards for bravery that the Lighthouse Board instituted. Ida Lewis of the Lime Rock lighthouse in Connecticut, Marcus A. Hanna of Cape Elizabeth, Maine, and C. E. Marr and E. H. Pierce of the Cuckolds, Maine, fog signal station are only a few of the keepers who were given awards for rescues at sea. The Bureau of Lighthouses later publicized such heroic acts through its *Lighthouse Service Bulletin.*

Although the work and life of the lighthouse keeper were filled with routine, the unexpected came in large doses. The need to rescue sailors often arose when the weather was most tumultuous. Birds in great flocks created problems, for it was not uncommon for them to be attracted by the light and fly into it, smashing the glass of the lantern and sometimes breaking prisms of the lens. At such times keepers would do all they could to divert the birds — from firing guns to putting up screens around the lantern. Because they were in such exposed positions, lighthouses suffered heavily from hurricanes and other storms. Equipment and buildings of the station would be damaged, and the history of the Lighthouse Service is dotted with instances when these terrors of nature killed or injured keepers and members of their families and, at least once, the keeper and her whole family.

Most stations permitted keepers' families to be with them and provided quarters for them. Such stations were often isolated, so loneliness and monotony dominated their lives. But it was not an unhappy life, for many wives and children of light keepers remember their lives fondly. We can look at this life — near the water, in a beautiful setting — romantically and think of it as being idyllic. Still, it must have been difficult on the wives and

Above: Interior of a keeper's house along the Atlantic coast in the 1880s. Left and below: Kitchen and bedroom of the old Point Loma lighthouse (1855), San Diego, refurnished to look as it did around 1885, six years before it was taken out of service.

Above: Landing supplies in 1904 at Fisherman's Cove for the keepers of the Farallon Island light station off the California coast at San Francisco. Right: More modern keepers — Coast Guardsmen with their mascot at the Anacapa Island light station (1923) off Ventura, Calif.

children. In the more isolated stations, such as on the islands off the coast of Maine, the keeper could regularly go ashore to pick up mail and supplies, but the wives had few such opportunities for social intercourse and the children sometimes had to miss school for long periods of time. Connie Small warmly recalls her life, but in her book *The Lighthouse Keeper's Wife* she writes of the vicissitudes of living at the more isolated stations and what had to be done to accommodate them.

The keepers tried to overcome these disadvantages and more often than not succeeded. They tried to swap assignments with other keepers to be closer to schools, or they boarded their school-age children — and sometimes the whole family — in town so that they could get an education. Teachers occasionally were brought to a station if there were enough students. Often the keepers had to make that extra exertion to get their children to school. The keeper of a Kennebec River light in Maine rowed his children across the river each morning, and Kate Walker, keeper of the Robbins Reef light (1883) off

Staten Island, transported her children each morning more than a mile to the shore in the late 1800s so that they could attend school.

Their families were important to the keepers, and perhaps the adversities they faced drew them together. On more than one occasion family members had to fill in for the keeper. The story of Abbie Burgess, who several times tended the light at Matinicus Rock (1857) off Rockland, Maine, while her father was stranded by storms, is legend, as is that of the 15-year-old boy who filled in for his father at the lonely Saddleback Ledge light (1839) off Vinalhaven, Maine (see both entries). At one-keeper light stations, wives often had to take on assistant keeper duties. The Lighthouse Board was not above taking advantage of a family in this way.

Many lighthouse families kept gardens for fresh vegetables and a cow for fresh milk; some keepers hunted ducks and other wildlife; and certainly most had access to an abundance of seafood. Life at a light station could have its up side.

Such a life for keepers and their families often was difficult, but for the most part they did not seem to mind. The keeper was the element that made the lighthouse system work, and after the 1850s it worked well because it had a corps of knowledgeable and dedicated keepers.

Keeper returning with provisions to the Egg Rock light off the coast of Maine after a five-day monthly leave.

ADMINISTRATION OF LIGHTHOUSES

When Congress in 1789 designated the Treasury Department to administer the newly centralized American lighthouse system, Secretary of the Treasury Alexander Hamilton took direct responsibility for lighthouses, but in 1792 he delegated his authority to the commissioner of revenue. A decade later Secretary Albert Gallatin took back the administration of lighthouses until 1813, the year he resigned; lighthouses then returned to the office of the commissioner of revenue until 1820, then they became the responsibility of the fifth auditor of the Treasury, one of the principal bookkeepers of the federal government.

One person occupied that office for the next 32 years. Stephen Pleasonton had no experience in maritime matters and was not noted as exceptionally intelligent, but he did have a reputation as being zealous in protecting the public dollar. As far as lighthouses are concerned, he did not spend the public dollar well, for although during his 32-year administration the number of navigational aids grew, the United States's lighthouses often were poorly constructed and had an inferior reputation; many ship masters and maritime businesses complained of the poor quality of the lights on light vessels and lighthouses. From time to time Congress expressed concern and launched an investigation. The reports that came back painted a picture of a lighthouse system that was considerably less than first class. But for 32 years Pleasonton fended off these attacks.

Although Pleasonton did not know much about lighthouses, he developed a relationship with Winslow Lewis, a retired ship captain who had a claim to such knowledge. Lewis was able to obtain most of the contracts for installing the lighting systems in lighthouses and more than a few contracts to construct light stations. Lewis's nephew, I. W. P. Lewis, a severe critic of his uncle and Pleasonton, alleged that Pleasonton had Winslow Lewis prepare the specifications for new lighthouses and then let him bid on the contracts.

The lighthouse system grew enormously during Pleasonton's administration. When he took over in 1820, there were 55 lighthouses. By 1838 the country had 204 lighthouses and 28 light vessels. Four years later the number grew to 256 lighthouses, 30 vessels, 35 beacons and nearly 1,000 buoys. By 1852 there were 331 lighthouses and 42 lightships.

The safety of mariners was not Pleasonton's highest consideration: economy was. Pleasonton also selected sites for lighthouses by appointing a local committee of pilots and mariners that often chose sites without regard for existing adjacent lighthouses or knowledge of the adequacy of the spot as a foundation for a light tower. Congress in 1847 did take away from him the construction of six lighthouses, turning them over to the Corps of Engineers. Finally, in 1851 Congress directed the secretary of the Treasury to establish a board to investigate the Lighthouse Service.

The board conscientiously approached its task and looked into all aspects of the administration, operation and condition of aids to navigation. In all the corners of the lighthouse establishment, the board found little to admire. It noted that the number of lighthouses had increased immensely during the 32-year administration of the fifth auditor, commending him for his zeal and faithfulness and "the spirit of economy which he has shown." The remaining 751 printed pages of the report contained material critical of the condition of the nation's lighthouses.

The board concluded that the administration of aids to navigation should be completely revamped and recommended that a lighthouse board be formed to manage them. The board also urged the adoption of the Fresnel lens. Congress quickly acted and on October 9, 1852, it created the nine-member Lighthouse Board. Congress had already gone on record in the appropriation act of 1851 as favoring Fresnel lenses.

For the next 58 years the Lighthouse Board administered aids to navigation, and credit has to go to its members for bringing order to the Lighthouse Service and raising it to the level of one of the finest in the world. One of the first steps the board took was to begin installing Fresnel lenses in all the new and existing

Top: Lamp shop work force in 1890 at the Staten Island depot, established by the Lighthouse Board to serve as the improved, central supply source for the lighthouse system. Above: Wharves at the Staten Island depot in 1912, with three lightships tied up.

lighthouses. By the time of the Civil War, the task was virtually completed.

To administer aids to navigation, the board created 12 districts, the first starting at the St. Croix River on Maine's northern border and the 12th embracing the Pacific coast. An inspector was appointed for each district, but within a few years the workload had become so heavy that an engineer was assigned to each district and the duties were divided between the two positions, with the engineer having repair and construction responsibilities and the inspector attending to administrative, personnel and inspection duties. A central supply depot on Staten Island was also set up, but in time each district developed its own depot, supplied from Staten Island, which received and tested the oil used in the lamps to see that it was of good quality.

The board began issuing annual *Light Lists* with information such as the location, description and type of light for each lighthouse. It also produced notices to mariners telling about newly lighted lighthouses. The fifth auditor had issued lists of lights, but they came out infrequently and presented lights chronologically, so that a navigator had to know when a lighthouse was erected to find its listing quickly. The board's listing was geographical. Today's *Light Lists* issued by the Coast Guard essentially follow the same system devised by the Lighthouse Board.

The board put its emphasis on providing an adequate navigational aid system. In addition to supplying the infinitely better Fresnel lens, it also increased the height of the towers so that the light would overcome a larger arc of the earth, thus permitting navigators to see the light sooner. Spares of everything were kept on hand. If a lightship had to leave its station for repairs, a relief vessel immediately replaced it. The board experimented with new fuels, developed better lamps and conducted tests on fog signals to understand how sound traveled over water. Joseph Henry, first secretary of the Smithsonian Institution, was a member of the board and chaired its Committee on Experiments. Most important, the board hired competent keepers, trained them and supplied written instructions on the duties of the light keeper.

The Lighthouse Board set the United States on the road to being a leader in navigational aids and raised its reputation from one of the worst to that of one of the best in the world. Although the board accomplished so much, it nevertheless in time became too cumbersome an administrative unit to manage navigational aids effectively.

In 1910 Congress reorganized the lighthouse system into the Bureau of Lighthouses with one person at its head. The first commissioner to head the new Bureau of Lighthouses was George Putnam, an engineer who retained this position for all but the last four years of the life of the bureau. The reorganization also changed lighthouse management from military to civilian, but Putnam took advantage of congressional authorization and had a Corps of Engineers officer assigned to each district to be responsible for repairs and new construction.

In 1910 the lighthouse system numbered 11,713 aids of all types, including approximately 1,200 lighthouses and 54 light vessels. In three years the total grew to 12,824, of which 1,462 were lights above the status of river post lights, 51 were lightships, more than 7,000 were buoys and 46 were tenders. Not only had Putnam inherited a growing organization, he also received a stable one with a large number of career employees, from whom he selected his district superintendents.

During Putnam's 25 years as commissioner, the Lighthouse Service continued to grow. By 1924 it was the largest such system in the world. By the time he retired in 1935 the total number of all types of aids to navigation had more than doubled from 1910. At the same time personnel decreased 20 percent, primarily because of technological advances such as the electrification of lighthouses, which required fewer people, and because of the increased automation of lights. Putnam presided over the growing use of electricity for buoys and fog signals and the introduction of the radio beacon, which served ship navigators as well as aviators and was his proudest achievement. He also implemented a retirement system for field employees.

Although America's lighthouse system over the years has come to be called the Lighthouse Service, no agency by this name has ever existed. The term "Lighthouse Service" had official status only during the life of the Bureau of Lighthouses. The name was not mentioned in the legislation establishing the bureau, but it soon began using this term for its employee newsletter, first issued in 1912. While this name came on the scene rather late, the tendency has been to apply it also to other periods of time, mainly because of its convenience in writing. There seems to have been no sense of cohesiveness among those who either managed or operated lighthouses before the advent of the Lighthouse Board in 1852, and, consequently, no comprehensive descriptive phrase for the lighthouse system came into use. The Lighthouse Board referred to itself as the U.S. Lighthouse Establishment, and on many aids to navigation produced by the board, such as fog bells, the letters U.S.L.H.E. will be found.

Sometimes the Lighthouse Service and the U.S. Life Saving Service get confused in the popular mind, and some people think that they are one and the same. Actually, they were distinct and rarely worked together; they did not come under the same organizational umbrella until 1939, when the lighthouse system became part of the Coast Guard. By this time the Life Saving Service, which was melded with the Revenue Cutter Service to form the Coast Guard in 1915, had become nonexistent as an entity.

In the Presidential Reorganization Act of 1939, aids to navigation were moved from their independent position to the Coast Guard. The employees of the Lighthouse Service were given the choice to remain in their civilian

Modern-day amenities at America's first light station, Boston Harbor, which was one of the last to be automated.

Coast Guard officials decommissioning the *Nantucket* lightship in 1984, the last to be retired.

status or convert to a military position at no loss in pay. About half chose each option.

Unquestionably, economies and increased navigational efficiency have been realized from the merger into the Coast Guard. Like its predecessors, the Coast Guard has taken advantage of advancing technology and applied it to navigational aids. It has introduced SHORAN (short-range navigation) and LORAN (long-range navigation) and has replaced all the lightships with either a "Texas tower"–type of structure or a large sea buoy. In recent years it has introduced a plastic lens, based on the Fresnel design but smaller, that is much less expensive but just as effective as the old lights and requires much less attention than earlier automated lights. Under the Coast Guard, the United States still ranks in the forefront of nations providing reliable, first-rate aid to the mariner.

FURTHER READING

A large number of books have been written about lighthouses, and these vary in quality and type. Two older ones are *Lighthouses and Lightships of the United States* (1917; 1933, Houghton Mifflin) and *Sentinels of the Coasts: The Log of a Lighthouse Engineer* (1937, W. W. Norton). Both are by George R. Putnam, longtime commissioner of the Bureau of Lighthouses, and are interesting and readable. F. A. Talbot's *Lightships and Lighthouses* (1913, J. B. Lippincott) is a world overview of lighthouses in the early part of this century. A superb survey is *The World's Lighthouses Before 1820* (1959, Oxford University Press) by David Alan Stevenson, a descendant of a famous Scottish family of lighthouse engineers. Edward Snow wrote a number of books on lighthouses. His *Famous Lighthouses of America* (1955, Dodd Mead) stands out among them. *America's Lighthouses: An Illustrated History* (1972, Stephen Greene Press; 1988, Dover Publications) by F. Ross Holland, Jr., is an overview of the history of lighthouses and lightships of the United States.

A number of good regional publications on lighthouses have been produced in recent years. One notable both for the writing and the photographs is Charles K. Hyde's *The Northern Lights: Lighthouses of the Upper Great Lakes* (1986, Two Peninsula Press). Another is James Gibbs's *Lighthouses of the Pacific* (1986, Schiffer Publishing), which covers the West Coast, Hawaii and Alaska. Robert de Gast's *Lighthouses of the Chesapeake* (1973, Johns Hopkins University Press), Love Dean's *Reef Lights: Seaswept Lighthouses of the Florida Keys* (1982, Historic Key West Preservation Board), and David L. Cipra's *Lighthouses and Lightships of the Northern Gulf of Mexico* (1976, U.S. Coast Guard) should be mentioned, along with David Stick's *North Carolina Lighthouses* (1980, North Carolina Department of Cultural Resources).

In the last few years a number of good histories of individual lighthouses have been published, such as Frank Perry's *The History of Pigeon Point Lighthouse* (1986) and Dennis L. Noble and T. Michael O'Brien's *Sentinels of the Rocks: From "Graveyard Coast" to National Seashore* (1979, Northern Michigan University Press). Memoirs of those who lived in lighthouses also are beginning to appear. Constance Small's *The Lighthouse Keeper's Wife* (1986, University of Maine), *Three Beams of Light* by Norma Engel (1986, Tecolote Publications) and *Living at a Lighthouse: Oral Histories from the Great Lakes* (1987, Great Lakes Lighthouse Keepers Association) are three of several that stand out.

Lightships have not been forgotten either. Willard Flint's *Lightships of the United States Government* (1989, U.S. Coast Guard) documents the history of each of the lightships that has served this country since 1820. Frederic L. Thompson's *The Lightships of Cape Cod* (1983, Congress Square Press) is a history of lightship stations around Cape Cod and the vessels that served there. (See also the Bibliography for additional titles.)

KEEPING THE LIGHTS

One could say with a considerable degree of accuracy that lighthouses today have become dinosaurs — not because the need for lights along our shores is gone, but because the need for the traditional light tower, built to support an illuminating apparatus operated daily by a light keeper, has changed. A good coastal light no longer has to come from a large and heavy Fresnel lens. Modern lights are just as powerful, but they are much smaller and lighter and are weatherproof and, consequently, require a small, simple and inexpensive platform, such as a steel skeleton tower or just a pole. Modern technology has not only dramatically reduced the size of the lights, it has also allowed them to operate without human attention for months at a time. Moreover, in the last 60 years the importance of lights has slowly declined, mainly because of the advent of radio and other electronic means of navigation. The introduction of the radio beacon in 1921 permitted a light vessel or light station to reach out several hundred miles to a passing ship. The station sent out an identification signal in Morse code, and ships equipped with a radio finder could determine the direction of the source of the signal. Later, radar permitted navigators to see the shore on a screen before it was sighted visually. Radar can extend about 20 miles to define a shoreline. Most important, radio beacons and radar gave navigators tools to determine their position when fog was too thick to see even the brightest light.

These technological advances have eliminated the need for traditional light stations and light towers, permitting the Coast Guard to eliminate personnel and decrease maintenance. As of 1989–90, all light stations under the Coast Guard's command were due to be automated. Lighthouses and fog signals now are of most benefit to operators of fishing boats and other small craft, as larger vessels are usually equipped with modern electronic accoutrements. In that sense, the lighthouse as we have known it for 250 years is a dinosaur.

Approximately 750 to 800 traditional lighthouses remain today, fewer than 500 of which are used by the Coast Guard. A preliminary survey of 750 lighthouses conducted by the National Park Service in early 1989 found that a third date from the 1876–1925 period, with somewhat fewer from 1826–75; only three percent were built before 1825. The five states with the most old towers were Michigan, New York, Maine, Massachusetts and California, with 90 to 40 each, followed by Florida, Wisconsin, Washington, Ohio, Maryland, Rhode Island and Hawaii, with between 40 and 20 each. About 400 of all the surviving lights were either listed in the National Register of Historic Places individually or as part of a historic district or were eligible for listing. About five percent, or 38 lighthouses, are part of National Park Service sites; a similar number are in state parks. Some

Opposite: Key West, Fla., light (1846) restored and reopened in 1989. Top: Lighthouse in poor condition in the late 1880s. Above: Some of the proud preservationists who helped revive the Key West landmark.

Nauset Beach lighthouse (1877), moved from Chatham to North Eastham, Mass., and now within the boundaries of the National Park Service's Cape Cod National Seashore. The site is one of dozens of lighthouses in national, state and local parks.

27 lightships built between 1904 and 1952 are still afloat, about a dozen converted into museums open to visitors, with five vessels located outside the United States. As more surveys and research are done by groups such as the state historic preservation offices, new figures can be added to round out what we know about these surviving sites. For example, new nominations of historic lighthouses to the National Register of Historic Places are being made as states and the Coast Guard complete their research.

SURPLUS LIGHTHOUSES

As light stations in the past became obsolete or generally surplus to the federal government's needs, they usually wound up in private hands or under the control of another government agency. Retired light stations frequently were sold at public auction to private buyers. A number of lighthouses in New England, the Great Lakes and the Gulf Coast areas have been privately owned for many years, some since the 19th century. This means of disposal began to decline in the 1930s, when national, state and local governments stepped up development of seashore parks. The then-emerging Cape Hatteras National Seashore, for example, obtained the surplus Cape Hatteras light station (1870) in 1936 and later received the one at Bodie Island (1872), except for the tower, which remained in service. With the growth in parks, fewer and fewer lighthouses ended up on the government's surplus list, because national, state and local government agen-

cies — in that order — had first call on surplus federal property. Today, in its seashore parks, the National Park Service has many of these former light stations; the Apostle Islands National Lakeshore in Wisconsin acquired six light stations when it was established in 1970. The U.S. Forest Service has a number of lighthouses in its forests, such as the Hiawatha National Forest in Michigan with three. The U.S. Fish and Wildlife Service has acquired lighthouses where some of its refuges have been created. States, counties and towns have established historical and recreational parks around surplus lighthouses and ancillary light station structures. New Jersey, for one, has three major lighthouses along its coast that are centerpieces of state parks. New England and the Great Lakes states also have been particularly active in this direction.

Increasingly, local historical groups have begun to lease or license lighthouses by entering into agreements with government agencies, under which they maintain and interpret the structures to the public. Some towns also have restored old lighthouses and converted them for civic and tourism uses. Universities and colleges have moved into light stations and adapted the buildings to their purposes, such as for a field laboratory. Sometimes local nonprofit groups are formed to make a bed-and-breakfast inn out of an old light station. American Youth Hostels has leased several former light stations and made them into low-cost accommodations for those traveling on a limited budget. These are just a few examples of the adaptive uses of former light stations.

East Brother Island light station (1874), Richmond, Calif., in the San Francisco Bay Area. Now converted into a sought-after bed-and-breakfast inn, the Stick Style structure received an award from the National Trust for its rehabilitation.

THE NEW KEEPERS

Although our old lighthouses have been supplanted by advancing technology, they still have a role to play in our lives. Lighthouses are historic structures — physical remains that remind us of the past and a way of life and also help us understand both better. Lighthouses enjoy a special place in our affections, and because they are historic there is much interest in preserving them. Today, a great deal of money and effort are going into the preservation of lighthouses, and many are being saved.

Those sites not receiving adequate care are ones in remote areas and offshore lights that are difficult to reach. Being off shore, however, does not preclude a lighthouse from receiving attention, for any number of lighthouses on distant islands in the Great Lakes, on ledges off the Rhode Island and Connecticut shores, and on rock islands along the Maine coast have attracted the interest of lighthouse enthusiasts. Sakonnet light (1884) on a ledge off Rhode Island at the mouth of the Sakonnet River will not receive any visitors, but local people came to have a deep affection for the light tower and raised the funds necessary to rehabilitate it. While remoteness does

Isolated Sakonnet light (1884) in Rhode Island, befriended by local preservationists.

not necessarily mean that a lighthouse cannot be saved, its chances decline with its distance off shore. No one has come forward yet with a proposal to save one of the pile reef lighthouses off the Florida coast or one of the caisson lighthouses in the Chesapeake Bay. Many lighthouses also are fighting losing battles with nature and may be beyond even the most ardent preservationists' skills (see the Epilogue).

Nevertheless, many lighthouses and their attendant structures are being saved today. And they are being preserved by diverse groups for equally diverse reasons.

The Coast Guard maintains those stations that have been automated — all, as of 1989–90 — but whose structures are still being used for housing or other official activities. The Coast Guard tries to care for its old lighthouses that still have active, although automated, lights. The needs in this direction are large and the funds available are small, because of the many missions of the Coast Guard and a less-than-opulent budget with which to accomplish them. Consequently, the Coast Guard, from time to time, receives criticism for its stewardship of lighthouses. In response to this concern, the Coast Guard in recent years has stepped up its preservation and maintenance efforts for lighthouses.

In terms of numbers, the Coast Guard still has responsibility for most of the country's lighthouses. As for old lighthouses that have been replaced by steel skeleton towers or ancillary structures that are not being used at an unstaffed light station, the Coast Guard has begun to lease them or transfer them outright to organizations and other government agencies. The vast bulk of these leased structures are being maintained by local historical groups; thus, the movement to keep our lighthouses is, in great part, a grass-roots effort.

The preservation of lighthouses and the human stories they embody has been a rising tide in this country for a long time. In the last decade or so, interest has accelerated dramatically, with the result that when a light station has been automated, a local historical group usually comes forward or is formed to obtain or lease the available structures to preserve them. Often a maritime museum is established, sometimes to convey the story of the particular lighthouse or, more often than not, to interpret the lighthouse and local maritime history.

The people who engage in these preservation efforts are a special breed. For the most part, they do not come from the general historic preservation community but, rather, have been drawn to preservation because of their attraction to lighthouses. They are dedicated and give much of their time to restore the structures and to present their story to the public. They make whatever money they can raise for the repairs go a long way, because the funds usually are spent only on materials. They often do the actual work themselves. Because of their dedicated efforts, these groups have not only preserved light stations that may have been left to molder, but they also have attracted artifacts and documents related to their lighthouses that probably would have been lost in

Above: St. Helena Island, Mich., light tower (1874) and dwelling about 1925. Right: View of the station in 1986, after it had been abandoned and left to decay. Note that its lantern was removed. Below: Workers repairing the roof of the dwelling in 1988, part of the restoration project spearheaded by the Great Lakes Lighthouse Keepers Association.

another generation or two. Although these preservationists have worked largely with the Coast Guard, individual groups have entered into agreements with other government agencies — on the state, local and national levels — to maintain and interpret light stations in their domain.

In addition to groups that rise up to save individual sites, three major lighthouse preservation groups, one regional and two national, have been formed. Each serves a useful purpose and does not duplicate the activities of the others.

The Great Lakes Lighthouse Keepers Association focuses its attention on the lighthouses of the Great Lakes. Although the association has devoted some of its energies to restoring light stations such as the 1873 light on St. Helena Island, Mich., it primarily acts as a coordinating organization, keeping its members informed of the activities of local lighthouse preservation groups, changes in the status of lighthouses, and new lighthouse books and other sales items. It conducts oral history programs, organizes an annual meeting and conferences on each of the Great Lakes, conducts an annual cruise and publishes a newsletter and books.

The U.S. Lighthouse Society is based in San Francisco but has a national focus. A nonprofit historical and educational organization, it encourages the preservation of old light stations and lightships and conducts regional tours of lighthouses about twice a year. It has completed the restoration of a lightship, the *WAL-605,* to be moored in the Bay Area. Its quarterly magazine, *The Keeper's Log,* usually carries articles on the history of lighthouses, biographies of key figures, excerpts from the old *Lighthouse Service Bulletin,* reports of lighthouse "inspectors" who relate news from their regions, book reviews and information on lighthouse-related products. The society also maintains a research library and photographic archives.

The Lighthouse Preservation Society, located in Rock-

Lightship WAL-605, painted with its last designation as a relief vessel for the West Coast. The lightship was restored by the U.S. Lighthouse Society to be opened for visitation.

Ten Pound Island light (1881), Gloucester, Mass. The conical tower has been relighted as a result of efforts by the city and preservationists including the Lighthouse Preservation Society.

port, Mass., has a national concern, but limits its activities to the preservation of lighthouses, technical assistance to local lighthouse preservation groups and government policy issues related to lighthouses. It persuaded Congress to create the $1-million annual Bicentennial Lighthouse Fund to spur the preservation of historic lighthouses in 1988–90. The Lighthouse Preservation Society is also working with government agencies to raise the profile of lighthouses and to make them more accessible to the public. Its quarterly newsletter is devoted to its activities on the national scene and the preservation of lighthouses in which it has been actively involved.

Many of the lighthouses preserved by local historical societies have small museums with lighthouse artifacts ranging from personal equipment of keepers to lenses. The quality of these museums and the depth of their collections are varied. Some lighthouses and keepers' quarters have been refurnished as they would have been during the stations' active years to give a picture of the life of the keepers and their families.

The best museum dealing with aids to navigation is the one established by Ken Black in Rockland, Maine. A retired Coast Guardsman who has had a longtime interest in lighthouse artifacts, he has assembled a good collection of lenses, fog signals and other items related to navigational aids. The two-story former dwelling, known as the Shore Village Museum, is literally crammed with relics. Black keeps track of activities related to lighthouses and occasionally issues newsletters that include notices of lighthouse books.

The Coast Guard Training School in Yorktown, Va., has a good collection of Fresnel lenses and is continuing to collect them, although it is not yet open to the public. Just outside the museum is a large display of variously colored and sized modern plastic lenses used for automating lighthouses, along with other aids to navigation. The Coast Guard Academy in New London, Conn., has a

Left: Ceremony dedicating and reopening the Yaquina Bay lighthouse (1871), Newport, Ore., after its 1976 restoration by the state. In 1946 residents opposed plans by the highway department to demolish it. Below: Rose Island light (1869), Newport, R.I., under restoration. The Rose Island Lighthouse Foundation raised money and led the effort to rehabilitate the abandoned surplus structure.

museum that includes many lighthouse items. The Coast Guard Museum Northwest in Seattle also contains objects related to lighthouses.

In Jacksonville Beach, Fla., Bill Trotter, an artist, has opened the American Lighthouse Museum, which contains lighthouse artifacts and memorabilia as well as paintings and models of lighthouses.

INCREASING VIGILANCE

The increasing public interest in lighthouses has forged greater sensitivity to these landmarks and their companions — the dwellings, oil houses, fog signals and other station buildings. In the past, keepers' houses have been demolished with little expression of concern from the public. But that condition is changing. Two recent incidents unexpectedly raised the wrath of the public. The first was the razing of the Deer Island lighthouse (1890) near Boston. The Coast Guard wanted to remove this brown conical tower on a caisson and replace it with a low-maintenance plastic pole light. As required by the National Historic Preservation Act of 1966 because the lighthouse was in the National Register of Historic Places, the Coast Guard consulted with the state historic preservation office. That office agreed with the request of the Coast Guard, which then demolished the old lighthouse. On the caisson, it erected a slim white pole topped by the new light. The Friends of Boston Harbor Islands and the boaters of the area were indignant that the historic lighthouse was torn down and derisively referred to the new light as the Tampon. The loss of the Deer Island light brought to the surface the hidden interest in preserving lighthouses. These galvanized citizens are providing the energy and concern that will bring public attention to other lights such as the Boston Harbor lighthouse (1783). Following its 1989 automation, it may become part of Boston Harbor State Park; a feasibility study has been undertaken to investigate appropriate management and use of this historic station.

In Maryland the same degree of wrath was expressed by a group of lighthouse admirers when the city of Baltimore, with the permission of the Coast Guard and the state historic preservation office, moved the Seven Foot Knoll screwpile lighthouse (1855) from its site in the Chesapeake Bay to the city's Inner Harbor. When the move was first proposed, local fishers and boaters objected to having the lighthouse taken away, saying that they needed such a large object as a daymark. The state and others listened to the concerns, but in the end rejected them and gave permission for the relocation to Baltimore for use as a museum. When the move took place, it opened old wounds and exposed a broader latent concern for old lighthouses. Delegate Ray Huff of Annapolis received many complaints from his constituents and others. He thus introduced in the Maryland

Seven Foot Knoll light (1855), a screwpile structure moved from the Chesapeake Bay to Baltimore for use as a museum despite protests from area mariners.

legislature a bill to form a commission to study the problem and make recommendations for preserving the lighthouses remaining in and around the bay. The bill generated even more lighthouse enthusiasts. With broad support, it passed both houses of the legislature in April 1989, several months earlier than Delegate Huff had anticipated, and was signed by Gov. William Donald Schaefer on May 25, 1989.

Throughout the history of the lighthouse system, lighthouses have been moved to escape erosion and other threats, and lighthouses that have been destroyed have been rebuilt. But these steps were taken to provide an active aid to navigation. This pattern was changed when Congress recently appropriated money to reconstruct the Great Point lighthouse on Nantucket, Mass. The original 1818 tower, successor to a 1784 light, had succumbed to erosion. The general preservation practice is to eschew reconstructions because so many deserving original historic structures are in need of preservation. Reconstructions are not historic structures — at best, they are memorials of past structures.

NAVIGATING PRESERVATION SHOALS

Certainly, those who start out to save a lighthouse today should have a somewhat easier time than their predecessors. The course has been sailed many times, and now "lighthouses" of information to show the way are available, whereas they were not even in existence less than 10 years ago. Primary sources of information are the three major lighthouse preservation organizations: the Great Lakes Lighthouse Keepers Association, the U.S. Lighthouse Society and the Lighthouse Preservation Society (see Information Sources). Each can give advice on initial steps to take and people to contact.

Nantucket's Great Point light (1818), before its loss to erosion in 1984 and its reconstruction in 1987.

Right and center: Deteriorated Round Island light (1895) near St. Ignace, Mich., in the Straits of Mackinac. Discontinued in 1947 and turned over to the U.S. Forest Service in 1958, the lighthouse seriously decayed until preservationists pressed for attention for this National Register site. Below: Original engineering drawings of the lighthouse, showing how it looked when built.

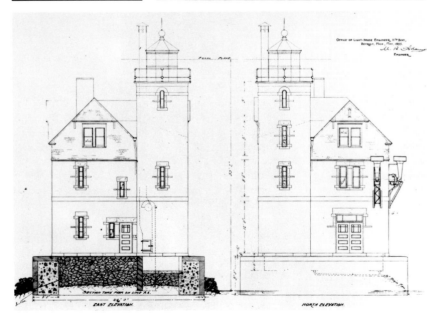

Another good source of information is your state historic preservation office (a list of these offices is available from the National Conference of State Historic Preservation Officers; see Information Sources). Appointed to carry out the state-federal preservation responsibilities under the National Historic Preservation Act of 1966, state preservation offices implement activities such as conducting surveys of historic resources, preparing statewide preservation plans, nominating properties to the National Register of Historic Places, reviewing federal projects for their effects on landmarks, administering properties and providing public programs.

An excellent publication for insights into the preservation, acquisition, management and use of lighthouse properties has been issued by the Island Institute of Maine. Compiled and edited by Deborah Davis, this handbook is entitled *Keeping the Light: A Handbook for Adaptive Re-Use of Island Lighthouse Stations*. Its infor-

Print of the Round Island light sold to raise preservation funds. Preservationists included the Friends of the Round Island Lighthouse and the Mackinac Island Historical Society, which worked with the Forest Service to restore the light.

mation has application to all light stations, not just those on islands or in Maine.

As outlined by *Keeping the Light* and other preservation sources, a number of key facts and steps should be kept in mind by anyone interested in becoming involved in lighthouse preservation:

■ *National Register of Historic Places.* Federal agencies such as the Coast Guard are required by law to nominate historic properties under their jurisdiction to the National Register of Historic Places, which is maintained by the U.S. Department of the Interior as the official list of the nation's historic sites worth preserving (now numbering 50,000). Properties listed in or eligible for the National Register receive certain protections from federal actions that might adversely affect them, including advance review of such plans by the Advisory Council on Historic Preservation.

To ensure that all historic lighthouses that should be in the National Register are nominated, many state historic preservation offices and the Coast Guard have recently increased efforts to survey and nominate them. Several states such as Massachusetts and Connecticut have submitted "thematic" nominations encompassing all their eligible historic light stations. Local groups may be able to further such efforts by identifying appropriate properties and assisting with research.

■ *Disposition of lighthouses.* The Coast Guard no longer sells surplus lighthouses to private citizens, but it may lease all or part of an unused light station, such as the keeper's cottage, to a suitable tenant that will open the site to public visitation. It first seeks federal, state or local government agencies, in that order, as lessees. Next in line are nonprofit organizations that propose an appropriate use, such as a museum, and that appear financially and otherwise capable of maintaining the property. Interested agencies or groups should contact the appropriate Coast Guard district office, a list of which is available from Coast Guard headquarters (see Information Sources). For those who wish to become involved with lighthouses owned by other agencies, it is best to start with the local administrator, such as the manager of a state park in which the lighthouse is located.

■ *Leasing versus licensing.* While the Coast Guard prefers to license the use of its surplus lighthouse properties, it has on occasion leased the properties outright. Under such leases, it makes the property habitable and asks a fair market rent. Under license arrangements, which may be for up to 30 years, occupants do not pay rent and may exchange their services for the use of the lighthouse. The Coast Guard in such a case does not rehabilitate or maintain the site.

■ *Authorized uses.* Although privately owned light stations have been converted to commercial uses such as bed-and-breakfast inns, the Coast Guard's current policy is not to license its lighthouses for profit-making uses. Museums and related activities may charge admission fees, but income must be used only to maintain the property. It is possible that more commercial leases, authorized under federal preservation law, may be undertaken in the future as more lighthouses need caretakers.

■ *Financial considerations.* Potential licensees should develop financial plans for rehabilitating, maintaining and interpreting a desired lighthouse. Their ability to carry out such a preservation project, using cash, volunteer efforts or a combination of these, is a crucial determinant in the Coast Guard's award of licensing agreements.

■ *Public access.* As federal property, the Coast Guard's light stations must be opened for public access under lease and license agreements. The exception would be those facilities, such as towers, still being used as active aids to navigation.

■ *Logistics.* In developing a plan to reuse a lighthouse, a number of logistical problems must be addressed because of the special nature of light stations — often located in isolated, maritime environments that may still house working navigational aids. Among these considerations are access itself, by water or difficult terrain; power supply to unused structures; water supply; wastewater and sewage treatment; sound insulation from working fog signals; and security.

■ *Liability.* Licensees must assume full liability for damage to the property from fire, theft, vandalism and other causes as well as for personal injury on the site.

■ *Rehabilitation and maintenance.* Rehabilitation work carried out on historic lighthouses listed in or eligible for the National Register should follow federal rehabilitation requirements. The Secretary of the Interior's Standards provide 10 key preservation principles and are supplemented with detailed guidelines for various levels of work, such as stabilization, rehabilitation and restoration. These and other generally followed preservation standards also call for protecting the entire complement of structures that may be found at a light station.

To help with some of the most pressing problems of identifying endangered lighthouses and stabilizing unused structures, Congress launched a multiyear Bicentennial Lighthouse Fund beginning in 1988, timed for the 1989 bicentennial of the federal government's administration of lighthouses. Developed under the leadership of Sens. George J. Mitchell of Maine and Donald W. Riegle, Jr., of Michigan, the fund provided $1 million a year for the states to use principally in making needed repairs to selected properties but also to conduct surveys of lighthouses not yet nominated to state and national landmarks registers. Awarded by the National Park Service through the state historic preservation offices, individual grants were matched by states and cities as well as private groups and other donors—and volunteers providing hands-on rehabilitation work.

The rising tide of interest represented by all these activities, by preservationists as well as the general public, shows that people feel comfortable with these old beacons and want to keep them around for at least another 200 years.

GUIDE TO THE GUIDE

T wo criteria initially guided the selection of the lighthouses to be included in this book: first, that the sites be listed in or eligible for the National Register of Historic Places and, second, that they be reasonably accessible to the public. Almost all the lighthouses and lightships in the National Register — the official inventory of America's most historic places—are here, but some other interesting and noteworthy examples have been added as well; many states are still in the process of surveying and nominating their deserving lighthouses to the National Register.

In the case of the second criterion, how could one develop a list of great American lighthouses and not include such offshore — but generally inaccessible — lights as Tillamook Rock in Oregon, a reef light or two along the Florida coast and a few of the remote lighthouses in Alaska? Some light stations also are still being used as quarters by Coast Guard personnel despite the planned automation of all lights in 1989–90, and these stations are closed to visitation. While access to such sites and other active towers may be limited or prohibited, some of these lighthouses are of such significance as to require inclusion in the book in any case; visitors still may be able to get close enough to permit a reasonably good view of the lighthouse. Because many of the sites presented here are still working lighthouses and others are open on limited schedules, travelers should check in advance about visiting hours. The grounds of some of the lighthouses are open on a less restricted basis, so the tower and other station buildings may be seen even if visitors cannot always go inside. And don't forget a last possible route, the one by which lighthouses and light vessels were originally meant to be seen: by water, as long as the boating is safe.

The lighthouse and lightship entries in the following guide section are organized into the six regions that have lights along their coasts and rivers. Within each region, the states, towns and entries are presented alphabetically. Locations indicate the nearest named city, town or vicinity; major islands and island groups are listed under their own names, while lesser-known points generally appear under the closest town for visiting, viewing or embarking to offshore sites. Because many of the lighthouses are in remote areas or small towns outside larger metropolitan areas, travelers first may want to review the index to find the lighthouses and lightships nearest the more well-known cities they plan to visit. One problem arises in preparing a guide to sites such as lightships, which—unlike most buildings—are movable. The lightship locations presented here are their moorings as we went to press; some of the vessels are seeking permanent berths, and others may be relocated in the future; thus, visitors should check beforehand.

Each entry highlights key details at the left or right. First to appear is the name or names by which the site has been known, with any secondary name in parentheses. For the sake of simplicity, each site name is given as "lighthouse" even though it may be known, for example, as "light station;" the few multiple and range lights are so indicated. Below the name are the more specific location and directions. The next item in some entries is the designer or builder; for most of the sites, this information has been lost, so far, to history. The last line shows the year in which the light station and, in many cases, succeeding towers went into service; each successive date indicates a new lighthouse on the site, but not repairs, relocations or increases in height.

Certain standard information in the entries themselves warrants explanation. The height of a light tower is measured from the ground to the top of the ventilator ball on the lantern. The height of the light itself is measured from mean high water to the focal plane of the light. Figures given for these heights are taken from modern *Light Lists*, published by the U.S. Coast Guard, if the tower is still standing. Differences often occur between these figures and those reported in 19th-century *Light Lists*. Throughout the text the term "light" is sometimes used interchangeably with the word "lighthouse," following the popular, abbreviated style. In most instances, a statement that a light has been moved usually means that a new site was selected for a new tower or lighting mechanism; of course, as the entries explain, in a few cases an existing tower or lantern actually was physically moved to a new location, sometimes to another light station some distance away. At the end of an entry's text, "NR" or "NR district" indicates that the site or its adjacent district is listed in the National Register individually or as part of a historic district; several sites are National Historic Landmarks, noted as "NHL," the highest level of national significance. The letters "ASCE" refer to a National Historic Civil Engineering Landmark of the American Society of Civil Engineers.

At the end of each entry, the bracketed information notes the ownership of the site. Some light stations have two owners. For example, the tower at the Bodie Island lighthouse in the Cape Hatteras National Seashore is owned by the Coast Guard, but the grounds and ancillary structures are owned by the National Park Service. Entries for sites leased or licensed by a separate organization note this fact, although for simplicity only the generic term "leased by" is used. (The Keeping the Lights chapter explains the differences between Coast Guard leases and licenses.)

May this book be your own beacon for enjoying America's great lighthouses.

NEW ENGLAND

Minots Ledge lighthouse, Cohasset, Mass., the second light constructed on this rocky, wave-swept site.

■ ■ ■ ■ ■ ■ ■ CONNECTICUT ■ ■ ■ ■ ■ ■ ■

BRIDGEPORT

■ **Black Rock Harbor**
Lighthouse
South end of
Fayerweather Island
1809, 1823

This early lighthouse guided ships into Black Rock Harbor, an important port because its deep water could take large sailing vessels. Rebuilt in 1823 after a hurricane demolished the original wood tower and dwelling, the lighthouse's 41-foot white octagonal stone tower was fitted with a fifth-order Fresnel lens after 1852. The tower remained in use until the light was deactivated in 1932. Over the succeeding years vandals damaged the structure, but in 1983 the Friends of Seaside Park began rehabilitation and have restored the lighthouse's appearance and secured it against further vandalism. The group also has been restoring the island as a nature preserve, creating trails for visitors. NR district. [City of Bridgeport]

NEW HAVEN

■ **New Haven Harbor**
Lighthouse
Lighthouse Park
End of Lighthouse Road
1805, 1840

Located on the east side of the entrance to New Haven Harbor, this lighthouse began service chiefly to guide ships into the harbor. The first light tower was made of wood, but because it was too short to be seen to the east, another tower took its place about 1840. This octagonal tower was not only taller but also more substantial, being made of stone. The light tower served until the Lighthouse Board decommissioned the light station in 1877. The old stone light tower somehow survived the subsequent years, and in 1949 the city gave it a coat of paint before Lighthouse Park was officially opened. In 1986 the lighthouse received a major refurbishing when workers cleaned its interior and repointed the stone joints. Today, it is the centerpiece of Lighthouse Park, a public bathing beach. [City of New Haven]

New Haven Harbor
lighthouse, the centerpiece of
the city's Lighthouse Park,
1932.

On display at the 1876 Centennial Exposition in Philadelphia, this lighthouse was moved to New Haven and installed on a caisson in the channel to mark a hazardous underwater rock ledge. The prefabricated cast-iron Second Empire–style lighthouse went into service on January 1, 1877. Fitted for many years with a fourth-order lens, the light continues to play an important role in guarding shipping against serious danger. The lantern now houses a modern plastic lens, and the light, 57 feet above the water, is automated. The station has been equipped in the past with a whistle fog signal, but today it has a foghorn. [U.S. Coast Guard]

■ **Southwest Ledge Lighthouse**
East side of main channel
1877

Southwest Ledge lighthouse in position on its caisson, 1951.

■■■■■■■■■■

NEW LONDON

To guide ships into and out of New London Harbor, the colony of Connecticut in 1760 erected a stone lighthouse on the west side of the entrance to the Thames River. Thirty years later, in 1790, the state of Connecticut turned over its lighthouses to the federal government, which replaced this light tower with an octagonal stone tower 11 years later. In 1838 an inspector's report called it an important light for shipping going into and out of the harbor of New London. The illuminating apparatus, the inspector noted, consisted of 11 lamps, each with a 13-inch reflector. In 1855 the Lighthouse Board installed a fourth-order lens in the 88-foot white tower. New dwellings were built for the keepers in 1863, the first fog signal went into service in 1874, and in 1912 the lens was lighted by acetylene gas until the change to electricity. The surviving dwelling is now in private ownership. The oldest lighthouse in Connecticut, the tower is still active. [U.S. Coast Guard]

■ **New London Harbor Lighthouse**
East end of Osprey Beach
Off Pequot Avenue
1760, 1801

The Lighthouse Board established this lighthouse to mark the ledge of rock on which it rests and the long shoal extending from it. Erected on a concrete pier, the lighthouse is a square three-story brick structure with

■ **New London Ledge Lighthouse**
East side of main channel
1909

New London Ledge lighthouse, a compact 20th-century light and dwelling with foghorns extending from its side.

granite trim and a mansard roof. The tower and lantern, fitted with a fourth-order lens, rise out of the center of the roof. After it was completed the lighthouse took over many of the duties of the New London Harbor light, which many ship masters believed to be inadequate. Still active, the light was automated in 1987. At present restoration and development of this offshore lighthouse are in the planning stage. [U.S. Coast Guard. Leased to New London Ledge Lighthouse Foundation]

NORWALK

■ **Sheffield Island Lighthouse**
Sheffield Island
By boat from Hope Dock in
South Norwalk
1826, 1868

The island's original 30-foot masonry tower served to mark the west entrance to the Norwalk River. The tower remained until 1868, when it was replaced by a gable-roof, two-story stone dwelling with a light tower on one end of the roof. This lighthouse served until about 1900, when the Lighthouse Board decommissioned it. Over the next eight decades, the lighthouse passed through several owners. In 1987 the Norwalk Seaport Association purchased it and now plans to restore the old structure and convert it into a marine museum. The lighthouse is open to visitors. A 30-minute boat ride from South Norwalk, Sheffield Island is part of a national wildlife refuge. [Norwalk Seaport Association]

STONINGTON

■ **Stonington Harbor**
Lighthouse
7 Water Street
1824, 1840

First erected on Windmill Point in 1824, a lighthouse remained there until 1840, when erosion threatened the site. The Treasury's fifth auditor had it torn down and relocated to the east side of the harbor. Attached to the stone dwelling, the 35-foot tower remained in service until 1889, when the Lighthouse Board replaced it with the Stonington Breakwater light. Some years ago the

Stonington Historical Society acquired the light tower and dwelling for use as a maritime museum. The lighthouse is now open daily, except Monday, from May to October. NR. [Stonington Historical Society]

Stonington Harbor lighthouse, 1929, now a maritime museum.

STRATFORD

The first lighthouse at this point consisted of a shingled frame light tower and a 1½-story frame keeper's dwelling. Located at the entrance to the Housatonic River, the light tower originally had a fixed light, but within a year lighting inventor Winslow Lewis fitted the lantern with 10 Argand lamps, each with a 16-inch parabolic reflector; the metal frame holding the lamps and reflectors rotated,

■ **Stratford Point Lighthouse**
South end of Stratford Point
Prospect Drive
1821, 1881

Stratford Point light station, 1951. The fog signal structure is in the foreground.

thus giving off a flashing light. In the 1850s the Lighthouse Board replaced this system with a Fresnel lens of the fifth order. After the Civil War the board, desiring a stronger light, installed two range lenses in a clamshell arrangement in the lantern. This light was not satisfactory, so the board replaced it with a third-order lens. In 1881 the Lighthouse Board replaced the old wood tower with a prefabricated conical cast-iron tower. By 1933 this tower was equipped with a fourth-order lens. The focal plane of the light, now automated, has always been 52 feet above sea level. For a number of years the tower has had a brown band around its middle. The 1881 dwelling still stands, as does a fog signal building constructed in 1910. [U.S. Coast Guard]

■ ■ ■ ■ ■ ■ ■ ■ MAINE ■ ■ ■ ■ ■ ■ ■ ■

BAR HARBOR

■ **Baker Island Lighthouse**
Frenchman Bay
Acadia National Park
1828, 1855

By 1907, 87 light stations guarded the coast and islands of Maine. Of these, 60-plus remain today although one-fourth of their keepers' dwellings have been lost. This lighthouse marked the entrance to Frenchman Bay and also served to warn mariners of the shoals around Little Cranberry Island. The Lighthouse Board had it rebuilt in 1855 because the old tower was beyond repair. The 1855 tower, still in use, is 43 feet tall, and the light's focal plane is 105 feet above sea level. William Gilley, a longtime resident of Baker Island, was the first keeper. For some reason he was dismissed after 21 years of service. Angered by this action, his sons stayed on the island and harassed the succeeding keeper, charging him landing and grazing fees. When the district lighthouse inspector heard of the keeper's tribulations, he notified the Lighthouse Board, which started legal action to remove the sons, who were considered squatters. The Gilleys countersued, claiming ownership of the island. Government attorneys discovered a defect in the title to the island dating to 1806. Unable to prove a clear title, attorneys effected a compromise whereby the government would retain 19 acres of land on which the light station stood, road access from the landing and pasturage for the keeper's cattle. Forty years later the question of trespassing again arose, but the courts affirmed the Lighthouse Board's use of the light station land, landing and right-of-way to the lighthouse.

Baker Island lighthouse. The fence around the tower defines the land still controlled by the Coast Guard.

The Coast Guard automated the light in 1966. It retained a small square of land around the tower because the light is still active and transferred the remainder of the property to Acadia National Park. The former keeper's dwelling, a 1½-story Cape Cod house with a wing, survives, along with an oil house and fuel shed from 1905. Baker Island is visited by many who come to the park, and during summer months park rangers conduct tours of the lighthouse. NR. [U.S. Coast Guard. National Park Service]

To mark the entrance to Northeast Harbor, the fifth auditor of the Treasury had a lighthouse erected on Bear Island. It served until 1889, when the Lighthouse Board replaced it with the present structure. This 31-foot masonry tower is sited high on the island, which placed the focal plane of its fifth-order lens 100 feet above the sea.

The station is intact and includes a gambrel-roof dwelling, boat house, oil house and fuel shed. When the Coast Guard decommissioned the light station in 1982, replacing it with a lighted buoy, it was turned over to the National Park Service as part of Acadia National Park. Several excursion boats from Northeast Harbor pass close by the island, giving visitors a view of the old light station. Public Law 99-420 of September 25, 1986, establishing permanent boundaries for Acadia National Park, stipulates that federal property on Bear Island "shall not be developed by the Secretary [of the Interior] in a manner which would provide for or encourage intensive visitor use." As a consequence, the National Park Service will not lease the lighthouse for private use but will permit visitors who land by private boats to hike individually to the site to view the light station's buildings and grounds. In keeping with the legislation, tour groups are not allowed to visit the site. NR. [National Park Service]

BOOTHBAY HARBOR

This lighthouse, rebuilt in the 1850s, serves not only to guide vessels entering the harbor but also to protect them from nearby dangerous shoals. The light was modified in 1888, because it caused some confusion to mariners and resulted in some vessels running onto rock ledges known as the Cuckolds. Originally equipped with a fourth-order lens, the recently automated light of the conical white tower is 61 feet above sea level. The light station, a popular one with boaters, is on the route of at least one excursion boat that gives tours of Boothbay Harbor. It also can be seen from the mainland. NR. [U.S. Coast Guard]

■ **Bear Island Lighthouse**
Northeast Harbor
Acadia National Park
Route 3
1839, 1889

Bear Island lighthouse and dwelling. The lighthouse was replaced by a buoy.

■ **Burnt Island Lighthouse**
West side of harbor entrance
By boat from
Boothbay Harbor
1821, 1850s

Burnt Island light station, nestled on a rocky island clearing in Boothbay Harbor.

CALAIS

■ Whitlocks Mill Lighthouse
Off U.S. 1 south
1909

This cylindrical brick light tower, lined on the interior with glazed brick, guided river traffic bound for the port of Calais and other commercial points farther inland along the St. Croix River, which separates Canada and the United States. The lighthouse replaced a lantern that had been attached to a tree since 1892. In addition to the 35-foot tower, the station consisted of a two-story stuccoed, gambrel-roof dwelling; pyramidal, shingled bell tower; and brick oil house and fuel shed. The lantern of the tower had a fourth-order lens whose green light was 32 feet above river level. When the light was automated, the Coast Guard sold all the structures except the tower. The light is still active. NR. [U.S. Coast Guard]

Above: Whitlocks Mill lighthouse, a river guide. Right: Dice Head lighthouse, c. 1900. Curtains in the lantern protected the lens from discoloration.

CASTINE

■ Dice Head Lighthouse
End of Fort St. George Road
1829, 1858

At the tip of the peninsula on the east side of the mouth of the Penobscot River is the Dice Head lighthouse, whose light guided shipping into the river and Castine Harbor. During changes in 1858, the original rubblestone tower was fitted with a fourth-order lens and encased with a new heptagonal, pyramidal tower made of wood. By the 1930s shipping had so decreased that the lighthouse was little more than a relic of the past. In 1937 the Bureau of Lighthouses closed the light station and moved the light to a new skeleton tower on the north side of the entrance to Castine Harbor. The old lighthouse still stands, recently restored with federal and matching funding. NR district. [Town of Castine]

ELLSWORTH

■ Bass Harbor Head Lighthouse
Mount Desert Island
Acadia National Park
Route 3 south to Route 102
1858

One of the most picturesque and photographed lighthouses in the state, visited by many who go to Acadia National Park, this lighthouse sits on a ledge on the southwest point of Mount Desert. Its mission was to assist vessels in entering the harbor. The 32-foot cylindrical tower, which is attached to the dwelling by a short

enclosed passageway, was fitted with a fourth-order lens whose focal plane was 56 feet above the water. The red light from this lens, now automated, still guides shipping into the harbor. NR. [U.S. Coast Guard]

Bass Harbor Head light. The metronome structure holds a mechanism to operate the bell.

FRENCHBORO

More than 20 miles from shore, this lighthouse served not only to warn sailors of the navigational hazard here but also to guide ships along this section of the coast. The first lighthouse on this rock, a stone dwelling with an octagonal wood tower at one end, lasted only 17 years. In 1847 a conical granite tower, designed by the noted Boston architect-engineer Alexander Parris, went into

■ **Mount Desert Lighthouse**
Mount Desert Rock
Alexander Parris
1830, 1847

service. This lighthouse served well through the years, although its distance from shore made a lonely existence for its keepers. George Putnam, longtime commissioner of the Bureau of Lighthouses, regarded this station as the most exposed in the United States. In addition to the tower, other structures on the rock include a clapboard double keepers' dwelling built in 1893, brick fog signal building dating from 1891 and frame boat house. In 1977 the Coast Guard automated the lighthouse, which remains active. NR. [U.S. Coast Guard]

GEORGETOWN

■ **Seguin Island Lighthouse**
By boat from Boothbay Harbor
South of Georgetown
1797, 1820, 1857

Seguin Island is located just south of the mouth of the Kennebec River, and on this island, just six years after lighting the Portland Head lighthouse, the federal government built the first island lighthouse in Maine. In 1819, however, a storm blew down the wood tower. The government constructed another lighthouse, this time of stone, and lighted it in 1820. In 1852, recognizing this tower as an important seacoast light, the Lighthouse Board recommended a first-order Fresnel lens for it. In 1857 the tower was rebuilt, and a first-order lens was placed in the lantern of the tower, the first in Maine. The white cylindrical granite tower is 53 feet tall but is 180 feet above sea level because of the high site. A short enclosed passageway connects a 1½-story brick keeper's dwelling to the tower.

The light continues to perform, as does the foghorn — noted for the strength of its sound in this foggiest of areas. Both light and horn are now automated. The Friends of Seguin Island plan to preserve the structures, assisted by the Bicentennial Fund, and open the island to the public. NR. [U.S. Coast Guard. Leased to Friends of Seguin Island]

Seguin Island light station, 1962, the first such island station in Maine.

ISLE AU HAUT

■ **Isle au Haut Lighthouse**
By ferry from Stonington
1907

This station is strongly suggestive of the one in Port Clyde at Marshall Point. Both light towers are brick with granite bases; a bridge connects each tower to the land; and both dwellings have gambrel roofs. The oil house at Isle au Haut, however, is brick, not granite as at Marshall Point. This station also has a stuccoed frame boat house and frame shed. Lighted December 30, 1907, the 49-foot tower, whose light is 48 feet above the water, served to guide the fishing traffic into the adjacent harbor of refuge. The Bureau of Lighthouses automated the light in 1934 and at that time sold all the buildings except the tower, which it kept. Recently, the dwelling was developed into a bed-and-breakfast inn. The light is still active. NR. [U.S. Coast Guard. Privately owned]

ISLESBORO

This lighthouse, a 39-foot square brick tower, went out of service in 1934. When local citizens learned that the lighthouse was to be decommissioned, they petitioned the Bureau of Lighthouses to turn over the tower to the town as a memorial to all those who went to sea from Islesboro. The bureau did so, and the light tower survives with its lantern. Until recently, just in front of it was a modern light. The two structures exemplified the story of the technological evolution in lighting lighthouses. The old and stolid brick tower with its lantern once held a fifth-order Fresnel lens illuminated by a flame that the keeper lighted in the evening and damped out the next morning. A few feet away was a simple, airy skeleton tower, part of it enclosed to hold batteries. Atop the tower was a small light, as effective as the old lens, powered by batteries kept charged by solar energy. If the bulb went out, another one automatically moved into position. But in 1988 the Coast Guard, at the request of local residents, moved the light back into the old lighthouse and removed the modern tower. NR. [Town of Isleboro]

■ **Grindel Point Lighthouse**
By ferry from
Lincolnville Beach
1851, 1874

KENNEBEC RIVER LIGHTHOUSES

In 1898 the Lighthouse Board completed five lights to guide ships up the Kennebec River to the major commercial center at Bath. These lighthouses continue to function. The first light after passing the mouth of the river is a small tower and fog bell on Fort Popham. Traveling upriver, several more traditional light stations are encountered in the following sequence:

The station has a shingled frame, octagonal light tower 23 feet tall and 41 feet above the river, as well as a two-story shingled keeper's dwelling, shingled barn, metronome-type bell tower and brick oil house. Occupied until 1959, when the light was automated, the station was transferred to the state a few years later by the Coast Guard. NR. [U.S. Coast Guard. State of Maine]

■ **Perkins Island Lighthouse**
Georgetown
East side of Kennebec River
1898

Squirrel Point light consists of an octagonal, shingled tower, 25 feet tall, shingled fog bell house with gable roof, two-story keeper's dwelling, barn, boat house and brick oil house, all built between 1898 and 1906. The keeper's dwelling, barn and boat house are now covered in vinyl siding. Like the other Kennebec River lighthouses, the white light tower's lantern held a fifth-order lens, whose

■ **Squirrel Point Lighthouse**
Phippsburg
Southwest end of
Arrowsic Island
Off Route 127
1898–1906

Above: Perkins Island light
station, Georgetown,
complete with light tower,
dwelling, oil shed and boat
house. Right: Phippsburg's
Squirrel Point light station,
with the fog bell building
attached to the light tower.
Below: Doubling Point range
lights, near Bath, showing the
walkway between the two
light towers.

focal plane was 25 feet above the water. Equipped today with a modern plastic lens, the lighthouse was automated in 1982. NR. [U.S. Coast Guard. Maine Maritime Academy]

Sometimes called the Kennebec River range light station, this site includes two white frame towers, each an octagonal tower 21 feet tall and illuminated with reflector lights, as well as a clapboard two-story keeper's dwelling and brick oil house. The main channel turns to the west near this station. The rear light is on higher ground than the front one, so that the focal plane of the front light is 18 feet and that of the rear light is 33 feet above the river. NR. [U.S. Coast Guard]

■ **Doubling Point
Range Lights**
Bath
Northwest end of
Arrowsic Island
East side of Doubling Point
1898

The main channel turns sharply to the north at this point, and the Doubling Point light marks this turn. The 35-foot octagonal pyramidal tower is covered in shingles and equipped with a fifth-order lens and is 23 feet above the river. Nearby are a 1½-story clapboard dwelling, frame shed and brick oil house. After passing Doubling Point, the navigator has a straight course to Bath. NR. [U.S. Coast Guard]

■ **Doubling Point Lighthouse**
Bath
Northwest end of
Arrowsic Island
West side of Doubling Point
1898

LUBEC

The most eastern light built during the fifth auditor's tenure, this station marks the Quoddy Roads and guides vessels along that section of the Maine coast. The first tower was in use until 1858, when the Lighthouse Board erected the present tower and dwelling and fitted the lantern with a third-order lens. The tower is 49 feet tall, and its light is 83 feet above sea level. With its distinctive red-and-white banding, it is a picturesque and photogenic lighthouse and, consequently, is one of the lighthouses more familiar to the public, often appearing in television commercials. The Coast Guard automated the light in 1988, to the objections of the last keeper. Quoddy Head State Park plans to interpret the station's history. NR. [U.S. Coast Guard]

■ **West Quoddy Head
Lighthouse**
Quoddy Head State Park
Route 189
1808, 1858

One of the state's best-known lighthouses, the West Quoddy Head light in 1956 after a light snow.

MILLBRIDGE

■ Petit Manan Lighthouse
2½ miles off
Petit Manan Point
By boat from Jonesport
1817, 1855

The first lighthouse on Petit Manan Island was 53 feet tall. Judged too short for the location, it was replaced by the Lighthouse Board in 1855 with a new granite tower 119 feet high. The focal plane of the tower's second-order lens was 123 feet above sea level, making this light the second highest on the coast of Maine. Petit Manan Island is subject to frequent fog and heavy storms. Winter storms in 1886 were reported so heavy that the top of this high light tower began to sway back and forth. The Coast Guard automated the light and foghorn in 1972. Pleasure boaters now visit the island, which is the responsibility of the Fish and Wildlife Service except for the light tower, which the Coast Guard still operates. NR. [U.S. Coast Guard. U.S. Fish and Wildlife Service]

Above: Petit Manan lighthouse, a tall granite tower. Right: Monhegan Island light station. This light tower replaced another sited elsewhere on the island.

MONHEGAN ISLAND

■ Monhegan Island Lighthouse
By ferry from Port Clyde
Alexander Parris (1851)
1824, 1851

Monhegan Island, whose recorded use goes back before the Pilgrims landed at Plymouth Rock, received a lighthouse in 1824. It was a relatively short granite tower positioned near the center of the island. The present tower was designed in 1851 by Alexander Parris. In 1857, when the Lighthouse Board replaced the lamps and reflectors with a second-order Fresnel lens, the tower was listed as 47 feet tall, but its location placed the focal plane of the light 178 feet above sea level. The gray conical tower has remained unpainted through the years, and in 1959 the Coast Guard automated the light. Monhegan Associates acquired the keeper's dwelling and ancillary structures at the station and made them into a museum devoted to the cultural and natural history of the island, including artifacts related to the lighthouse. NR. [U.S. Coast Guard. Monhegan Associates]

PEMAQUID POINT

Located on the west side of the entrance to Muscongus Bay, this picturesque and popular lighthouse has a conical tower made of stone. When it was fitted with a fourth-order lens in the 1850s, the tower was 38 feet tall and the light, sited on a bluff, was 79 feet above sea level. The Lighthouse Board replaced the dwelling in 1857 with a 1½-story clapboard structure that still survives. The Bureau of Lighthouses automated the light in 1934, and some years later the town acquired the dwelling and other ancillary buildings of the station. The dwelling now houses the Fisherman's Museum, which includes lighthouse artifacts. NR. [U.S. Coast Guard. Town of Pemaquid Point]

■ **Pemaquid Point Lighthouse**
Route 129 from Damariscotta to Route 130
1827

PORT CLYDE

Marking the entrance to Port Clyde Harbor, this lighthouse served the considerable traffic associated with fishing activities, shipbuilding and the commercial ice industry of the port. The light tower is similar to the one at Isle au Haut. Located at the water's edge on an outcropping of boulders, the white conical tower is made of brick and its base of cut granite. The lantern for many years held a fifth-order lens whose focal plane was 30 feet above the water. The tower, with its base, is only 31 feet tall. A wood bridge resting on granite piles connects the light tower to the land. A gambrel-roof dwelling, near the land end of the bridge, and a granite oil house survive. The Coast Guard has licensed the grounds and keeper's quarters to the St. George Historical Society, which plans to establish a museum on the maritime history of the St. George Peninsula. NR. [U.S. Coast Guard. Leased to St. George Historical Society]

■ **Marshall Point Lighthouse**
Route 131 from Thomaston
1832, 1857

Marshall Point light station before automation. The bell tower and boat house flanked the bridge.

■ Cape Elizabeth (Two Lights) Lighthouse

Adjacent to Two Lights
State Park
Off Route 77
1828, 1874

Twin lights on Cape Elizabeth, 1915. The tower in the foreground remains active.

■ Lightship Nantucket (LV-112)

Commercial Street at
Main Wharf
1936

PORTLAND

This site on the mainland just south of Portland — considered by the Lighthouse Board as one of the most important on the East Coast — was once well known for its twin lights, but in 1924 the Bureau of Lighthouses decided to end the use of all multiple-tower light stations. With that announcement came an uproar of protest from the maritime community. The two lights had been a familiar site along the coast for nearly 100 years. The protests, however, fell on deaf ears, and the west light winked off. Although one light is gone, local residents continued to call this site Two Lights, and the name is commemorated in the 41-acre state park adjacent to the light station.

Two rubblestone towers, one equipped with a flashing Argand light and the other with a fixed light, went into service in 1828. These lights served both to guide shipping along the coast and to mark the entrance to Casco Bay and Portland Harbor. In 1851 an inspection of the station revealed that the towers were well built "but greatly neglected." In 1874 the Lighthouse Board erected two conical cast-iron towers, 300 yards apart, to replace the stone towers. The two 67-foot white towers with lights, one fixed and one flashing, 129 feet above sea level, served together until 1924. The east tower, with its second-order lens, has continued in service, and today it and the fog signal are automated. The west tower was sold in the 1970s and is on private land. The two-story keeper's quarters near the east tower is still in use, but as a private residence. One keeper, Marcus A. Hanna, became a hero of the Lighthouse Service in 1885 when he rescued two seamen whose schooner had wrecked on the rocks near the station in a raging snow storm. A fashionable residential section now surrounds the towers. NR. [U.S. Coast Guard. Privately owned]

"The Shoals of Nantucket are known and dreaded by every navigator on the Atlantic seaboard . . . ," noted an 1843 report to Congress. Tumultuous seas that could snap an anchor chain and thick, often-present fog that could obscure a lightship and make it a victim of an approaching ship were two hazards that a lightship crew faced on the station marking the south end of the Nantucket Shoals, which saw heavy traffic daily. The first ship assigned to the station, in 1854, was blown off and onto Montauk Point, N.Y., 18 months later by a December storm, resulting in extensive repairs. Its replacement, an exceptionally sturdy ship, was often blown off station — once it wound up in Bermuda — and reputedly left an estimated 25 mushroom anchors on the Nantucket Shoals. Other vessels assigned to the area experienced similar treatment. In 1931 the Bureau of Lighthouses assigned *Lightship No. 117* to this station, but in January 1934 the American liner *Washington* bumped into it. Four months later, in a thick fog, the British liner *Olympic*, sister ship of the *Titanic*, rammed the lightship with such severity that it sank with seven of its 11-member crew.

The *Olympic*'s owners had to pay for the lightship and compensate survivors of the lost crew.

The replacement for this ship was *Lightship No. 112.* Constructed in Wilmington, Del., in 1936, *No. 112,* a double-hulled vessel, spent its career on the Nantucket Shoals, except for a three-year period during World War II when it was fitted with guns and tended the submarine nets surrounding the harbor. When this duty ended it returned to its station on Nantucket Shoals. A 149-foot lightship with a beam of 32 feet and displacement of 1,110 tons, it remained on station until 1975, when the Coast Guard repaired the ship. Later in the same year it decommissioned the lightship and gave it to the town of Nantucket, Mass., where until 1984 it operated as a floating museum. In that year the town leased the lightship to Nantucket Lightship Preservation, which in 1985 took it to Boston for extensive repairs. Since then it has traveled to various ports on the Atlantic coast, where it is open to the public. The ship winters in Portland. [Nantucket Lightship, Inc.]

The Portland Head light, in its picturesque setting, must be the most often painted and photographed lighthouse in the country. The white conical stone and brick tower, 80 feet tall, is set on a headland on the southwest side of the entrance to Portland Harbor. The fog signal house sits in front of the tower, right on a point of land. A brick structure, apparently the former oil house, abuts the tower and houses a small museum displaying lighthouse objects. A wood structure built onto the rear of the keeper's quarters joins the oil house to make an enclosed passageway from the house to the light tower. The dwelling, with white clapboards on the first floor and shingles on the second, exudes the essence of New England. Closer examination, however, reveals that the

WLV-612 heading out to sea to the Nantucket Station. This vessel succeeded *LV-112,* which now serves as a floating museum and winters in Portland.

■ **Portland Head Lighthouse**
Fort Williams State Park
Route 77 to Shore Road
1791

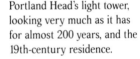

Portland Head's light tower, looking very much as it has for almost 200 years, and the 19th-century residence.

clapboards and the shingles are made of metal, probably installed over the last decade or so.

When Massachusetts, which then embraced what is now the state of Maine, turned over its lighthouses to the federal government in 1790, the Portland Head light was only a partially built tower. Congress appropriated $1,500 to complete the lighthouse, and in 1791 its light went into service, the first tower completed by the new government. In 1855 the Lighthouse Board had the tower lined with brick and a metal spiral stairway installed in the tower. At the same time the board placed a fourth-order lens in the lantern. Ten years later the board reinstalled the second-order lantern and lens on the tower to warn mariners away from Alden's Rock and Bulwark Shoals. In 1883 the board reinstalled the fourth-order lens, but two years later reversed itself and returned the second-order lens. No changes have occurred since. The tower today is essentially as it was when it was built. The Coast Guard plans to turn over the buildings, except the lighthouse, and the grounds to the town of Cape Elizabeth, which intends to open the site to the public. NR. [U.S. Coast Guard]

ROCKLAND

■ **Matinicus Rock
Lighthouse**
6 miles south of
Matinicus Island
By ferry from Rockland to
Matinicus Island, then
by boat
Alexander Parris (1848)
1827, 1848, 1857

One of the most isolated light stations on the Maine coast, Matinicus Rock lighthouse was described in the 19th century as having "neither tree nor shrub and hardly a blade of grass.... The surface is rough and irregular and resembles in a large way a confused pile of loose stone. Portions of the rock are frequently swept by the waves which move the huge bowlders [sic] into new position." The light station was established in 1827 with twin wood towers, which were replaced in 1848 by two granite towers designed by the noted Boston architect Alexander Parris. At the same time workers constructed a granite dwelling. Nine years later the Lighthouse Board replaced these two towers with granite ones 80 feet apart. Today, the bases of the 1848 towers can be seen at either end of the keeper's dwelling. Although the Lighthouse Board

considered these important lights suitable for first-order lenses, when the lamps and reflectors were replaced, the board installed third-order lenses in the 48-foot towers. After the Bureau of Lighthouses discontinued multiple lights at stations in 1924, the deactivated tower lost its lantern. One lens was left in the active tower and remained in use until 1983, when the light was automated. This lens then was removed and sent to the Lighthouse Museum in Rockland.

Twin light station on Matinicus Rock, c. 1890s, one of the most isolated locations along the Maine coast.

The island was for a long time the home of Abbie Burgess, probably the best-known light keeper on the Maine coast. Her dedication epitomized the conscientious lighthouse keeper, and she first exhibited her spirit in 1859 at the age of 17 when her father went ashore, leaving her to care for her invalid mother and three sisters. Unexpectedly, a storm arose, stranding her father on the mainland. The storm raged for four weeks, but each night she and her sisters activated the light in the lantern of each of the twin towers. Waves swept across the island, flooding the dwelling and forcing the beleaguered light tenders to seek refuge in the light towers. Still, the four young women never failed to exhibit the light each evening. A little over a year later, the sea again became roiled while the father was absent, and once again the girls tended the light each evening. But this time they nearly ran out of food, being reduced toward the end to one cup of cornmeal and one egg each day. In 1861 Abbie married Isaac H. Grant, the son of her father's successor. For 14 years the couple lived on Matinicus Island. Four children were born to them here, one of whom, a two-year-old, died and was buried on the island. The family transferred to the Whitehead light in Tenants Harbor in 1875, where Abbie Grant was assistant keeper until 1889. Toward the end of her life, Abbie asked that her tombstone be in the shape of a lighthouse. She died in 1892, and years later after her death, New England lighthouse historian Edward Snow placed such a marker over her grave at Spruce Head Cemetery on the nearby mainland. Occasional tours are led to the island to view the puffins that nest here. NR. [U.S. Coast Guard]

■ **Owls Head Lighthouse**
Lighthouse Park
Route 73 south
1825, c. mid-19th century

Marking the entrance to Rockland Harbor, this white granite tower is 26 feet tall. But its location on a high promontory raises the focal plane of the light to 100 feet, which makes it visible 16 miles out to sea. The present tower is probably not the original one and may date from the mid-19th century. Owls Head was one of the last light stations in the country scheduled for automation in 1989. This picturesque station in a beautiful setting reminds us once again why Maine is called the Lighthouse State. NR. [U.S. Coast Guard]

Right: Owls Head light station with its fog signal house in the foreground. Below: Rockland Breakwater lighthouse at the end of its jetty in Rockland Harbor.

■ **Rockland Breakwater Lighthouse**
Jameson Point
Waldo and Samoset Roads
1888, 1902

Located at the end of a half-mile long jetty in Rockland, this lighthouse was erected in 1888 and rebuilt in 1902 to guide vessels into Rockland Harbor. It replaced a post light that had been put at the end of the pier in 1888. The present light is atop a white square tower at the corner of the fog signal house, which is joined to the keeper's dwelling. These structures rest on a square granite pier. The light and fog signal are now automated and still active. The Rockland Lighthouse Museum has leased the dwelling from the Coast Guard and has opened it to the public. NR. [U.S. Coast Guard. Leased to Rockland Lighthouse Museum]

STOCKTON SPRINGS

■ **Fort Point Lighthouse**
Fort Point State Park
1836, 1857

Located on the west side of the mouth of the Penobscot River, this 31-foot square brick light tower has for many years been painted white. Much of the exterior brickwork was replaced after being damaged when workers sand-blasted the tower to remove old paint. A two-story dwelling is attached to the tower by a short enclosed passageway. For many years the fog signal was a bell, but in recent years a horn has been in service. The old fog bell tower and the bell, minus the striking apparatus, are on display on the grounds of the light station. One of the last staffed light stations in the country, it was automated in 1988. The light station, with the exception of the tower, is to be turned over to the state to be made part of Fort Point State Park, site of the remains of Fort Pownall, a 1759 colonial fortification. [U.S. Coast Guard. State of Maine]

TENANTS HARBOR

Abbie Burgess Grant and her husband transferred from Matinicus Rock lighthouse off Rockland to this light station in 1875. Both served here for many years and in 1889 retired from this light, after Abbie wrote of dreading the day when she could no longer climb the old granite tower. The lighthouse is located on the west side of Penobscot Bay and served to guide shipping to the various ports of the area as well as traffic traveling along this section of the coast. The 41-foot conical tower was erected in 1852 to replace a tower built on this island 48 years earlier. The other structures at the station, including the 1½-story keeper's dwelling, built on the foundation of the original stone dwelling, and the brick oil house, date to 1891, when the brick service room was added to the tower. The brick fog signal building went up three years earlier. Automated in 1982, the light is still active. NR. [U.S. Coast Guard]

■ **Whitehead Lighthouse**
East side of Whitehead Island
1804, 1852

Whitehead light station. The masonry tower here replaced another at this location. The fog signal is in the foreground.

VINALHAVEN

In the Penobscot Bay area, this lighthouse marks the western entrance to the Fox Island Thorofare. Today, the light serves ferry and fishing boat traffic, as well as yachting activities. The 20-foot cylindrical masonry tower has a fourth-order lens whose light is 39 feet above sea level. In addition to the tower the light station consists of a fog signal (originally a bell, but now a horn), dwelling

■ **Brown's Head Lighthouse**
Northwest end of
Vinalhaven Island
By ferry from Rockland
1832, 1857

and short enclosed passageway that connects the tower and dwelling. The Coast Guard automated the light in 1987. At that time it licensed the light station to the town of Vinalhaven. The old fog bell is cared for by the Vinalhaven Historical Society, which has plans to open the station to visitors. NR. [U.S. Coast Guard. Leased to Town of Vinalhaven]

Brown's Head light station on the island of Vinalhaven, with its metronome-shaped fog signal building at the opposite end from the tower.

■ Saddleback Ledge
Lighthouse
Between Vinalhaven and
Isle au Haut
Alexander Parris
1839

Saddleback Ledge lighthouse, located on a rocky isolated island. The barricade offered little resistance to the worst storms.

Saddleback Ledge light station is considered one of the most lonely stations on the coast of Maine. It sits on a soilless island between Isle au Haut and Vinalhaven. Keepers, anxious to see something green growing, would haul sacks of soil to the site, knowing that the first storm would wash the earth away. The light tower, designed by the architect Alexander Parris, is a conical granite structure 42 feet tall. The light emanating from the tower's fourth-order lens was 53 feet above sea level. The dwelling is now gone, leaving only the tower on the island. Still active, the light was automated in the 1960s.

The weather in the area can be stormy and unpredictable. Before one keeper could return from shore, a storm arose that lasted for 21 days. The keeper's 15-year-old son remained on the island, climbing the spiral stairway each night and lighting the lamp in the lens. And each night his father, who knew that there was little food at the station, peered toward the island to see if the light had been lighted, for this meant that his son was all right. Three weeks passed before the sea calmed enough for the keeper to row back to the island, where he found his son in a weakened condition.

Keepers were beset by more than weather. In 1927 a storm swept across the island, bringing a flock of ducks and drakes. Some crashed into the lantern, breaking panes of glass. "Just when I thought the cannonading had ceased," said the keeper, "one big sea drake struck the plate glass in the tower lantern. . . . When he struck he broke up the works. Before he stopped he put out the light and broke prisms out of the lens. The bird weighed 10 pounds." After repairing the light, the keeper noticed a pile of sea birds at the base of the tower. He put those that were just dazed in the boat house to recover, and the next day they departed.

Boat landings are difficult on Saddleback Ledge. Even

keepers have had boats turn over. Pleasure boats sail past the island, and lobster fishers from Matinicus will carry passengers on a tour of area lighthouses, including this light. NR. [U.S. Coast Guard]

YORK

Often called the Nubble light, this station's official name has always been Cape Neddick. The lighthouse was erected on a little island, or nubble, just off Cape Neddick. Lined on the interior with brick, the white conical iron-plated light tower is 41 feet tall, but from its high vantage point on the small island, the light from the fourth-order lens achieves a focal plane 88 feet above sea level. A dwelling, brick oil house, enclosed passageway connecting the tower and dwelling, and fog signal complete the complex. Located near a popular resort area, Cape Neddick is considered by many to be an outstanding example of a picturesque lighthouse. The station received much attention on national television when it was recently automated. At low tide visitors once could walk to the island just as keepers did, but officials considered this activity unsafe and stopped it. The town of York plans to take over the light station and open it to the public. NR. [U.S. Coast Guard. Town of York]

■ **Cape Neddick (Nubble) Lighthouse**
Off U.S. 1A at York Beach
End of Nubble Road
1879

Cape Neddick's lighthouse, dwelling and metronome-shaped bell tower.

■ ■ ■ ■ ■   MASSACHUSETTS   ■ ■ ■ ■ ■

ANNISQUAM

In 1801 a lighthouse went into service on Wigwam Point, the east side of the entrance to Annisquam Harbor, off Ipswich Bay and west of Rockport. Ninety-six years later the light tower was replaced with a 41-foot white cylindrical tower whose flashing white light is 45 feet above sea level. The fifth-order lens was replaced by a fourth-order one in 1972, and at that time the light was electrified. The light and the foghorn, both now auto-mated, are still active. Although altered over the years, the frame 1½-story clapboard dwelling at the station

■ **Annisquam Harbor Lighthouse**
Wigwam Point
Entrance to Annisquam Harbor
1801, 1897

Annisquam Harbor light tower, the second for this site.

dates to 1801; the stone oil house, too, was built at about the same time. The Coast Guard still uses the station for housing. Access to the adjacent beach is through Coast Guard property. NR. [U.S. Coast Guard]

BOSTON

■ **Boston Harbor Lighthouse**
Boston Harbor
Little Brewster Island
1716, 1783

This lighthouse was built on the site of the first lighthouse in the United States. In the early 18th century, as shipping traffic increased in the Boston area, merchants became concerned that vessels carrying their goods have safe entry into the port. They petitioned the General Court of Massachusetts for a "Light Hous and Lanthorn on some Head Land at the Entrance of the Harbor of Boston for the Direction of Ships and Vessels in the Night Time bound into the said Harbor." A committee appointed by the legislature quickly recognized the necessity for a navigational aid and recommended that a lighthouse be placed on Beacon Island (now Little Brewster Island) at the entrance to the harbor. The court ordered the erection of a lighthouse at the recommended location, and on September 14, 1716, the keeper displayed the light for the first time. The light station consisted of a tall masonry tower, two-story dwelling and several small sheds. The light in the lantern was supplied by either candles or lamps. To pay for the operation of the light, the court levied tonnage dues on cargo going into and out of the harbor. In 1719 the court placed a cannon on the island to serve as a fog signal, the country's first.

George Worthylake, the first keeper, was paid a relatively small salary but was able to supplement his income by also working as a pilot. Two years later Worthylake and his family drowned in a boating accident. Benjamin Franklin, then a young boy, commemorated the catastrophe in his poem "Lighthouse Tragedy."

In the 1750s the wood portions of the lighthouse burned, and on several occasions lightning struck the tower. The General Court refused to put a lightning rod

Boston Harbor's stone light tower, its second-order lens in place, and shingled dwelling. This light station is the site of the nation's first lighthouse.

on the tower, thinking "it vanity and irreligion for the arm of flesh to presume to avert the stroke of Heaven." Later, however, it did install one. At the beginning of the Revolution, to prevent the signal from benefiting British vessels, American troops removed the lamps from the lighthouse's lantern and set fire to the structure. British attempts to repair the tower were rebuffed by American forces. On June 13, 1776, as they evacuated Boston, the British blew up the tower.

At the end of the war, the Massachusetts legislature appropriated funds to rebuild the lighthouse on the island. There is no evidence that any materials from the old lighthouse were used in the new one, an 89-foot white conical stone tower with a second-order lens whose light is 102 feet above sea level. This lighthouse was operated by the state until June 1790, when it was turned over to the federal government. The lighthouse keeper continued to work as a pilot, and an 1838 inspection report complained that the keeper was neglecting his light-keeping duties for his alternate job.

During the first half of the 19th century several changes occurred at the station. The tower's wood stairs were replaced with metal ones. The cannon remained the fog signal until the late 1840s, when a fog bell was installed at the station. Also, 21-inch English reflectors were placed on the lamps in the lantern, and the lighthouse developed the reputation as having the best reflector lights of any in the United States. With the establishment of the Light-house Board in 1852, repairs were made to the tower and it was raised 14 feet. Where repairs were required in the stone tower, the workers patched with brick. The fog signal was updated in the 1870s with a more modern trumpet and later a siren. Today, the station has a foghorn. Scheduled for automation in August 1989, this was to be the last staffed lighthouse in the country. NHL. [U.S. Coast Guard]

■ Long Island Head
Lighthouse
Boston Harbor
North end of Long Island
1820, 1900

In 1820 this lighthouse went into service on the north end of Long Island to help vessels pass safely into Boston's inner harbor. Rebuilt several times, the light tower by 1900 was a 52-foot white brick structure and had a 3½-order lens whose light was 120 feet above sea level. The tower was connected to the dwelling by a covered passageway. Automated in 1918, the light is still active, although it did go out of service for a three-year period starting in 1982. The Coast Guard reactivated it with solar power and a modern plastic lens that emits a flashing white light that can be seen for six miles. Access to the light station by land is virtually prohibited because of the presence of the city's prison hospital between the mainland and the lighthouse. In the future Boston Harbor ferries plan stops at the light station. NR. [U.S. Coast Guard]

Above: Long Island Head light station in Boston Harbor, now operated with solar power. Right: Cleveland Ledge lighthouse, a caisson type with a striking modern design, reflecting the architecture of the 1940s.

BOURNE

■ Cleveland Ledge
Lighthouse
2 miles off shore
1943

This handsome Art Moderne lighthouse may seem somewhat out of place in Massachusetts, but it reflects a style of architecture in vogue when it was designed and constructed, the last traditional lighthouse built in

Massachusetts. This caisson lighthouse has a cylindrical light tower rising out of a Moderne two-story dwelling. The light of its fourth-order lens is 74 feet above the sea. Still active, the light tower has been equipped with a plastic lens and was automated in 1978. NR. [U.S. Coast Guard]

CAPE ANN

Before the Revolution, Massachusetts erected twin towers on Thacher Island, just off the mainland at Cape Ann. These lighthouses were the 11th and last of the colonial lighthouses. Each tower was 45 feet tall with a light 90 feet above sea level. The first keeper was a Tory, and at the beginning of the Revolution local citizens forced him out of his job, rendering the light inoperative during the war. The lights were reactivated after the hostilities, and in 1790 the state turned over the light towers to the federal government. Later equipped with 11 lamps and 21-inch reflectors, these towers made up a light station that the Lighthouse Board in 1852 considered "very important." The board later ordered the construction of two new towers to replace the original ones. Made of granite, these towers went into service in

■ **Cape Ann Twin (Thacher Island) Lighthouses**
Thacher Island
By boat from "T" Wharf in Rockport
1771, 1861

1861. Each was 124 feet tall, with lights in their first-order lenses 166 feet above sea level. The last twin light station, these lights continued in operation until 1932, when the Bureau of Lighthouses deactivated the light on the north tower. In 1980 the Coast Guard automated the remaining light and the fog signal.

In 1919 the lighthouses on Thacher Island were instrumental in averting a tragedy of potentially monumental proportion. The S.S. *America,* returning from Europe with President Woodrow Wilson and his staff aboard, was unknowingly steering for Thacher Island in a thick fog. At the last minute the sound of the fog signal at the Cape Ann light station was heard aboard the ship,

Twin towers on Thacher Island, off Rockport, built in 1861 to replace the colonial lighthouses.

and the captain altered course in time to prevent disaster.

Today, the light station is changed somewhat from its original appearance, because some of the structures associated with the north tower have burned. The single and double dwellings at the south tower survive, as do the fog signal building, boat house at the landing and tramway that connected the various elements of the station. Around 1967 the Coast Guard turned over the north half of the island to the Fish and Wildlife Service, with which the town of Rockport manages that half of the island. In 1980 the Coast Guard entered into a lease arrangement with the town for the south half of the island. Thacher Island Association, a nonprofit organization, was formed to care for the leased property. Today, a retired couple representing the association resides on the island in the old keeper's dwelling. They greet visitors to the island, maintain the buildings and keep trails clear. The island can be reached during the summer months by a small boat from the "T" Wharf in Rockport. [U.S. Coast Guard. U.S. Fish and Wildlife Service. Leased to Town of Rockport]

CHATHAM

■ **Chatham Lighthouse**
Bridge Street near
Main Street
1808, 1830s, 1863, 1877

The first aid to navigation at this harbor on Cape Cod consisted of two towers, each made of wood. In the 1830s these structures were replaced by two towers made of brick. In 1863 the south tower was rebuilt. In the late 1870s, because of erosion, the towers and the remainder of the station began to fall into the sea. The Lighthouse Board had no choice but to move the light station to the other side of the coast. In 1877 it erected two cast-iron towers, 100 feet apart, to replace the old ones, as well as a shingled double keepers' dwelling and brick oil house. In 1923 the Bureau of Lighthouses moved the south tower to Nauset Beach near North Eastham to take the place of the last of the Three Sisters lights (see North Eastham entries). Today, the 48-foot white conical north tower still stands and sends out its beam, 80 feet above sea level. NR. [U.S. Coast Guard]

Chatham light station in 1951, with its single remaining tower, and its predecessor twin lights with bird-cage lanterns on another part of the coast.

In 1823 the federal government erected the first light-house at Monomoy Point, which is at the south end of Monomoy Island, a thin island (actually two islands end to end) extending out about eight miles from Cape Cod at Chatham. The light tower was rebuilt in 1855 and again in the 1870s. By 1922 the tower had been painted white and a passageway built between the tower and the keeper's dwelling. In 1923, when the twin lights of Chatham were reduced to one, the Monomoy Point light rose in importance for a brief period. But the Bureau of Lighthouses decided that the single light at Chatham was an adequate aid for vessels navigating through the area and discontinued the Monomoy Point lighthouse the same year. The lighthouse and the land fell into private hands.

When the Monomoy National Wildlife Refuge was created in 1977, the lighthouse became the property of the Fish and Wildlife Service, which has made considerable repairs to the tower and dwelling, some with support from the Bicentennial Fund, and will be undertaking more in the near future. Currently, the Cape Cod Natural History Museum is negotiating with the Fish and Wildlife Service to place natural and historical exhibits in the buildings and to bring small groups to the island for nature hikes and other educational programs. The only way to get to the island now is by boat, but landing at the island is discouraged for those who are not familiar with these dangerous waters. The Fish and Wildlife Service also may limit access to the island. NR. [U.S. Fish and Wildlife Service]

■ **Monomoy Lighthouse**
Monomoy Island
Monomoy Point
1823, 1855, 1870s

COHASSET

Minots Ledge and its neighboring reefs east of Quincy and south of Hull have been the scene of numerous wrecks, but not until the 1840s was serious consideration given to placing a lighthouse here. The two lights built successively at Minots Ledge represented engineering feats because of the rocky, wave-swept location. In the spring of 1847 work began at the difficult site to erect an iron pile lighthouse, a type selected because its openness would give much less resistance to the waves. Work could be done only in calm weather for only two or three hours a day when the tide was low, exposing the rocks. Drilling the holes for the nine iron legs, 10 inches in diameter, proceeded slowly. By the fall of the following year the workers had the legs secured in place and braced with iron rods. The engineer decided to omit the lower bracing; he believed that it would lessen rather than add to the tower's strength. When the legs were completed, they were capped with an iron platform on which the keepers' quarters were built. The workers then placed a lantern containing 15 lamps and reflectors on the roof of the quarters.

The new lighthouse went into service on January 1, 1850, and shortly thereafter the principal light keeper expressed concern about the structure's stability. When nothing was done, he resigned. His successor at first

■ **Minots Ledge Lighthouse**
Off shore southwest
of Cohasset
1850, 1860

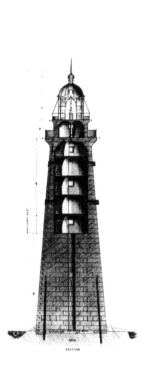

Cross section of the 1860
Minots Ledge lighthouse,
drawing of the original iron
pile light erected on the
stormy site and the newer
lighthouse c. 1900.

disparaged the first keeper's fears, but in time he, too, came to believe that the tower lacked adequate stability. In April 1851, at the beginning of a storm, the keeper left the lighthouse in the care of his two assistants. Although he tried to return the next day, the seas were too heavy, and the storm continued to build. Nearly a week later the townspeople heard the insistent ringing of the lighthouse's fog bell, and then it stopped. When the storm cleared, the people on the shore could see that the lighthouse was gone; it had broken at the place where the engineer had eliminated the bracing. The bodies of the two keepers were eventually recovered.

For the next nine years a lightship guarded these dangerous reefs. Meanwhile, in 1855 the Lighthouse Board had begun erecting a granite conical tower on the site of the former lighthouse. Storms impeded the work, but finally the workers prepared the base to receive the foundation stones, which were cemented to the rock. Slowly the tower rose higher and higher above the water until, with its lantern, it was 97 feet tall. The light from its second-order lens was 85 feet above sea level. It was test-lighted in August 1860 but did not begin regular service until November 15, when the keepers reported for duty. In time it became known as the lovers light, because of the one, four, three sequence of its flash. Since that time the lighthouse has served well, withstanding all storms. In 1947 the Coast Guard automated the light, and in 1983 it was converted to solar power. NR. ASCE. [U.S. Coast Guard]

DUXBURY

Located on the north side of the channel that leads to Duxbury, Plymouth and Kingston, this 47-foot brown conical light tower began service in 1871. It was equipped with a fourth-order lens whose light was 35 feet above sea level. Known locally as the Bug Light, it is now automated. Both the light and the foghorn are still active. In the mid-1980s the Coast Guard for economic reasons decided to remove the upper portion of the lighthouse, which contained the living quarters. Local preservation-

■ **Duxbury Pier Lighthouse**
End of pier in
Duxbury Harbor
1871

Duxbury Pier lighthouse, a conical light tower known as the Bug Light, because it is small and low in the water. Here, too, curtains once protected the lens.

ists, upset by this decision, formed the Bug Light Preservationists and persuaded the Coast Guard to let them restore the upper portion. They made repairs and painted the structure for a relatively small amount of money — about $20,000 for materials — which they raised themselves. The preservationists now have a license from the Coast Guard to maintain the lighthouse. [U.S. Coast Guard. Leased to Bug Light Preservationists]

FALMOUTH

■ **Nobska Point Lighthouse**
Woods Hole Harbor
Nobska Road
1829, 1876

A lighthouse was first established at the entrance to Woods Hole Harbor in 1829 to serve as a guide to the harbor and to guard vessels against shoals in the area. In 1876 the Lighthouse Board replaced the light with an iron cylindrical tower whose interior was lined with brick and built a 1½-story dwelling. Painted white, the 40-foot tower was equipped with a fourth-order lens whose light was 87 feet above sea level. Today, the light station consists of the tower and dwelling (now clad in vinyl siding), another frame house built in 1900, a brick oil house and brick structure for the radio beacon. The light was automated in 1985 and is still active. The residences are now being used by Coast Guard personnel. NR. [U.S. Coast Guard]

Nobska Point light station with its iron tower from 1876.

GLOUCESTER

■ **Eastern Point Lighthouse**
Gloucester Harbor
East end of Eastern Point
Near the Dog Bar
Breakwater
1832, 1890

Originally, the light on Ten Pound Island in Gloucester Harbor guided fishing vessels home to the harbor. As the light could not be seen until the ships had already found the entrance, the fifth auditor of the Treasury had a lighthouse built in 1832 at Eastern Point, a rocky projection on the east side of the entrance to the harbor. The light tower served until 1890, when the Lighthouse Board ordered a new one built on the foundation of the old one. This 36-foot white brick conical tower supports a fourth-order lens whose flashing white light is 57 feet above sea level and can be seen at a distance of 13 miles. A small service room is attached to the tower, and a long enclosed passageway connects the tower with a two-story dwelling and the fog signal building. A brick oil house

Eastern Point light station, erected after the Ten Pound Island light to provide better guidance to mariners.

stands off to the side, and a steel skeleton tower supports the radio beacon. Until recently the Coast Guard staffed the light station, but it is now automated and closed to the public. NR. [U.S. Coast Guard]

This lighthouse, first opened in 1821, served as a guide to Gloucester Harbor for 60 years. In 1881 the Lighthouse Board ordered it rebuilt. The new tower was a 30-foot brown conical masonry structure whose fifth-order lens is 44 feet above the water. Winslow Homer spent summers in Gloucester, and this lighthouse appears in many of his paintings, as it does in the work of Fitzhugh Lane. The tower remained in service until 1968, when a skeleton structure was built nearby to hold the light. The old tower has received federal restoration aid, and, at the request of the city, the Coast Guard planned to move the light back to the historic lighthouse in 1989. NR. [City of Gloucester]

■ **Ten Pound Island Lighthouse**
Gloucester Harbor
Ten Pound Island
1821, 1881

Ten Pound Island light station in Gloucester Harbor.

MARBLEHEAD

Established in 1838 on Marblehead Neck at the entrance to Marblehead Harbor, this lighthouse was low but adequate for the times. As the years passed, the surrounding area became more developed and the light was obscured. The Lighthouse Board's first solution to the problem was to erect a tall mast and hang a lantern on it. This approach worked until the early 1890s, when the board was prodded into seeking money for a new and

■ **Marblehead Neck Lighthouse**
Off Beacon Street
1838, 1895

Marblehead Neck lighthouse, an iron skeleton tower, c. 1912.

taller tower. In 1895 the board erected an iron skeleton pyramidal tower 105 feet tall. The focal plane of its light was 130 feet above sea level, well above the surrounding construction. When the severe hurricane of 1938 caused the light in the light tower to go out, the keeper drove his car to the tower and hooked up the car battery to the light, thus keeping it on through the night. This light, now automated, is still active, serving vessels coming into the harbor as well as those traveling north and south. The tower, painted brown with a black lantern, is all that remains of the station, together with the oil house. The land surrounding the station is now the property of the town, which has created a park here. A small patch of land on which the tower stands is still owned by the Coast Guard. NR. [U.S. Coast Guard. Town of Marblehead]

MARION

■ **Bird Island Lighthouse**
Bird Island
South of Butler Point
By boat from Marion
1819, 1889

Built on Bird Island northeast of New Bedford, at the east entrance to Sippican Harbor off Buzzard's Bay, this station's first light tower, made of stone, was 25 feet tall, with the focal plane of its revolving light 35 feet above sea level. Nearby stood a stone dwelling for the keeper. In 1889 the Lighthouse Board erected a new tower and equipped it with a fourth-order lens. The tower was 37 feet tall, and its light was 37 feet above sea level. The hurricane of 1938 swept away all the structures of the station except the light tower. In 1939 the Bureau of Lighthouses decommissioned the light and sold it to the town of Marion. The tower was restored by the Sippican Historical Society, which now maintains it with the town. NR. [Town of Marion]

MARTHA'S VINEYARD

■ **East Chop Lighthouse**
Oak Bluffs
Lighthouse Road
1877

Sited on the east side of the entrance to Vineyard Haven to guide steamers and other vessels into the harbor, this lighthouse replaced one operated privately for many years. The 40-foot white conical cast-iron tower has Italianate details, reflecting a popular style at the time of its construction. In recent years the light has been automated and fitted with a modern plastic lens. In the 1940s the Coast Guard tore down the station's ancillary buildings and gave the land they rested on to the town of Oak Bluffs for use as a park. NR. [U.S. Coast Guard]

East Chop light station, c. 1924. Only the light tower remains.

The first lighthouse at Gay Head, a wood octagonal tower 47 feet tall, began service in November 1799. In 1852 the Lighthouse Board noted that the lantern contained a revolving light with 10 lamps, each with a 14-inch reflector. Although the light was 172 feet above sea level, it did not serve the seagoing traffic well, being "... obscured about three-fourths of the time." The board thought that the lighthouse was a prime candidate for a first-order lens, as the light's importance "is not second to any on the eastern coast." The board had a new brick tower built and installed a first-order lens on December 1, 1856, one of the first Fresnel lenses used in the country. Through the years the light has served well as a guide for Boston-bound traffic to the entrance to the Vineyard Sound and as a seacoast light. Perhaps most important, it marks the Devils Bridge Rocks.

Gay Head gets its name from the varied colors of the cliffs that flow down to the ocean. Most people appreciated the beauty of the colors, but to at least one keeper they were a liability: "Clay ochre and earth of various colours from which this place derived its name," he said, "ascend in a sheet of wind from the high clifts and catch on the glass of the light-house, which requires to be often cleaned on the outside. . . ." He had to haul water for more than a mile and a half, he said, because ". . . I catch some rain water and it is true that many times I empty it coloured as red as blood with oker blown from the clifts."

In 1953, the Coast Guard gave Gay Head's first-order

■ **Gay Head Lighthouse**
West end of
Martha's Vineyard
Lighthouse Road
1799, 1856

Gay Head light, c. 1890s, on which one of the first Fresnel lenses in the country was installed.

lens to the Dukes County Historical Society of Edgartown. The lighthouse is now automated and uses a modern apparatus to send out its beam. Only the tower now remains; the Coast Guard removed all ancillary structures. NR. [U.S. Coast Guard]

MATTAPOISETT

■ Ned Point Lighthouse
End of Ned Point Road
1837, 1888

On the northeast side of the entrance to Mattapoisett Harbor, the fifth auditor of the Treasury built a lighthouse to guide ships into the harbor and to warn them of the hazards in the area, which is on Buzzard's Bay northeast of New Bedford. An 1851 inspection of the rubblestone lighthouse found a poor lighting system, a "badly built" light tower and a leaky dwelling, although the tower had been freshly whitewashed. Rebuilt in 1888, the new white tower, 39 feet tall, had a fifth-order lens whose light was 41 feet above sea level. Now automated, the light is still active.

All that remains of the station today is the tower and oil house. In 1930 the Coast Guard floated the dwelling to the Wings Neck light station across Buzzard's Bay on Cape Cod. In 1958 it sold all of the station's land, except for the plot with the tower, to the town of Mattapoisett, which created a park around the light tower. NR. [U.S. Coast Guard. Town of Mattapoisett]

NANTUCKET

■ Brant Point Lighthouse
West entrance to
Nantucket Harbor
End of Brant Point
1746, 1759, 1774, 1783, 1786,
c. 1788, 1825, 1856, 1901

The second lighthouse in this country was established in 1746, when, at the behest of local ship captains, the Nantucket government had a cheaply built beacon light placed on Brant Point on the south side of Nantucket Harbor. Fire destroyed it in 1758, and the town rebuilt it the next year. This structure stood until 1774, when "a most violent Gust of Wind that perhaps was ever known there" destroyed it. The town again replaced the light, and this time it lasted just nine years before it burned. The even smaller beacon built in 1783 proved unsatisfactory because of its dim light — called a "bug light" by mariners. In 1786 the town put up another light that a storm leveled in two years. Sometime between 1788 and 1795, when Nantucket turned over the lighthouse to the federal government, the town erected a more substantial

Brant Point lighthouse, the last of many constructed for this location.

tower that lasted until 1825, when this lighthouse was dismantled and a frame tower on a dwelling constructed. An inspection in 1838 revealed that the light was poor because of the smoked interior of the lantern, smoked chimneys of the lamps and black and spotted reflectors. This lighthouse continued to deteriorate, and in 1853 the Lighthouse Board recommended that it be replaced.

In 1856 the board built a new brick tower, 47 feet tall, at the west entrance to Nantucket Harbor; its lantern held a fourth-order lens. During the latter half of the 19th century the Nantucket Harbor channel shifted, thus reducing the effectiveness of the light. In 1900 the board erected a new cylindrical wood tower on the extremity of Brant Point and lighted it on January 31, 1901. This tower is still in operation and is considered the lowest light in New England — the focal plane of its red light is only 26 feet above sea level. Its companion at the site is a horn fog signal. The 1856 dwelling and tower (minus its lantern) are still standing. NR. [U.S. Coast Guard]

The Sankaty Head lighthouse was judged one of the best and most solidly constructed lighthouses in the country by the Lighthouse Board investigation in 1852. It had been built just two years previously to guard vessels against some recently discovered shoals some distance off the island. From the beginning it was equipped with a second-order Fresnel lens whose beam, 158 feet above sea level, was bright enough, according to one fisherman, by which to bait a hook "in the night season." The customs collector reported that some sailors "call the Sankaty Head light the 'Rocket light,' others the 'Blazing star.'" Its light was rivaled only by the lights of the towers at the highlands of the Navesink in New Jersey, which also had Fresnel lenses. The investigators found that the lamp in the lens burned only about as much oil as "required for a small beacon-light in any of our rivers and harbors, fitted with ten lamps and reflectors." Benjamin F. Isherwood, later to achieve fame as an engineer for the Navy, had supervised the manufacture of the lens for the

■ **Sankaty Head Lighthouse**
Siasconset
Off Polpis Road, 1 mile north of Siasconset
Cabet King
1850

Sankaty Head lighthouse, c. 1890, an especially well-constructed tower that has needed little repair.

light tower. The contractor, Cabet King, built the tower of "hard brick" set in cement, beginning five feet below the surface of the ground and going to 53 feet above. Atop the brick he laid six feet of granite, to which he added a lantern nine feet tall. The Lighthouse Board's judgment has been confirmed by the fact that it has not been necessary to rebuild the 70-foot tower to this day. This seacoast light, now automated, continues to function. The tower, painted white with a wide red band about its middle, also serves as a good daymark. NR. [U.S. Coast Guard]

NEW BEDFORD

■ **Butler Flats Lighthouse**
Clark's Point
Off East Rodney French
Boulevard
1804, 1898

This caisson lighthouse was constructed to replace the square lighthouse erected on Clark's Point in 1804. The site chosen was mud flats; the builder had to scrape away the mud to get to hardpan on which to rest the iron caisson. Filling the cylinder with rock and cement, he created a platform for the conical white tower. The new light was exhibited on April 30, 1898, at which time the old Clark's Point light went out of service. The light of the fifth-order lens was 53 feet above sea level. Automated in 1978, the light is still active through an agreement with the city of New Bedford, which maintains the light as a private aid. The lighthouse is in the river and is best seen from Clark's Point. The old Clark's Point light tower, now owned by the city, has been rehabilitated and can be seen atop Fort Taber, which is open to the public. NR. [U.S. Coast Guard. City of New Bedford]

Butler Flats light tower, a caisson lighthouse built on mud flats.

■ **Palmer Island Lighthouse**
New Bedford Harbor
Charles M. Pierce
1849

Because of the narrowness of the channel into the inner harbor of New Bedford, New England's premier 19th-century whaling port, in 1849 the Treasury Department had a lighthouse placed on Palmer Island, on the west side of the harbor entrance. This white conical tower, built by Charles M. Pierce, a mason, was 39 feet tall, and its light, which later came from a fourth-order lens, was 34 feet above sea level. A fog bell supplied a signal during times of reduced visibility.

The light tower is no longer active. The city of New Bedford has a special attachment to the old structure, which is featured on the city's seal, and now owns it. In 1966 vandals set fire to it, gutting the interior and destroying the later additions to the structure. Local preservationists believe that the tower could now be restored to its original appearance. Although located in the harbor, the tower is attached to land by a stone accessway. NR. [City of New Bedford]

NEWBURYPORT

In 1788 the Massachusetts legislature authorized the building of two light towers on the north end of Plum Island to serve as range lights. Over the years these towers were moved about because of erosion and the shifting bar at the mouth of the Merrimac River. In 1874, for example, the towers were moved back 75 feet because of the threat of erosion. Construction started in 1887 on a stone tower to replace the front range light structure, but before it was completed the river had shifted again and work ceased. The rear range light was rebuilt in 1898 and fitted with a fourth-order lens. This white conical tower, 35 feet tall, is the only one that remains. In 1981 the lantern received a modern plastic lens and its light, 50 feet above the sea, was automated. The Coast Guard has retained the tower and the land on which it sits and transferred the remainder of the land to the Parker River National Wildlife Refuge. NR. [U.S. Coast Guard. U.S. Fish and Wildlife Service]

■ **Newburyport Harbor Lighthouse**
Plum Island
Northern Boulevard
1788, 1898

NORTH EASTHAM

This lighthouse has lived two lives—the first in Chatham and its second here. In 1923 the Bureau of Lighthouses moved the north tower of the 1877 Chatham twin lights (see Chatham lighthouse entry) to Nauset Beach to replace the last wood tower of the set known as the Three Sisters (see next entry). This conical cast-iron tower is 48

■ **Nauset Beach Lighthouse**
Nauset Light Road
Off U.S. 6
1877

Nauset Beach light in 1944, moved from Chatham in 1923.

feet tall and for years had a fourth-order lens; the focal plane of its light was 114 feet above sea level. The lens was moved in more recent years to the Salt Pond Visitors Center in the Cape Cod National Seashore. The light tower, which for a number of years has been painted red and white, is now automated. The keeper's frame dwelling with shingle siding also survives. NR. [U.S. Coast Guard]

■ **Three Sisters Lighthouses**
Nauset Beach
Cable Road
Off Ocean View Drive
Winslow Lewis (1838)
1838, 1892

The Boston Marine Society, believing that a navigational aid at Nauset Beach was needed to guide small, shore-hugging vessels past the Nauset Shoals, petitioned Congress for a three-light aid that would not be confused with other lights nearby. As requested by the society, Congress appropriated $10,000 specifically for a three-light navigational aid, America's only such station. Winslow Lewis obtained the contract from the Treasury's fifth auditor for less than $7,000, and his crew proceeded to build three short brick towers and a two-story brick house. During construction the workers often ignored the building specifications. The construction supervisor refused to accept what he considered poor work but was directed by his superiors to do so. Lighted in 1838, Lewis's Argand lamps and parabolic reflectors served until 1858, when they were replaced by sixth-order lenses. Fifteen years later these were replaced by larger, fourth-order lenses.

In time erosion threatened the light towers, and in 1892 the Lighthouse Board had three wood towers built, each 29 feet tall to the top of the lantern. These replaced the brick towers, which eventually succumbed to erosion but whose foundations are occasionally visible when winter storms scour the beach. This solution was not permanent, for by 1911 these towers faced the same danger as their predecessors. This time the Bureau of Lighthouses decided to move the center tower to a safer place near the keeper's wood dwelling, built in 1875, and to remove the other two lights from service. The single tower, now with a flashing light, began operation on June 1, 1911. This wood tower continued to function until 1923, when the bureau closed it and lighted the iron tower moved from Chatham, now called the Nauset Beach light.

In 1918 the Bureau of Lighthouses sold the paired wood towers to a Cape Cod couple who used them as a

Three Sisters lights, the only such multiple-light station in the country.

residence, eventually incorporating them into a larger home. The last of the "sisters" was sold with its lantern, and the new owner built a one-story residential addition to it. The Cape Cod National Seashore acquired the paired towers in 1965 and eventually removed the residence that had been joined to them. In 1983 it obtained and moved the third tower to the site of the other two. The park currently plans to arrange the Three Sisters in their original configuration at a site on Cable Road and display them as an interpretive exhibit. NR. [National Park Service]

PLYMOUTH

Sometimes called the Gurnet light, this light station traces its ancestry to a colonial lighthouse erected by the Massachusetts legislature on Gurnet Point on the north side of the entrance to Plymouth Bay. Built in 1769, the light was little better than the one at Brant Point on Nantucket. This first beacon set a pattern for twin lights on this point: the structure was 20 feet long, 15 feet wide and 20 feet high, with a lantern on each end containing two lamps. However, the towers were too close together to be effective. In 1778 a stray cannonball struck the lighthouse but did not damage the lights, and repairs were made after the war. In 1790 the state turned over the lighthouse to the federal government, and with it came a woman light keeper, perhaps the first in the federal service. The lighthouse burned in 1801. The local citizens erected a temporary single-light beacon at the same site, and in 1802–03 the government built twin towers so that navigators would not confuse this site with the single-light station at Barnstable. The new 22-foot towers were 30 feet apart, and their lights were 70 feet above sea level. The station also had a white dwelling and a foghorn. In 1842 the towers were rebuilt; these structures were white octagonal pyramidal towers, each 39 feet tall with a

■ **Plymouth (Gurnet)**
Lighthouse
Gurnet Point
South of Green Harbor
1769, 1803, 1842

Plymouth light station, where land has been cut away to raise the height of the tower. The fog signal building is on the embankment's edge.

fourth-order lens whose light was 102 feet above sea level. Like their predecessors, they were too close together to be effective. Over time their importance declined because of the decrease in marine traffic.

With the opening of the Cape Cod Canal in 1914, the lights resumed importance as a coastal aid, but in 1924 the Bureau of Lighthouses discontinued one of the lights when it phased out multiple lights. The remaining light is still in service, and the residence still stands. The U.S. Lighthouse Society has licensed the site from the Coast Guard. It can be reached by a five-mile hike over a sandy beach or by boat. NR. [U.S. Coast Guard. U.S. Lighthouse Society]

PROVINCETOWN

■ Race Point Lighthouse
Cape Cod National Seashore
Race Point Road
Off U.S. 6
1816, 1876

Despite the fact that the tip of the Cape Cod peninsula had been the site of many shipwrecks, a lighthouse was not established here until 1816, and another 36 years passed, with more wrecks, before a fog signal was added to the station. The Lighthouse Board tore down the original conical white rubblestone tower in 1876 and put up a new one made of iron plates lined on the interior with brick. The 40-foot tower, painted white, had a fourth-order lens whose light was 41 feet above sea level and visible for 12 miles. Even with this lighthouse, navigating the area is still dangerous, and many ships have continued to pile up on nearby shoals and beaches. The light is still active and is now judged to be visible for 16 miles. A foghorn is present for times of reduced visibility. The light station is now within the bounds of the Cape Cod National Seashore, although the light station property is still under the jurisdiction of the Coast Guard. The Coast Guard, however, permits visitors to walk around the grounds. NR. [U.S. Coast Guard]

Original Race Point light around 1870 and the newer light station in 1956, surrounded by a network of trails left by dune buggies.

Surviving Bakers Island light tower and dwelling before automation.

SALEM

The federal government erected a lighthouse at this point to replace a daymark set here in 1791. The station, at the entrance to Salem Harbor, consisted of a dwelling with a white conical light tower at each end. It remained a twin-light station until sometime around 1870, when one of the lights was eliminated. A fog bell was later added, and through the years the fog signal was updated — to a siren in the 1930s and a horn today. Now, only one tower and the dwelling remain, but the light is still active. NR. [U.S. Coast Guard. Leased to Bakers Island Association]

■ **Bakers Island Lighthouse**
Entrance to Salem Harbor
1798

Derby Wharf, built just before the Revolution, is the symbol of Salem as a port, particularly during the years when it was heavily engaged in overseas trade. For many years the Bakers Island light served as a guide to mariners entering Salem Harbor. But in the 19th century, better lights were needed to guide vessels into the inner harbor, and in 1870 Congress appropriated money for lights at Derby Wharf, Hospital Point and Fort Pickering. In January 1871 a temporary light was placed on a warehouse near the end of the wharf, and workers soon began erecting a square 25-foot-tall lighthouse, 12 feet on each side, at the end of Derby Wharf. In the spring of the year the light tower went into service, its lantern emitting a red light. The focal plane of the fifth-order lens was 25 feet above the water. By the time the lighthouse was constructed, the port of Salem was in its declining years, but the fishing and coastal trade remained active, and the lighthouse continued to serve a need. The size of the lens in its lantern changed from time to time. In 1906 it received a larger, fourth-order lens, which was replaced four years later by a sixth-order lens; by 1932 the now-electrified light had a 300-millimeter lens. The color of the tower also changed. Originally painted red, it received a white coat in 1922 and has remained that color since.

   In 1977 the Coast Guard discontinued the light and two years later turned over the tower to the National Park Service as an addition to the Salem Maritime National Historic Site, of which Derby Wharf is a part. The Friends of Salem Maritime restored the old light tower, persuaded the Coast Guard to relight it in 1983 and with

■ **Derby Wharf Lighthouse**
Salem Maritime National Historic Site
Derby Street
1871

Derby Wharf lighthouse, once an important guide to Salem Harbor.

the Peabody Museum of Salem and the park, collaborated in preparing an exhibit on the lighthouse's history, which was placed at the tower. The two lights erected along with Derby Wharf are still active: the square brick Hospital Point tower is a range light (its Stick Style dwelling has served as the residence of the commandant of the First Coast Guard District), and the Fort Pickering light is maintained as a private aid to navigation. NR. [National Park Service]

SCITUATE

■ Scituate Lighthouse
Cedar Point
End of Lighthouse Road
1811

Scituate's striking octagonal light tower and bird-cage lantern.

As a result of pressure from fishing and other marine interests for a lighthouse to guide vessels into Scituate's harbor, in 1810 Congress appropriated $4,000 to build a lighthouse here. The local citizens argued among themselves for a year before they agreed on siting the lighthouse at Cedar Point, on the north side of the entrance to the harbor. Lighted on September 19, 1811, the granite octagonal tower was 25 feet tall excluding the lantern, with the light 35 feet above sea level. In addition, a 1½-story, 24-foot-square wood dwelling was built. To make the light visible at a greater distance and aid vessels heading for Boston Harbor, the tower was raised 15 feet in 1827. On this brick addition, the workers placed a new and larger lantern and inserted four large windows on the seaward side so that the lighthouse could exhibit a white light over a red light. The white light came from lamps and reflectors in the new lantern, while the red light came from lamps and reflectors below. The lights were not satisfactory because at a distance they appeared to merge, causing some confusion to navigators. An inspector in 1838 criticized the light, and in 1841 the fifth auditor of the Treasury had the lamps and reflectors rearranged and the red pane on the lower lamps replaced with red chimneys. By 1852 both lights were red, and two years later both were white. The following year the Lighthouse Board added a Fresnel lens, which served for five years. In 1860, with the completion of the Minots Ledge lighthouse north of here and in accordance with congressional direction, the board decommissioned the station. Although the fishers of the area urged that the lighthouse be reactivated, the Lighthouse Board responded only by placing a lantern at the end of a newly constructed breakwater in 1891.

Over the years local groups attempted to purchase the property from the Lighthouse Board so that the old light station could be preserved, but these efforts, for various reasons, were not successful. Finally, in 1917, the town of Scituate succeeded in purchasing the light station from the government, and the Scituate Department of Parks restored it in the 1920s. During its active years, the station had grown to include, in addition to the dwelling, an enclosed passageway between the tower and the dwelling, shops and ancillary structures; most of these have been retained. The Scituate Historical Society manages the site and opens it to the public on certain days in the summer. NR. [Town of Scituate]

TRURO

Also known as the Cape Cod light, this light station, first built in 1798 on the highlands near Truro, was the first on Cape Cod. Its main mission was to light the area between Nantucket and Cape Ann. The 45-foot tower had to be rebuilt in 1833 and again in 1857. At the time of the last construction, the Lighthouse Board placed a first-order lens on the tower to make it more visible to mariners. This light was usually the first one sighted by ships from Europe bound for Massachusetts Bay. When electrified, the light measured 4-million candlepower. The present white cylindrical tower is 66 feet tall, but the focal plane of its light is 183 feet above sea level. The station had a fog signal and later a radio beacon. The keeper's dwelling is a 1½-story Queen Anne–style house, and the assistant keeper had a modern ranch-style residence. In 1945 the first-order lens was replaced by aerobeacons. The dwellings are still used by the Coast Guard, which permits visitors on the grounds of the station and is developing plans to display the lens's clockwork system. The station is encompassed by the Cape Cod National Seashore. NR. [U.S. Coast Guard]

■ **Highlands (Cape Cod) Lighthouse**
Highlands Road
Off U.S. 6
1798, 1833, 1857

Highlands lighthouse in 1859. The tower today is very much the same.

■ ■ ■ ■ ■ ■   NEW HAMPSHIRE   ■ ■ ■ ■ ■ ■

PORTSMOUTH

In 1821 White Island, one of the Isles of Shoals located just over five miles off the New Hampshire coast, received a lighthouse. Made of stone, this tower was 87 feet tall. It served until 1859, when a new tower, made of brick two feet thick, was erected and fitted with a second-order lens whose focal plane was 82 feet above sea level. This cylindrical tower, 58 feet tall and now painted white, has

■ **Isles of Shoals Lighthouse**
White Island
1821, 1859

Isles of Shoals light station off Portsmouth. The covered walkway permitted less hazardous trips to the tower along the rocky embankment.

over the years served to guide vessels along this coast and into Portsmouth Harbor. Fog signals at the station have included a bell, siren and horn. A passageway runs from the tower to the original oil house. The keeper's dwelling is still standing. Now automated, the light continues in service. The light station, except for the tower, will go to the New Hampshire State Parks in the future. Access at present is by private boat only. NR district. [U.S. Coast Guard]

■ **Portsmouth Harbor
(New Castle) Lighthouse**
New Castle Island
Adjacent to Fort Constitution
1771, 1804, 1877

In 1771 the colonial government erected a lighthouse at Portsmouth Harbor to guide vessels into the harbor. Because Portsmouth was a principal shipbuilding port during the Revolution, this light saw a number of vessels sail out of the harbor to take part in the struggle for independence; John Paul Jones, for example, took command of the *Ranger* here in 1777. The Portsmouth Harbor tower survived the Revolution easily, and in 1791 the state turned over to the government the tower and "one and three-quarters acres of a neck of land in New Castle, on Great Island, at the entrance of Piscataqua River,

Portsmouth Harbor lighthouse, the third constructed for this location.

commonly called Fort Point." By 1804 the original wood tower had deteriorated, compelling the government to put up a new one, also of wood, on a granite foundation. In 1838 an inspector reported that the 80-foot octagonal lighthouse was in "fine order," and in 1851 the investigating board found the tower in good condition but noted that the tower was lighted with lamps and spherical reflectors "old and much worn" and the interior of the lantern was "very dirty." Although the old lighthouse served for 73 years, in 1877 the Lighthouse Board built an iron tower on the foundation of the 1804 tower. A new dwelling for the keeper had been built five years earlier. The white light tower still stands, emitting a green flashing light, the focal plane of which is 52 feet above sea level. The keeper's dwelling also survives. The light station is adjacent to Fort Constitution, which is open to the public. NR district. [U.S. Coast Guard]

■ ■ ■ ■ ■ ■   RHODE ISLAND   ■ ■ ■ ■ ■ ■

BLOCK ISLAND

To serve traffic entering Long Island Sound and traffic heading for Narragansett Bay as well as to guard ships against the long sand bar at Sandy Point, the Treasury's fifth auditor had a lighthouse built here. The first lighthouse, in 1829, was 45 feet tall. Erosion threatened it, and in 1837 the fifth auditor had the light moved one-fourth mile back. In 1851 the Lighthouse Board noted that this tower had two fixed lights but that they "appeared only as one light"; the investigators also considered the light to be "inferior." The board had another tower erected in 1857, but in a decade it, too, was considered useless. In 1867 the board rebuilt the light

■ **North Lighthouse**
New Shoreham
Sandy Point
1829, 1857, 1867

North light's sturdy masonry construction, emulated at several sites including Plum Island (N.Y.) and Sheffield and Great Captain islands (Conn.).

tower and dwelling. The new dwelling was a gray granite two-story structure with a one-story granite addition that served as the kitchen. The light tower, painted brown, rested on one end of the dwelling's gable roof and held a fourth-order lens whose light was 58 feet above sea level. The Coast Guard electrified the light in the 1940s and automated it in 1955. Fifteen years later the light was discontinued and replaced with a light on a skeleton tower. The Fish and Wildlife Service acquired the lighthouse in 1973 and used it for a decade. Since the early 1970s the town of New Shoreham, working through its North Light Commission, has been trying to keep the old structure in good repair, using support from the Bicentennial Fund to restore the lantern and keeper's quarters. Several ferries from such places on the mainland as Newport, New London, Galilee and Providence make runs to Block Island. NR. [Town of New Shoreham]

■ **Southeast Lighthouse**
Mohegan Bluffs
Southeast point of
Block Island
1873

A handsome Gothic Revival structure, this octagonal pyramidal red brick light tower, which is attached to the 2½-story brick dwelling, is 67 feet tall and houses a first-order lens that emits a green light. Because of the tower's siting on Mohegan Bluffs, the focal plane of the light is

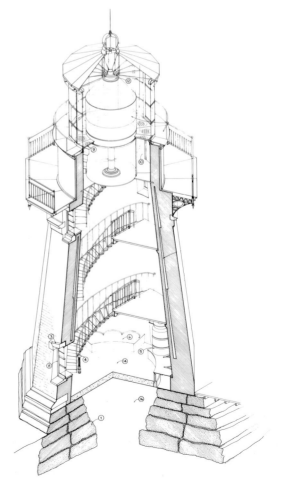

Cross section of Southeast light. Granite blocks form the foundation, topped by a concrete floor. A cast-iron stairway climbs to the lantern's platform, where hexagonal glass lights bring daylight to the watch room and vestibule below. The tower is capped by a ventilator with a lightning rod.

201 feet above sea level. But the bluff is eroding, and the edge is getting dangerously close to the tower and dwelling. The Coast Guard, the Block Island Historical Society and the National Trust for Historic Preservation have worked together to study moving the light to a safer location, aided by a grant from the Bicentennial Fund. When a new light is placed in a skeleton tower at the light station, the Coast Guard plans to turn over the old light tower, dwelling and other ancillary structures to the Block Island Historical Society. The project has been on hold until the question of who is going to own the site is resolved. [U.S. Coast Guard]

JAMESTOWN

Beavertail light is situated on the south end of Conanicut Island, which is in the center of the entrance to Narragansett Bay; consequently, it marks both the east and west passages into the bay. Beavertail, a 58-foot wood tower, was the country's fourth lighthouse. When it burned a few years after construction, colonial masons in 1753 erected a 64-foot rubblestone tower to replace it. The lighthouse's principal purpose at the time was to serve traffic going to Newport, one of the largest and busiest ports in colonial America. The British burned this tower in 1779, but after the war, in 1783–84, the state repaired and put it back into operation. In 1793 Rhode Island turned over the lighthouse to the federal government. The keeper's dwelling collapsed in 1815, and the government built another one, which an inspector 22 years later said was poorly put together. In 1851 the Lighthouse Board reported that the tower was the "worst built tower yet seen; built of soft shale [and the] tower inside and out [is] in wretched condition. . . ." Despite these adverse comments, the tower had been standing for a century and had survived injury at the hands of the British.

■ **Beavertail Lighthouse**
South end of
Conanicut Island
End of Beavertail Road
1749, 1753, 1856

Beavertail light, a square granite tower, the third lighthouse built for the site.

The board had a new light tower built in 1856 and installed a third-order lens that emitted a fixed white light. This 52-foot square granite tower was attached to a keeper's dwelling built at the same time; both still survive. The tower received a fourth-order lens in 1899, and at that time the light was changed to a flashing light. Now automated, the light is still active. The lantern, electrified in 1931, has been glazed with green plexiglass to give off a green light. Nearby is an assistant keeper's house of 1898. Both residences are made of brick and have been stuccoed and painted white. The station has been leased to the Rhode Island Parks Association, a nonprofit organization that plans to install a maritime museum in the structure. NR. [U.S. Coast Guard. Leased to Rhode Island Parks Association]

■ **Dutch Island Lighthouse**
South end of Dutch Island
Bay Islands State Park
1827, 1857

The federal government established a light on Dutch Island west of Conanicut Island in 1827 and had it rebuilt 30 years later. This second structure was a 42-foot square brick tower attached to a keeper's dwelling that was erected at the same time. Its purpose was to guide ships into Dutch Island Harbor as well as through the west entrance to Narragansett Bay. The light was automated in 1947, and shortly thereafter the Coast Guard tore down the dwelling. In 1979 the Coast Guard removed the light from service and eventually turned it over to the Rhode Island Department of Environmental Management to become part of Bay Islands State Park. Since then, the Friends of Dutch Island have come forward to preserve the lighthouse. The light tower and oil house are all that remain of the old light station. NR. [Rhode Island Department of Environmental Management]

Dutch Island light station near Jamestown, equipped with a bell on the tower, c. 1884. The dwelling no longer exists.

NARRAGANSETT

Marking the west side of the entrance to Narragansett Bay and the north side of the east entrance to Block Island Sound, this light station was established in 1810 with the building and lighting of a 35-foot wood light tower. In 1816, after a storm had destroyed this tower, a stone tower was built on the site. This tower served until 1857, when the Lighthouse Board had an octagonal pyramidal tower of granite block erected. The tower was 51 feet tall, and its light was 65 feet above sea level. To make it a distinctive daymark, the board later had the upper half of the tower painted brown and the lower half white. The dwelling, once attached to the light tower, is now gone. The Coast Guard automated the light in 1954. Still active, it is on the grounds of the Coast Guard station. Public access is limited. NR. [U.S. Coast Guard]

■ **Point Judith Lighthouse**
Point Judith
1470 Ocean Road
Route 108 south
1810, 1816, 1857

Point Judith light, now part of a Coast Guard station. The octagonal tower also acts as a distinctive daymark.

Castle Hill lighthouse, a fortresslike tower confronting the sea. A fog bell is attached just below the tower's gallery.

NEWPORT

Built into the side of a rock ledge at the water's edge, this conical 34-foot light tower, made with heavy rough granite blocks, began service in 1890. The style is Richardsonian Romanesque, and there is some evidence that the famous architect H. H. Richardson may have designed the lighthouse. The upper half of the tower has been painted white; the bottom is unpainted. The flashing red light from its fifth-order lens was 42 feet above sea level. When the 1938 hurricane destroyed the dwelling and the other structures of the light station, the decision was made not to rebuild them. The Coast Guard automated the light in 1957. NR. [U.S. Coast Guard]

■ **Castle Hill Lighthouse**
Castle Hill
West end of Newport Neck
Off Ocean Avenue
1890

Ida Lewis Rock lighthouse, one of very few lights named after persons.

■ **Ida Lewis Rock (Lime Rock) Lighthouse**
Newport Harbor
Wellington Avenue
1854

Originally known as the Lime Rock lighthouse, this site honors a great American light keeper. Ida Lewis came to the lighthouse as a young girl when her father became keeper. After her father's death she became keeper, and during the course of her 34-year career she rescued a number of people. As her fame spread she received honors, awards and medals, and she was visited by many prominent people, including President Ulysses S. Grant. She was, unquestionably, the best-known light keeper of her day, and she burnished the image of the light keeper to a high luster. On her death in 1911, the Bureau of Lighthouses changed the name of the lighthouse to the Ida Lewis Rock light station.

The lighthouse consisted of a Greek Revival dwelling with a hipped roof and 13-foot tower, attached to the northwest corner of the dwelling. In 1927 the bureau removed the lens from the lantern and placed an automated beacon on a skeleton tower in front of the lighthouse. The next year it sold the lighthouse to the Ida Lewis Yacht Club. The light on the skeleton tower continued in service until November 1, 1963, when the Coast Guard deactivated it. Later, the yacht club obtained permission from the Coast Guard to put a light back in the old lantern and maintain it as a private aid to navigation. Although adaptively used by the yacht club, the building is virtually unaltered from the time that Ida Lewis lived here. NR. [Ida Lewis Yacht Club]

■ **Newport Harbor Lighthouse**
North end of Goat Island
1823, 1838, 1865

Although the fifth auditor of the Treasury in 1823 established a 30-foot octagonal lighthouse on Goat Island at the entrance to Newport Harbor, the light was succeeded in 1838 by a lighthouse erected on a nearby breakwater. In 1851 the 1823 tower was disassembled and moved about 10 miles to Prudence Island at Portsmouth (see Prudence Island lighthouse entry). In 1865 the Lighthouse Board replaced the 1838 tower on Goat Island with a 35-foot octagonal tower of rough-cut granite blocks painted white. The light tower had a dwelling attached to it, but in 1922 a submarine struck the residence, damaging it so severely that the Bureau of Lighthouses tore it down. Still active, this light was automated in 1963. Recently, the area between the coast and the lighthouse was filled, creating a small grassy park that affords easy access to the lighthouse. NR. [U.S. Coast Guard]

Rose Island light station, deactivated in 1971 but subject of a major restoration project.

In its active years this 35-foot tower with its fourth-order lens guarded vessels from the dangerous shoals north of Newport Harbor. But changes in the channel caused by the Newport Bridge in 1969 demanded new aids to navigation, so the lighthouse was deactivated in 1971. A frame dwelling with a mansard roof and octagonal tower, which rises from the roof, the lighthouse is at the water's edge, and most of the station's ancillary structures remain. Newport and the Rose Island Lighthouse Foundation have restored the old lighthouse, with help from the Bicentennial Fund, including the exterior, multicolored slate roof, first floor and stairs to the lantern, which are being returned to their 1912 appearance. The second floor will be modern quarters for a "keeper" who will protect the lighthouse from vandalism. The tower was due to be relighted for the 1989 bicentennial and opened to the public. Visitors will be able to get to the 16-acre island (to be part of the state park system) by boat from Fort Adams. NR. [City of Newport]

■ **Rose Island Lighthouse**
Southwest point of
Rose Island
By boat from Fort Adams
1870

PORTSMOUTH

In 1851 workers disassembled the 1823 light tower on Goat Island in Newport Harbor, transported the materials about 10 miles to Prudence Island at Portsmouth and rebuilt the tower. The old octagonal light tower, 30 feet tall, exhibited its light at its new location on January 17, 1852. The original lantern, still in place and transported with the tower, is a bird-cage type that is quite rare today. This light served to guide ships along the east passage of Narragansett Bay. The light station once had its full complement of structures, including a clapboard dwelling, but the hurricane of 1938 swept the house and the other structures into the water, killing the keeper's wife and her son, a former keeper and two guests. The

■ **Prudence Island**
Lighthouse
East side of Sandy Point
1823

Prudence Island light near Portsmouth, surrounded by the devastation of the 1938 hurricane. The bird-cage lantern is supported by metal framework.

keeper himself almost drowned but managed to survive when a wave swept him back to shore. The administrators decided not to rebuild the station and automated the light in 1939. About 1961 a foghorn was placed on the gallery of the lantern. NR. [U.S. Coast Guard]

WARWICK

■ **Warwick Lighthouse**
1350 Warwick Neck Avenue
1827, 1932

The first lighthouse on Warwick Neck, a wood tower on a stone dwelling, was erected in 1827. By 1889 the dwelling was in poor shape, so the Lighthouse Board built another nearby. It remodeled the house into a barn, and this structure served as the lighthouse until 1932, when an iron light tower was erected. This cylindrical cast-iron light tower has the distinction of being the last traditional lighthouse built in Rhode Island. The light was originally closer to the shore, but the hurricane of 1938 undermined the 51-foot tower, and the administrators had it moved 50 feet to the north the next year. The light is scheduled for automation in 1990. NR. [U.S. Coast Guard]

Warwick lighthouse, the last traditional-style light in Rhode Island.

WATCH HILL

Located on the north side of the east entrance to Fishers Island Sound, the first tower at this point near the Connecticut state line had a light that was 73 feet above sea level. It served until 1856, when the Lighthouse Board replaced it with a 45-foot square granite tower attached to a square dwelling. The light of its fourth-order lens was 61 feet above sea level. The Coast Guard automated the light and foghorn in 1986. Both are still active. The Watch Hill Improvement Society has leased the unused parts of the light station and plans to establish a museum that will exhibit the history of the station and the nearby coast. [U.S. Coast Guard. Leased to Watch Hill Improvement Society]

■ **Watch Hill Lighthouse**
Watch Hill Point
Route 1A from Westerly
1807, 1856

Watch Hill light station consisting of a square granite tower, dwelling, foghorn building, fuel shed and garage.

■ ■ ■ ■ ■ ■ ■ VERMONT ■ ■ ■ ■ ■ ■ ■ ■

SHELBURNE

Located originally on Lake Champlain, a mile from Colchester Point, the Colchester Reef lighthouse warned southbound ships en route to Burlington of three dangerous shoals that lay in the way. In constructing the lighthouse on the shoals, the workers first built a square granite pier that served as the base of the lighthouse. On the pier they built a square house with a mansard roof and a square tower rising from one end. Davits on an end of the granite base held a boat used by the lighthouse keeper to go ashore when necessary. In time this lighthouse became the best known on the lake. The lighthouse continued in use until 1933, when it was decommissioned. It lay deteriorating for nearly 20 years and then was acquired by the Shelburne Museum. In 1952 the museum moved it, piece by piece, from its foundation in the lake to the mainland, where workers reassembled it on the grounds. The museum positioned it close to the old Lake Champlain steamer *Ticonderoga*. Today, the old structure is a lighthouse-maritime museum featuring an exhibit on the shipwrecks of Lake Champlain. [Shelburne Museum]

■ **Colchester Reef Lighthouse**
Shelburne Museum
Off U.S. 7 south
1871

MID-ATLANTIC

Thomas Point Shoal lighthouse, near Annapolis, Md., the last screwpile light still in its original location in the Chesapeake Bay. Rocks at the lighthouse base prevent ice from doing irreparable damage to the structure.

■ ■ ■ ■ ■ ■   DELAWARE   ■ ■ ■ ■ ■ ■

FENWICK ISLAND

■ **Fenwick Island Lighthouse**
Route 54 at Maryland border
1859

Authorized by Congress in 1856 to fill in a dark space between the Assateague, Va., light to the south and the Cape Henlopen, Del., light to the north, this station was not lighted until August 1, 1859. It is positioned almost squarely on the Mason-Dixon Line, which divides Maryland and Delaware. The Lighthouse Board had the tower fitted with a third-order Fresnel lens whose focal plane was 83 feet above sea level. The octagonal masonry tower is 87 feet tall and is painted white, its original color. Today, the light is automated and still active. The Friends of Fenwick Island Lighthouse have recently restored and opened the old tower and maintain a small museum in its base. At the light station is the marker that commemorates the beginning of the work of the English engineers Mason and Dixon; on one side is the coat of arms of William Penn and on the other is that of Lord Delaware. NR. [U.S. Coast Guard. Leased to Friends of Fenwick Island Lighthouse]

LEWES

■ **Delaware Breakwater Lighthouse**
East end of breakwater
behind Cape Henlopen
Off Route 18
1885

This lighthouse eventually took over most of the duties of one of the colonial lighthouses that succumbed to erosion: the Cape Henlopen light, built in 1767 at the behest of Pennsylvania business interests. Made of fieldstone, the octagonal tower was rather short for a coastal light. The British burned it during the Revolution, but shipping companies repaired and relighted it in 1784. The site turned out to be a poor one as the area was subject to wind erosion. In 1852 the Lighthouse Board considered the tower well built but recognized the problem of erosion, noting that a sand dune was moving toward the tower. In 1856 the board fitted it with the largest Fresnel lens, a first order, and over the next 30 years continued the fight to save the tower from the sand. At times the wind would blow the sand away from the foundation, so the engineers would put in plantings to anchor the sand. At other times the wind would move the sand toward the station; by 1863 the sand was up to the second story of the keeper's dwelling, prompting the Lighthouse Board to build new quarters. Sometimes the ocean contributed to the problem, as in 1883, when the water from a storm lapped at the tower's foundation.

Prompted in some degree by the continuing erosion and fears of losing the light, but much more by the needs of the nearby harbor of refuge, the board decided to erect a new lighthouse on the Delaware Breakwater. This light was actually part of a larger complex later designated a National Harbor of Refuge. Beginning in the first quarter of the 19th century, maritime interests urged a place where ships could seek safety behind Cape Henlopen during severe weather. After a study by prominent military engineers who recommended a large refuge, Congress in 1825 authorized construction of the breakwater and an icebreaker pier. Work began three years later and was completed in 1839. A lighthouse was placed on the west end of the breakwater to mark the entrance to the harbor. Over the years the harbor of refuge grew in use and complexity. To provide greater safety for vessels, Congress authorized closing the gap between the breakwater and the icebreaker pier. Because the usefulness of the lighthouse at the former west end of the breakwater had diminished substantially, the Lighthouse Board had another lighthouse built at the east end of the breakwater. This Delaware Breakwater light from 1885, a brown conical tower 56 feet tall, could be seen on the sea side as well as the harbor side of Cape Henlopen. The focal plane of its light was 61 feet above sea level. Eleven years later, Congress authorized an expansion of the refuge with a new breakwater and several icebreaker piers. On completion of this work, named by Congress the National Harbor of Refuge, the Lighthouse Board marked the entrance to the harbor with a lighthouse. Damaged in 1920, this lighthouse was replaced in 1926 by the present structure on the south end of the harbor of refuge breakwater. It is a brown caisson-type lighthouse with a white conical tower, black lantern housing a fourth-order lens and light 72 feet above mean high water.

In the meantime, a ship wrecked near the old Cape Henlopen lighthouse shortly after the 1883 erosion threat and caused sand to build up around the structure. That was but a brief respite, for the erosion pattern resumed; by 1885 the tower was once again threatened. The battle against nature continued for four decades until, in 1924, the Bureau of Lighthouses was so fearful of the imminent demise of the tower that it relocated the light to a skeleton tower 700 feet inland. Finally, on April 13, 1926, a severe storm toppled the old lighthouse. Shortly afterward the bureau deactivated the light and let the Delaware Breakwater lighthouse, the Harbor of Refuge lighthouse and the nearby lightships officially take over the historic tower's work. NR district. [U.S. Coast Guard]

Below left: Cape Henlopen light, a 1926 victim of erosion. The old colonial light had a helical-bar lantern and screen to prevent birds from harming the lens. Below: Delaware Breakwater lighthouse in 1925.

■ **Lightship Overfalls**
(WLV-539)
Lewes-Rehoboth Canal
Between Shipcarpenter and
Mulberry Streets
1938

Lightship Overfalls, when it
was still on duty off the New
England coast at the Boston
station.

During its 35 years of active duty, this lightship served at
several stations on the East Coast, including Boston, its
longest assignment. A steel double-hulled ship built at
Rice Brothers Shipyard in East Boothbay, Maine, the
vessel is 116 feet long, with a beam of 25 feet and a draft of
12 feet. Launched in 1938, the vessel first was assigned to
the Boston station, off the entrance to the harbor. Later,
the lightship was moved to the Pollock Rip, Mass., and
Cornfield Point, Conn., stations before the Coast Guard
decommissioned it in 1973. The Lewes Historical Society
acquired the vessel shortly afterward and renamed it the
Overfalls, for the lightship station a short distance from
Lewes Harbor. It is displayed now as a museum ship.
NR. [Lewes Historical Society]

MILFORD

■ **Mispillion Lighthouse**
End of County Road 203,
off Route 36
1831, 1859, 1873

Located at the mouth of the Mispillion River, this
lighthouse guided vessels from the Delaware Bay into the
river. It was particularly important during the day of
sailing vessels when trade in the area was heavier. The
first lighthouse here was lighted in 1831, but it was taken
by erosion. A second was activated in 1859. The third
lighthouse built here in 1873 is a two-story L-shaped
wood dwelling in the Carpenter Gothic style. The tower,
also of wood, rose out of the dwelling at the junction of the
wings. This lighthouse served until 1929, when the
Bureau of Lighthouses decided that an automated light
would be satisfactory and moved to this site the steel
skeleton tower from the Cape Henlopen light, which is
still maintained by the Coast Guard.

In 1932 the Bureau of Lighthouses sold the lighthouse
and the new owners built a restaurant near it. The
lighthouse survived with its metal lantern in place, but
the structure became rundown. Elements of its original
design, such as the ornamentation on the gable ends,

remained intact, however. The present owners are in the process of restoring the lighthouse as part of a marina development, using Bicentennial Fund support. The grounds are open to the public, and the lighthouse will be opened when restoration is finished. The old structure stands as the last wood lighthouse in Delaware. NR. [Privately owned]

PORT PENN

To aid the movement of shipping traffic along the Delaware River from the bay to Philadelphia, the Lighthouse Board installed several range light stations, each with two lights. The front one was low and the rear one much higher, so that a navigator could distinctly see one light over the other and know the ship was in safe water. One of the first range light stations on the Delaware was at Port Penn, erected in 1877. Dredging of the river in 1904 altered the channel, thus making the Port Penn station virtually useless. To better serve traffic, the Lighthouse Board established the Liston range lights and in 1906 moved the rear light, an iron skeleton tower with a shaft containing a spiral stairway to the lantern, from the Port Penn station 1½ miles to the Liston station. In 1907 a two-story keeper's residence, as well as a barn and oil house, was added to the site, and seven years later a similar but smaller assistant keeper's dwelling was built. This lighthouse, with the 5-million candlepower light from its second-order range lens 176 feet above the river, served as the rear light for this station. The light was automated in the mid-1930s. Not long afterward, the Bureau of Lighthouses sold the residences and outbuildings to private individuals. This rear light and the front one, 45 feet high, are still active. Today, the light station complex, just off the road, looks essentially as it did during its active years. NR. [U.S. Coast Guard]

■ **Liston Rear Range Lighthouse**
Route 2, ½ mile east of Route 13
1877

Liston rear range lighthouse, a skeleton tower with keepers' dwellings.

■ ■ ■ ■ ■ ■ ■   MARYLAND   ■ ■ ■ ■ ■ ■ ■

ANNAPOLIS

■ **Thomas Point Shoal**
Lighthouse
Chesapeake Bay at entrance
to South River
1875

Perhaps the most photographed lighthouse in the Chesapeake Bay, the Thomas Point Shoal lighthouse is the last screwpile structure left on its original site in the bay. It went into service on November 27, 1875, to replace a light on the shore at Thomas Point at the entrance to the South River. The Lighthouse Board thought that a light on the shoal would better serve the shipping traffic in the bay. A screwpile with a hexagonal 1½-story building perched on the spidery legs, the light's lantern rises out of the center of the building. During its early years floating ice tipped over the fourth-order lens in the lantern. In time heavy riprap was placed around the lighthouse to fend off the ice. With its red roof and white sides this picturesque lighthouse is a fine example of its type. The light and fog signal, both now automated, are still active. This was the last staffed lighthouse in the Chesapeake Bay. NR. [U.S. Coast Guard]

BALTIMORE

■ **Lightship Chesapeake**
(No. 116; WLV-538)
Harborplace
Off Pratt Street near
Gay Street
1930

Lightship Chesapeake, on
station in 1965.

This steel-hulled light vessel, 133 feet, 3 inches long with a beam of 30 feet and a draft of 12 feet, 6 inches, displaces 630 tons. The light vessel has two masts, with the after-mast carrying the light beacon. It has two mushroom anchors; its primary one comes out of the stem, and the secondary one is stowed at the main deck with its chain running out of a hawsehole on the starboard side just abaft, or behind, the stem. After it was readied for sea in Charleston, S.C., the Bureau of Lighthouses assigned it to the Fenwick station, off Fenwick Island near the Maryland-Delaware border. It served there until 1933, when the bureau moved it to the Chesapeake station, off the mouth of the Chesapeake Bay, where it remained, except for a tour of duty with the Navy in World War II, until

1965. At that time a new "Texas tower"-type lighthouse went into service on that station. The Coast Guard moved the lightship to the Delaware station, off the mouth of the Delaware River, and in 1970 the Coast Guard replaced the lightship with a large navigational buoy and decommissioned the vessel the next year.

Shortly thereafter, the National Park Service acquired the lightship with the dual purpose of opening the historic ship to the public and using it in its environmental education program for school children. The lightship occasionally made trips to the Chesapeake Bay to teach students about the maritime environment. In 1981 the National Park Service loaned the vessel to the city of Baltimore for 25 years for display at the city's Harborplace. Berthed near the U.S.S. *Constellation,* the red-hulled lightship with the word *Chesapeake* painted in large block letters on both its sides is open to the public. The ship retains its structural integrity, with only a few changes having been made since its launching, principally when the Coast Guard decommissioned the vessel and removed the foghorn, wood wheel and radio equipment. [National Park Service]

The oldest surviving Chesapeake Bay screwpile light, Seven-Foot Knoll has been moved to a museum setting. Its plain circular design reflects a type common at the time of its construction. The one-story structure, made of iron plates with the light tower resting on the center of its rather flat pyramidal roof, is painted barn red and rests on the screwpile framework. During its active years, the lighthouse had a fourth-order lens and a bell for a fog signal. The lighthouse was originally positioned at the mouth of the Patapsco River, the pathway for shipping traffic bound for Baltimore Harbor, but has been inactive for a number of years. Following rehabilitation, the lighthouse — in remarkably sound condition — is to be operated for the city by the Lady Maryland Association. [U.S. Coast Guard. Loaned to City of Baltimore]

■ **Seven-Foot Knoll Lighthouse**
Pier 5 at Inner Harbor
Off Pratt Street at
Concord Street
1855

ELK NECK

This lighthouse, which principally served traffic going to and from the Susquehanna River, is located at the southern tip of Elk Neck, at the head of the Chesapeake Bay between the Elk and Northeast rivers. The masonry tower is just 38 feet tall, but the site on which it rests is 100 feet above the bay; consequently, the focal plane of its light is 129 feet above sea level. The last keeper at the lighthouse was the last civilian woman keeper in the Chesapeake Bay and the nation. When she retired in 1947, the Coast Guard automated the light. To eliminate a target for vandals, the Coast Guard tore down all the outbuildings and destroyed the brick stairway in the tower. The light is still active, but trees have grown up around the tower so that it is partially obscured. In a game preserve, it is accessible to the public. [U.S. Coast Guard]

■ **Turkey Point Lighthouse**
Elk Neck State Park
Route 272, off Interstate 95
1833

HAVRE DE GRACE

■ **Havre de Grace (Concord Point) Lighthouse**
Concord Point
End of Lafayette Street
1827

Located at the mouth of the Susquehanna River in the old bayport town of Havre de Grace, this light is the oldest on the Chesapeake Bay and went into service with a veteran of the War of 1812 as its keeper. A short white tower 43 feet tall whose light was 39 feet above the water, it is no longer active and has been leased to the Friends of Concord Point Lighthouse, a nonprofit organization that preserves the old structure and displays it to the public. The town recently acquired the keeper's house, which the Friends will restore and exhibit with the help of a grant from the Bicentennial Fund. Its restoration is part of a multimillion-dollar redevelopment of Havre de Grace's waterfront. Plans call for the keeper's house to become the area's information center. NR. [Town of Havre de Grace. Leased to Friends of Concord Point Lighthouse]

Above: Havre de Grace light at night in 1941. Right: Point Lookout light and double keepers' dwelling in 1928.

ST. MARYS CITY

■ **Point Lookout Lighthouse**
End of Route 5
Adjacent to Point Lookout
State Park
1830

This lighthouse, located at the north entrance to the Potomac River, originally was a small house with a lantern protruding from the roof, the light of which was 20 feet above the ground. Later, the house was enlarged and increased to two stories, thus raising the lantern 16 feet. The square white dwelling has a hipped roof, and the lantern is positioned on the front side of the roof just below the peak. This lighthouse is no longer active, having been replaced by a light on a nearby skeleton tower. The Navy owns the structure, but the state of Maryland hopes to include it in the adjacent Point Lookout State Park. [U.S. Navy]

ST. MICHAELS

■ **Hooper Strait Lighthouse**
Off Route 33
1867, 1879

Hooper Strait, at the entrance to Tangier Sound, for a number of years had a lightship, but after the Civil War the Lighthouse Board decided to replace it, along with many other lightships in the Chesapeake Bay, with a screwpile lighthouse. Completed on September 14, 1867, this lighthouse served for a decade when it succumbed to its biggest nemesis — floating ice, which carried the

structure away. By the time the lighthouse tender found it, the lighthouse was five miles south of its station. The tender's crew was able to salvage the lantern and lens and some other property. Two years later the board erected another screwpile structure on the site, with a hexagonal, six-room 1½-story house. Each of the first-floor rooms had a 200-gallon water tank that received runoff from the roof, providing water for everything, including drinking. This second lighthouse, with its fifth-order lens, survived the years and cold winters of the Chesapeake Bay. In 1954 the Coast Guard automated the lighthouse and later declared it surplus. The Chesapeake Bay Maritime Museum acquired the structure and moved it to the museum in St. Michaels in 1967. NR district. [Chesapeake Bay Maritime Museum]

Hooper Strait screwpile light at the Chesapeake Bay Maritime Museum.

SOLOMONS

In 1828 the fifth auditor of the Treasury ordered the erection of a lighthouse at Cove Point, which marks the north entrance to the Patuxent River. Shipping interests had early realized that the point needed a lighthouse, not only to serve north and south traffic in the Chesapeake Bay but also to guide southbound vessels headed for the

■ **Cove Point Lighthouse**
End of Cove Point Road, north of Solomons
1828

Cove Point light station, with a conical lighthouse typical of those that rim the Chesapeake Bay. It is equipped with a bell and foghorn.

Patuxent River. The tower was a conical masonry structure 51 feet tall. After the Lighthouse Board came into being in the 1850s, a fourth-order Fresnel lens was placed in the tower. In recent years the light has been automated. The dwellings of the station are still in use by Coast Guard staff and their families who have been assigned to other installations nearby. The light station is not open to the public but the site is accessible and the station can be viewed from just outside the surrounding fence. NR. [U.S. Coast Guard]

■ **Drum Point Lighthouse**
Calvert Marine Museum
Off Route 14
1883

Drum Point, on the north side of the entrance to the Patuxent River, was long recognized as a site needing a navigational aid, if for no other reason than to warn vessels of the shoal that extends from this point. The first appropriation for such a light was made in 1864, but for some reason—and uncharacteristically—the Lighthouse Board failed to use the money. Eighteen years later Congress voted another appropriation, and this time the board acted, placing a screwpile lighthouse a little more than 100 yards off the point and in 10 feet of water. Work on the structure began on July 17, 1883, and 33 days later, on the evening of August 20, the keeper touched the lucerne to the wick of the lamp in the fourth-order Fresnel lens and the light winked on. Seven 10-inch legs tied together by cross braces formed the support framework for the lighthouse. On the end of each leg was a flange, or blade, three feet across, which was screwed into the bay bottom. On the framework was built a 1½-story hexagonal structure that served as the keeper's home. On top of this structure was the lantern, with its gallery, or walkway. The focal plane of light from the lens was 47 feet above sea level. The lighthouse and its keepers served

Drum Point lighthouse, another screwpile light moved to a museum location.

well, if unspectacularly, the shipping in the bay.

The point slowly accreted over the years, and by 1962 the spindly legged structure was completely out of the water at low tide. In that year the Coast Guard decommissioned the lighthouse, and it lay idle, deteriorating, for the next 12 years until the Calvert County Historical Society acquired the structure and made arrangements to have it moved two miles upriver to the Calvert Marine Museum in 1975. The old lighthouse was placed at the edge of the water on the museum grounds, and work began on the restoration of the structure, which had suffered from vandalism. Ultimately, the restorers returned the lighthouse to pristine condition, and many local citizens enthusiastically helped refurnish it as it had been in its active years. The lighthouse is open to the public. NR. [Calvert Marine Museum. Calvert County]

VALLEY LEE

Located on the Potomac River 14 miles upstream from its mouth, this 35-foot white brick conical tower guided shipping along the river for approximately 125 years before it was deactivated. Its fourth-order lens flashed a white light. The station later continued to serve as housing for Coast Guard personnel. Recently, the Coast Guard transferred the site to St. Marys County, which has no immediate plans for it but has rented the dwelling to an individual in exchange for upkeep of the structures. NR. [St. Marys County]

■ **Piney Point Lighthouse**
Off Piney Point Road, south of Valley Lee
1836

Piney Point light station on the Potomac River, with its fog signal building at right.

■ ■ ■ ■ ■ ■ NEW JERSEY ■ ■ ■ ■ ■ ■

ATLANTIC CITY

Dr. Jonathan Pitney, the "father of Atlantic City," traveled a long and frustrating 20-year road trying to get a lighthouse for the Absecon Island vicinity, which had a long history of shipwrecks. In the 1840s a Navy officer, authorized by Congress, conducted a study to determine the need for a lighthouse at this site. Despite Pitney's voluminous documentation of ship disasters, the officer recommended against building a lighthouse. Pitney

■ **Absecon Lighthouse**
Vermont Avenue at Pacific Avenue
Maj. Hartman Bache and Lt. George G. Meade
1857

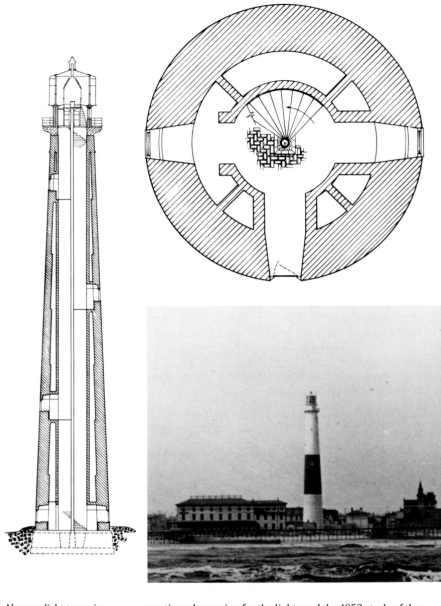

Absecon light tower in Atlantic City around 1891. The cross sectional drawings include the tower and the base indicating a brick floor.

continued pressing for the light, and the 1852 study of the country's lighthouses urged that a lighthouse be placed at this point because "the coast here is very low and difficult to distinguish." Finally, Congress appropriated money for the lighthouse. The work was begun by Maj. Hartman Bache, who was to play a crucial role in lighting the Pacific coast, but was finished by Lt. George G. Meade, who was later to lead the federal forces in the Battle of Gettysburg. Meade built a lighthouse that was 171 feet tall and that, in keeping with its role as a primary seacoast light, had a first-order Fresnel lens in its lantern. The brick tower rested on a granite base. On January 15, 1857, the keeper lighted the oil lamp in the lens for the first time. The new light immediately proved its value, for in the first 10 months of its existence on this coast, where shipwrecks had been "frequent and appalling," there was not a single wreck. To make the light tower a better daymark, the Lighthouse Board in 1872 had the tower painted white with a wide red band around its midsection. In 1898 the board changed the white sections to orange and the red section to black.

The Bureau of Lighthouses discontinued the light in 1933 and replaced it with an electric light on Atlantic City's Steel Pier. The old light tower lay idle for a number of years, and the keeper's dwelling and other buildings disappeared. In 1948 the Coast Guard transferred this landmark to the city, and in 1963 the city council appointed a citizens committee to restore it. The committee succeeded in its effort, relighting the lighthouse and establishing a reception center that was a replica of the light keeper's home and a museum. In more recent years the site has fallen into disrepair, and a local museum association has stepped forward to assist the state, which now owns the property, in restoring the light tower and its site. NR. [State of New Jersey. Atlantic City Coastal Museum]

BARNEGAT LIGHT

Located 45 miles south of Sandy Hook, this light station, with its 40-foot tower, was established apparently to serve primarily as a guide to the inlet. In the 1852 lighthouse report the light on the tower came in for considerable criticism, in part because ship captains who wanted a coastal light at the site criticized the existing tower serving the inlet. Under good conditions, one skipper said, the light could be seen 10 miles, but if the weather was at all hazy one could not tell whether the light was from a lighthouse or a ship. Another referred to the light as being "but an indifferent one . . . frequently mistaken for a vessel's light. . . ." Although it planned to install a first-order Fresnel lens at this lighthouse, the board put in one of the fourth order, probably because the tower could not support the size and weight of a first-order lens. Indeed, when Lt. George G. Meade examined the tower in 1855, he found it to be poorly constructed.

Noting the number of shipwrecks scattered around the area, Meade recommended that a coastal light be established here. In 1857–58 the board erected a new light tower, 161 feet tall, and fitted it with a first-order lens whose focal plane was 175 feet above sea level. The keeper lighted the big lens on January 1, 1859. The light served well through the years, but, with the initiation of the Barnegat lightship in 1927, the light was automated and reduced in candlepower. In 1944, realizing that the lightship was fulfilling the tower's function, the Coast Guard discontinued the light and eventually turned over the tower to the state to be used in a park. It had already given the state all the other buildings. Today, the tower is viewed each year by thousands of visitors to the beach and is climbed by a good percentage of them. Erosion came close to claiming the light tower, but the state dumped heavy riprap at the base of the lighthouse, and that effort seems to be successful in protecting the old structure. NR. [State of New Jersey]

■ **Barnegat Lighthouse**
Barnegat Inlet
North end of Long
Beach Island
Lt. George G. Meade (1859)
1835, 1859

Barnegat lighthouse as illustrated in 1865 in *Frank Leslie's Illustrated Newspaper.*

CAPE MAY

■ Cape May Lighthouse
Cape May Point
Route 109 west
1823, 1847, 1859

The Cape May lighthouse today is like most of the coastal lights along the East Coast below New England: sited on low ground so that, to get the light high enough to be seen at sea, a tall masonry tower is necessary. The government built the first lighthouse here in 1823 and rebuilt it in 1847. In 1859 the Lighthouse Board erected the present tower, a 170-foot white tower with a red lantern, which serves also to guide ships into the Delaware Bay. The focal plane of its 600,000-candlepower flashing white light is 165 feet above sea level. Two white keepers' dwellings are near the tower. Still active, the light has been automated. The Mid-Atlantic Council for the Arts licensed the light station from the Coast Guard and is currently restoring the dwellings. NR. [U.S. Coast Guard. Leased to Mid-Atlantic Council for the Arts]

Right: Tall masonry tower of the Cape May lighthouse with a lifeboat station in the foreground in 1951. Below: Navesink light station, where the first Fresnel lenses in the country were installed in the original twin towers. The striking Romanesque fortification replaced the earlier two lights.

HIGHLANDS

With twin rubblestone towers, this light station was established on the highlands to mark the western entrance to New York Harbor. Cmdr. Matthew C. Perry, at the direction of Congress, brought the first Fresnel lenses to this country, and these were mounted on the twin towers at Navesink in 1840. In its 1852 investigation the Lighthouse Board reported that these lights were "the best on the coast" and were "vastly superior to the Sandy Hook light, at equal and at greater distances." By 1857 the twin towers were in poor condition, and the Lighthouse Board decided to replace them. It erected 73-foot brownstone towers, one octagonal and one square, connected by a brownstone dwelling. The lantern on each of the towers was fitted with a first-order lens, with the focal plane of each light 246 feet above sea level. The keepers lighted these new lights on May 1, 1862. In 1883 the lights became the initial first-order lenses to use mineral oil. In 1898 the Lighthouse Board installed an electric arc bivalve lens in the south tower, the first electrically powered primary light in this country and, at 25-million candlepower, the most powerful. (The Statue of Liberty was the first electrically lighted lighthouse in the country, but its light was only a harbor guide.) At the time of the electrification of the south tower, the board took the north tower out of service.

Over the years the south tower light lost some of its importance as a navigational aid and was reduced in power, eventually to 5,000 candlepower. The Coast Guard automated the light in 1949, decommissioned the station in 1953 and the following year turned over the property to the borough of Highlands for development as a historic site. Today, the state of New Jersey owns and operates the site and has established a museum of the history of lighthouses and the U.S. Life Saving Service, which had its beginning at Sandy Hook. Its interpretive program tours are focused on the lighthouse. NR. [State of New Jersey]

■ **Navesink (Twin Lights) Lighthouses**
Off Route 36
1828, 1862

This 85-foot octagonal rubblestone tower is the only surviving lighthouse of the colonial period and thus is the oldest lighthouse in the United States. Built by Issac Conro, it has survived for 225 years and is still guiding navigators. Although it is located in New Jersey, this structure was known as New York City's lighthouse because the money to construct it was raised in New York and the tonnage dues used to maintain it were collected in the port of New York. American forces tried to destroy the lighthouse during the Revolution because they feared that it would aid the British, but this sturdy tower resisted these efforts. After the war the lantern was repaired and the light put back into service. The Lighthouse Board in 1852 reported that it was one of the three best masonry lighthouses in the United States; it also noted that the 18 Argand lamps and 21-inch reflectors made the lighthouse adequate as an entrance light. In 1856 the board installed a third-order Fresnel lens in the lantern,

■ **Sandy Hook Lighthouse**
Gateway National
Recreation Area
Route 36
By boat from Pier 11
in New York City
Isaac Conro
1764

permitting the lighthouse to serve a broader purpose than just as an entrance light. The light, 88 feet above sea level, could be seen 15 miles. The first siren fog signal was installed here in 1868.

Later, Fort Hancock was established at Sandy Hook, and as this military reservation expanded, it surrounded the light station. Today, much of the old Fort Hancock is in the Sandy Hook unit of the Gateway National Recreation Area. The lighthouse is still active and under the control of the Coast Guard. The keepers' dwellings, on the other hand, have been included within the park. The park rangers interpret the lighthouse to the public; the grounds are accessible, but the tower is not. NHL. [U.S. Coast Guard. National Park Service]

Below: Sandy Hook light, the oldest surviving lighthouse of the colonial era and thus the oldest lighthouse in the country. Below right: Hereford Inlet light, an unusual Stick Style light.

NORTH WILDWOOD

■ **Hereford Inlet Lighthouse**
Central Avenue between
First and Chestnut Streets
1874

Marking the entrance to Hereford Inlet, an important harbor of refuge for small coasting vessels, this lighthouse has a Stick Style frame dwelling, part one story and part two stories. The square light tower, with its fourth-order lantern and lens, rose out of the one-story portion to a height of 57 feet. The light, 53 feet above sea level, was originally a fixed white light but was changed to a flashing red and white one in 1897. The Coast Guard decommissioned the lighthouse in 1964 and transferred it to the state's marine police, and the light was moved to a white skeleton tower. In 1983 the old structure was conveyed to the town. Volunteer efforts restored the former navigational aid and permitted North Wildwood to open the station to the public during the summer. At the urging of the town, the tower's light has been reinstalled. NR. [Town of North Wildwood]

SALEM

■ **Finn's Point Rear
Range Lighthouse**
Supawna Meadows National
Wildlife Refuge
Fort Mott and
Lighthouse Roads
1877

Built at the same time as the Liston rear range light at Port Penn, Del., this light also served the same purpose— to guide naval traffic around the islands and shoals of the Delaware River. The light was a 100-foot black pyramidal skeleton tower with a cylinder containing the stairway, and its light, when active, was 99 feet above the river. The light was automated in 1939, and in 1951 the Coast Guard discontinued it. The rear range light is now a part of Supawna Meadows National Wildlife Refuge; the front range light has not survived. In 1981 local citizens formed the Save the Lighthouse Committee and successfully persuaded Congress to appropriate money to refurbish the tower. Work was completed by the end of the year. The lighthouse is open the third Sunday of each month from April to October from 12 to 4 p.m. Volunteers are available to answer questions. NR. [U.S. Fish and Wildlife Service]

SEA GIRT

This lighthouse is a brick, two-story, L-shaped dwelling with a square brick light tower nestled into the intersection of the wings. The first radio fog beacon was installed here in 1921, in part to aid ships approaching New York Harbor. By the 1930s Sea Girt Inlet was deep enough for small fishing boats drawing no more than two feet of water and then only at high tide. By 1945 the lighthouse's usefulness had long since passed, and the Coast Guard took it out of service and turned it over to the town. Attempts in 1981 to sell it spurred the Sea Girt Lighthouse Citizens Committee to come to the old structure's rescue. The committee began the efforts to restore the lighthouse and accomplished the task by fund raising and volunteer work. It is scheduled for use as a local civic building. [Town of Sea Girt]

■ **Sea Girt Lighthouse**
Beach Boulevard and
Ocean Road
1896

Sea Girt lighthouse, a light in a suburban seaside location.

■ ■ ■ ■ ■ ■ ■   NEW YORK   ■ ■ ■ ■ ■ ■ ■

BROOKLYN

Established to guide steamers to the Coney Island iron piers and New York's garbage scows to their dumping grounds, this lighthouse was originally a rear range light. A white steel skeleton structure, the 68-foot tower is a square pyramidal shape. By 1896 the front light was no longer of use, so the Lighthouse Board took it out of service. The board then had the structure removed and the land sold at public auction. Except for a short period

■ **Coney Island Lighthouse**
Norton Point
Off Surf Avenue between
46th and 47th Streets
1890

Coney Island lighthouse, a steel skeleton tower, in 1945. Until 1988, the tower was tended by a civilian keeper.

Above: Esopus Meadows lighthouse, a navigational aid that guided vessels around mud flats in the Hudson River. Right: Hudson City lighthouse, another guide to the mud resting on the bottom of the Hudson River.

during the Spanish-American War, the rear light, which has a flashing red light, has remained in service. Its automation in 1988 ended the career of the last civilian lighthouse keeper. [U.S. Coast Guard]

ESOPUS

Built on a circular granite pier, Esopus Meadows replaced an earlier lighthouse that was beyond repair because of the constant battering by the ice. Located near the middle of the Hudson River, the light guided vessels around the mud midriver. Somewhat similar in design to the brick Hudson City lighthouse, this 1½-story wood structure has a red mansard roof; the light tower rises out of the river side of the dwelling. The focal plane of the light was 58 feet above river level. The Coast Guard automated the lighthouse in 1965, and the structure began a slow decline. A few years later it moved the light to a nearby steel tower. The Saugerties Lighthouse Conservancy plans to restore the lighthouse, which is accessible by water only. NR. [U.S. Coast Guard]

■ **Esopus Meadows Lighthouse**
West side of Hudson River
1839, 1872

HUDSON

Halfway between Hudson and Athens, this lighthouse is listed in the Coast Guard's *Light List* as being at Hudson, an old whaling port about 100 miles upriver from New York City. The light was put up to guide ships around the Middle Ground Flats, in the center of the river at Hudson. The builders first erected a limestone pier, or base, and on this foundation built a 1½-story red brick dwelling with a mansard roof. The square light tower, attached to the house, holds a fifth-order lens whose light is 48 feet above river level. Stone quoins and lintels give distinctiveness to the tower and dwelling. Exterior detailing reflects the Second Empire style.

■ **Hudson City (Hudson-Athens) Lighthouse**
Southwest end of
Middle Ground Flats
in Hudson River
1874

In recent years the Coast Guard has automated the light. Local citizens have formed the Hudson-Athens Lighthouse Preservation Committee and have leased the lighthouse from the Coast Guard. The building is in reasonably good condition but needs some restoration work. The committee intends to maintain the structure and open it to the public. NR. [U.S. Coast Guard. Leased to Hudson-Athens Preservation Committee]

KINGSTON

Built near the confluence of the Hudson River and Rondout Creek, Kingston light went into service on August 25, 1915, replacing an 1880 lighthouse whose effectiveness had been reduced by dikes that altered the entrance to the port of Kingston. The builders poured a concrete pier and on it erected a buff-colored brick 2½-story dwelling with an attached 48-foot light tower of the same material. The light of the fourth-order lens in the tower's lantern was 52 feet above river level.

■ **Kingston (Rondout II) Lighthouse**
Kingston Point
Hudson River and Rondout Creek
1880, 1915

The Coast Guard has automated the lighthouse,

Kingston lighthouse, at the intersection of Rondout Creek and the Hudson River. A fog bell is atop the portico.

replacing the Fresnel lens with a modern plastic lens. In 1984 it entered into an agreement with the Hudson River Maritime Center, an organization devoted to preserving the history of the Hudson River. Although an examination revealed the old lighthouse to be basically sound, the center determined that it needed some repairs; the state of New York, Hudson River Heritage Task Force and city of Kingston collaborated to undertake the work. Part of the dwelling was refurnished to depict the life of a keeper and his family, and exhibits on the history of the Hudson and its lighthouses were placed in the building. It is open to the public on weekends during the summer and fall. Today, the lighthouse is popularly known as Rondout II. NR. [U.S. Coast Guard. Leased to Hudson River Maritime Center]

LONG ISLAND

■ Cedar Island Lighthouse
Sag Harbor
Cedar Point County Park
1839, 1868

The first Cedar Island lighthouse was replaced in 1868 by this more substantial structure, designed to guide vessels into Northwest Harbor from Gardiners Bay. The light was particularly useful to whalers headed for Sag Harbor. Erected on a masonry pier, the granite two-story dwelling was L-shaped with a square 40-foot granite tower nestled in the intersection of the wings. The tower was fitted with a fourth-order lens whose light was 44 feet above sea level. By 1900 the water was wearing away three-acre Cedar Island, and although the Lighthouse Board placed riprap along the shore, the erosion continued. The Bureau of Lighthouses moved the light in 1934 to a skeleton tower on a breakwater at the island and closed and put the old lighthouse up for auction in 1937. The 1938 hurricane filled in the water area separating the island from Cedar Point. The light had several private owners before it was acquired by Suffolk County in 1967 for use as a park. Few repairs have been made, the light has been vandalized, and at one point a fire severely damaged the roof and interior. Since 1984 the structure has been in the hands of the Suffolk County Historical Trust, which would like to restore it. [Suffolk County]

Located at the end of Eatons Neck on the east side of the entrance to Huntington Bay, this lighthouse served as a guide not only to ships entering the bay but also to those passing through this section of Long Island Sound. John McComb, Jr., who constructed the Montauk Point and Cape Henry, Va., lighthouses, was awarded the contract to build this one. As with the other two, he built this one well, for it has survived almost two centuries. Made of fieldstone, the 73-foot octagonal pyramidal tower has required repairs from time to time, the most extensive occurring in 1868. Its lantern probably was first lighted with spider lamps, but in time the Treasury's fifth auditor equipped it with 12 Argand lamps and 13-inch reflectors. In 1856 the lantern received a third-order Fresnel lens. The first fog signal was a bell, but in 1868 a "syren" fog signal was authorized, because of the coastal traffic and because "it marks the entrance to Lloyd's Harbor, an important place of shelter, principally to sailing vessels." In 1904 a "first call automatic siren" fog signal was installed. Today, the station has a foghorn. Now automated, the lighthouse, whose light is 144 feet above the water, is still active. The station is used as quarters for Coast Guard personnel. NR. [U.S. Coast Guard]

■ **Eatons Neck Lighthouse**
Asharoken
End of Lighthouse Road
John McComb, Jr.
1799

The first lighthouse on this site was an 89-foot octagonal stone tower, fitted with 14 Argand lamps and 21-inch reflectors, which served to mark the eastern entrance to New York Harbor. In 1852 the national lighthouse investigating committee noted that the range of these lamps and reflectors would not exceed 14½ miles; it was "clearly necessary" that the height of the tower be increased and "the most powerful lens apparatus that can be procured" be placed in it. The height of the old tower was not increased; rather, the Lighthouse Board ordered that a new and taller tower be erected and instructed the engineer to tear down the old tower and dwelling and use the salvageable stone in the new construction.

In 1857–58 a 167-foot brick light tower, located 200 yards from the old tower, and a new stone keeper's dwelling were built. On November 1, 1858, the keeper lighted the new lamp and first-order Fresnel lens, whose

■ **Fire Island Lighthouse**
Saltaire
Fire Island National Seashore
Off Route 109 near Robert Moses State Park
1826, 1858

Fire Island lighthouse, a striking daymark with a newly restored keeper's dwelling. An 1898 view shows the lighthouse in the distance with a life-saving station in the foreground.

focal plane was 167 feet above sea level. The Lighthouse Board regarded this lighthouse as the most important one on the coast for transatlantic steamers bound for New York. The steamers set course for this light, which generally was the first one they saw on the coast; it was also their departure point for the trip to Europe. To make it a better daymark, the board had the tower painted black and white, with the top and third bands being black. In 1912, to protect the brick, the Bureau of Lighthouses encased the tower in a thick coat of cement, which over the years became more of a problem than a cure.

The new Fire Island lighthouse was a key element in making the approach to New York Harbor accessible and safe, and through the years the lighthouse fulfilled its intended function well. But advancing technology rendered it obsolete, and in 1973 the Coast Guard deactivated it. The light station, whose remaining structures are the light tower and stone dwelling, has been included within the bounds of the Fire Island National Seashore. An archeological dig has exposed the remains of the foundation of the first light tower. The Fire Island Lighthouse Preservation Society, a local group working with the National Park Service, has raised $1 million to restore the old lighthouse and dwelling and to convert the dwelling into a maritime museum. NR. [National Park Service. Fire Island Lighthouse Preservation Society]

■ **Montauk Point Lighthouse**
Montauk Point
Route 27
John McComb, Jr.
1797

John McComb, Jr., who built the first Cape Henry light in Virginia, erected this lighthouse on a bluff at Montauk Point, the eastern tip of Long Island. The tower, 108 feet tall and made of "Chatham freestone, fine hammered," and the bluff raised the light to 160 feet above sea level. The light served both the coastal traffic, particularly ships going to and from Europe, and vessels entering and leaving Long Island Sound. The Lighthouse Board

Montauk Point lighthouse, marking the eastern extremity of Long Island.

considered this lighthouse "a very important light" and ranked it 10th of the 38 lighthouses in the country needing first-order lenses. The lighthouse served well, but by the 1960s erosion threatened it. To date, controls have slowed the erosion. The Coast Guard automated the light in September 1986. It also allowed the Montauk Historical Society to maintain the structures and grounds and operate the small museum that had been there during Coast Guard days. The society opens the site to the public on a daily basis. NR. [U.S. Coast Guard. Leased to Montauk Point Historical Society]

NEW YORK CITY

This red conical steel-plated tower, the first lighthouse encountered by navigators journeying up the Hudson River, is located under the George Washington Bridge. It was erected in 1920, replacing two red stake lights that had been here since 1889. The light of its 40-foot tower was 61 feet above the river. With the building of the bridge in 1931, which had a light on it to guide river traffic, the light tower became obsolete, so the Coast Guard put the light tower up for sale. A children's book, *The Little Red Lighthouse and the Great Grey Bridge,* published about this time, stirred such a storm of protest that the Coast Guard decided in 1951 to offer the tower to the city's Department of Parks and Recreation. The city accepted and made the "little red lighthouse" a part of Fort Washington Park. NR. [City of New York]

■ **Jeffrey's Hook Lighthouse**
Fort Washington Park
Off Riverside Drive under the George Washington Bridge
1889, 1920

Above: Jeffrey's Hook light, literature's "Little Red Lighthouse." Left: *WLV-613,* the last lightship assigned to Ambrose Station.

■ **Lightship Ambrose (LV-87; WLV-613)**
South Street Seaport Museum
Pier 16, East River
1907

Now preserved as part of the South Street Seaport Museum, this red steel-hulled, 683-ton lightship has an overall length of 135 feet, 9 inches, a beam of 29 feet and a draft of 12 feet, 1 inch. Built in Camden, N.J., in 1907 to specifications for first-class light vessels, it had two steel masts, each of which held a light. The light on the main mast was used when the light on the foremast had to be lowered so that its lamps could be replenished with oil. In the early 1930s both masts were fitted with a 375-millimeter lens and 1,000-watt lamp. About the same time the steam engine was replaced with a diesel engine.

Upon completion, *Lightship No. 87* was assigned to Ambrose Channel and marked the southern entrance to New York Harbor. In addition to storms and other natural phenomena, the lightship had to face a higher degree of risk of collision, because this was the nation's busiest port, and on occasion it was hit. *No. 87* served at this station until 1932, when it was replaced by a newer lightship. It then became the relief light vessel for Lighthouse District 3 based at Staten Island and served in that capacity until 1936, when the Bureau of Lighthouses assigned it to the Scotland station off Sandy Hook, N.J. Replaced in 1964 once again by a newer lightship, *No. 87* was assigned as a Coast Guard exhibit at the 1964 World's Fair. Afterward, it went to Curtis Bay in Baltimore, where it remained until 1968, when the Coast Guard transferred it to the South Street Seaport Museum in New York City. Today, the vessel is in a good state of preservation and is open to the public daily. NHL. [South Street Seaport Museum]

NORTH TARRYTOWN

■ **Tarrytown Lighthouse**
South of Kingsland
Point Park
Off Riverside Drive
1883

The Lighthouse Board placed this conical steel lighthouse at this point to warn navigators of the Tarrytown Shoals along the Hudson River. Built on a stone pier, the white tower is similar to the Robbins Reef lighthouse on Staten Island. The first three floors are living quarters; the fourth floor has a bedroom and workshop, while the fifth is the watchroom. The first and watch room floors have walkways but only the first-floor walkway is covered. The lighthouse was staffed until 1957, when the

Tarrytown light, a steel caisson lighthouse, before automation.

Coast Guard automated the light. Four years later it deactivated the light station, which is now part of Kingsland Point Park and is connected to the mainland by a bridge. NR. [Westchester County]

SAUGERTIES

■ **Saugerties Lighthouse**
Hudson River and
Esopus Creek
End of North Dike
1836, 1869

Built at the confluence of the Hudson River and Esopus Creek, Saugerties light went into service in 1869, replacing a deteriorated stone lighthouse from 1836. Elise Barry, who had an important role in preserving the Hudson River lighthouses, described the new lighthouse

as a two-story brick Italianate structure whose dwelling "forms a fat ell around the tower and is situated on a stone pier or caisson." The Coast Guard's *Light List* characterized it more simply as a "drab square tower in southeast angle of dwelling." The lantern on the tower contained a sixth-order lens, the smallest Fresnel lens.

The Coast Guard closed the station in 1954, when it moved the light to a nearby steel tower and automated it. Over the next two decades the lighthouse fell into poor repair. The Saugerties Lighthouse Conservancy is attempting to restore the lighthouse, but it is in poorer condition than first thought. The group, however, has begun stabilizing the pier, with the eventual goal of opening it to the public. Federal support from the Bicentennial Fund has been matched by state and private grants. NR. [U.S. Coast Guard. Leased to Saugerties Lighthouse Conservancy]

Saugerties light, the focus of an intense restoration effort.

STATEN ISLAND

The original lighthouse here, supported by a masonry base built on the reef, guarded ships against the reef on the west side of the main channel into the inner harbor of New York. In 1883 the Lighthouse Board replaced this

■ **Robbins Reef Lighthouse**
St. George
New York Harbor
1839, 1883

Robbins Reef lighthouse, with the New York City skyline in the distance.

structure with another, similar one close by but on a different part of the reef. This lighthouse, too, had a stone base with a tower built on it and was fitted with a fourth-order lens. Another structure, which served as quarters, circled the light tower like a doughnut. From 1886 until 1919, Kate Walker served as keeper of this light. Appointed after the death of her husband, the former keeper, and after several men had turned down the job, she estimated that she saved 50 lives during her tenure, mostly fishers whose boats, caught in sudden storms, crashed on the rocks of Robbins Reef. She raised two children at the lighthouse, rowing them a mile to Staten Island each day so they could go to school. When she retired, Walker was 73 years old. The light tower at Robbins Reef has for many years been painted brown on the lower half and white above. The light is still active but is not open to public visitation. The Staten Island ferry passes close by, however. [U.S. Coast Guard]

STONY POINT

■ **Old Stony Point Lighthouse**
Stony Point Battlefield Historic Park
Off U.S. 9W north
1825, 1925

Set on a promontory overlooking the Hudson River, this octagonal fieldstone tower guided ships past Stony Point for a century when a new lighthouse replaced it. The old stone dwelling was taken down at the same time, as a new residence was erected near the new tower. A unique feature of the original tower is its bird-cage lantern, one of perhaps only five that have survived. In 1945 the old stone tower was made part of the battlefield park. The 1925 structure is a black pyramidal skeleton tower, 29 feet tall, still active today. NR. [Palisades Interstate Parks Commission]

■ ■ ■ ■ ■ ■   PENNSYLVANIA   ■ ■ ■ ■ ■ ■

PHILADELPHIA

■ **Lightship Barnegat (No. 79; WAL-506)**
Penn's Landing
Delaware River at Market Street
1904

Lightship No. 79 is the oldest iron-hulled light vessel in the country and was part of a five-ship contract let by the Lighthouse Board to the New York Shipbuilding Company of Camden, N.J. Of those five, the only other one that survives is *No. 83*, on display in Seattle. Displacing 631 tons, *No. 79* was a 116-foot-long steam-powered vessel with a beam of 28 feet, 6 inches and a draft of 12 feet, 7 inches. It was equipped with two 3,600-pound mushroom anchors, one from the stem and the other from a hawsehole on the starboard side just abaft, or behind, the stem and stowed at the railing. This two-masted ship was fitted with two lights, the principal one on the foremast and the auxiliary one on the main mast.

The Lighthouse Board assigned the ship to the Five Fathoms Bank station off Cape May, N.J., and it remained there until 1924. After two years as a relief lightship, the vessel received a permanent assignment to the Barnegat station, seven miles off Barnegat Inlet, N.J., and it remained there, except for a tour of duty with the Navy in World War II as a guard ship at Cape Henlopen, Del.,

until 1967, when the Coast Guard retired it from the station. From then until 1975 *Lightship No. 79* was on display at the Chesapeake Bay Maritime Museum in St. Michaels, Md. The Heritage Ships Guild of the Ports of Philadelphia acquired the vessel in 1975 and moved it to Philadelphia, where it was used to train guild members in the skills necessary to operate the ship. In more recent years it has been open to the public as a historic ship. With its diesel engine installed in 1931, the ship is still operational. [Heritage Ships Guild of the Ports of Philadelphia]

Lightship Barnegat on station off Barnegat Inlet, N.J.

■ ■ ■ ■ ■ ■ ■ ■ VIRGINIA ■ ■ ■ ■ ■ ■ ■ ■

ALEXANDRIA

Designed to improve inland navigation by guiding vessels bound up the Potomac River to the ports of Alexandria, Georgetown and Washington, Jones Point light is a cottagelike 1½-story wood dwelling with a round iron lantern rising from the center of its gable roof. Additional structures included a privy and shed to store buoys, for the keeper had the additional responsibility of tending the buoys in the vicinity of the lighthouse. By the end of the Civil War the lamp in the fifth-order lens had been converted to gas, but in 1900 the Lighthouse Board converted it back to an oil lamp. At that time a ruby-colored glass tube was placed around the lamp, changing the color of the light to red. In 1919 the Bureau of Lighthouses automated the Jones Point light by converting the lamp to the use of acetylene gas.

Seven years later the bureau recognized that the river channel had shifted and the lighthouse was no longer of

■ **Jones Point Lighthouse**
Jones Point Park
Off U.S. 495 near the
Woodrow Wilson Bridge
1855

Jones Point lighthouse, a
cottagelike structure.

much use. At that time it erected a steel skeleton light tower 100 yards away. In 1926 the government also deeded the old lighthouse to the Daughters of the American Revolution, and for a number of years that organization maintained and used it. During World War II the Army took over the site, and at the end of the war returned the lighthouse to the DAR "in a state of total disrepair." In 1964 the DAR transferred the lighthouse and land to the National Park Service, which restored the exterior of the structure and made it the centerpiece of Jones Point Park. Disappointed that a full restoration was not accomplished, the DAR is now working to raise funds for the lighthouse's complete rehabilitation. On the site is the south cornerstone from the 1791 survey that created the District of Columbia and originally included Alexandria. NR. [National Park Service]

CHINCOTEAGUE

■ **Assateague Lighthouse**
Chincoteague National
Wildlife Refuge
Route 175, off U.S. 13
1833, 1867

The need for a seacoast light between Cape Charles, Va., and Cape Henlopen, Del., had been recognized since colonial days. Finally, in 1831 Congress authorized the lighthouse, and in 1832 the government acquired a 50-acre tract of marsh and sand hills sprinkled with vegetation. In an unusual move Stephen Pleasonton, then the Treasury's fifth auditor in charge of lighthouses, advertised in Boston for a contractor to build the structure. The low bidder, from Massachusetts, shortly began erecting the lighthouse, which was in operation by the end of January 1833. In 1851 the lighthouse investigators found that the lantern of this masonry light tower was equipped

Assateague lighthouse, a
well-known landmark in the
Chincoteague National
Wildlife Refuge.

with only 11 lamps, each with a 14-inch reflector, and that the tower was inadequate in height, making the lighthouse a poor seacoast light. The inspectors recommended that the tower be increased to 150 feet and that a first-order Fresnel lens be installed in the lantern, improvements essential for warning navigators of the shoals that extended up to 12 miles off shore.

On the eve of the Civil War, Congress finally made an appropriation to provide a proper seacoast lighthouse at Assateague, but with the advent of the war the money was impounded. At the end of the hostilities the Lighthouse Board urged that the government proceed with replacing the old tower, and in 1866 work began on a new one. When work halted for the winter, the new brick conical tower stood at 95 feet. Work resumed in March, and by the end of summer the tower was completed and the lantern in place. Toward the end of September the lens was installed and adjusted, and on October 1, 1867, the keeper exhibited the light for the first time. The tower was 142 feet tall, and the focal plane of its light was 154 feet above sea level. The nearby duplex served as a residence for the keepers. By 1890 two assistant keepers had to share one side, and in 1892 the Lighthouse Board remodeled the quarters into three six-room apartments. In 1910 a brick bungalow was added. With the introduction of electricity to the light station in 1932 and a concommitant reduction in staff, the Bureau of Lighthouses sold the old dwelling, keeping the 1910 one, which still stands on the site. The light station is within the bounds of the Chincoteague National Wildlife Refuge. The light tower has been automated and is still active. NR. [U.S. Coast Guard. U.S. Fish and Wildlife Service]

HAMPTON

This octagonal pyramidal tower, built on the north side of the entrance to Hampton Roads near Fort Monroe, is the second oldest lighthouse on the Chesapeake Bay. Its light is 54 feet above the water. The light tower was damaged badly during the Civil War; indeed, it was within sight of the battle between the *Monitor* and the *Merrimack*. After the war it was restored to its original condition. Still active, this lighthouse is a short distance from Fort Monroe and its grounds are open to the public. NR. [U.S. Coast Guard]

■ **Old Point Comfort Lighthouse**
Fort Monroe
Off Interstate 64
1802

Old Point Comfort lighthouse, showing the walls of Fort Monroe in the background bordering a moat.

MATHEWS

■ **New Point Comfort Lighthouse**
Mobjack Bay
End of Route 14
1805

Patterned on the Old Point Comfort light tower but a few feet taller, this lighthouse went into service on the northeast side of the entrance to Mobjack Bay, where it also served traffic going up and down the Chesapeake Bay. The octagonal sandstone tower is 63 feet tall, and the light from its fourth-order lens, 58 feet above the water, could be seen 13 miles. The lighthouse investigators in 1851 found that the light was run by a retired sea captain and a black female slave. During the Civil War, the Confederates disabled the light, which remained inoperative for the duration of the war. Relighted after hostilities had ended, the lighthouse was staffed until 1919, when it was automated. The Coast Guard decommissioned it in the 1950s, replacing it with a lighted buoy. The lighthouse, now in the hands of Mathews County, was restored in 1981 and dedicated to those from the area who died at sea. Additional repair money has come from the Bicentennial Fund. The light is now accessible only by boat. NR. [Mathews County]

PORTSMOUTH

■ **Lightship Portsmouth (No. 101)**
Water Street
1916

A well-preserved vessel, this steel-hulled ship was built in 1916 at Wilmington, Del. The 360-ton ship is 101 feet, 1 inch long, 25 feet at the beam and has a draft of 11 feet, 3 inches. This lightship incorporated many design refinements and is considered a more mature version of the modern light vessel. It was the first such vessel to have a single light mast, which, located amidships, is large and hollow and rises out the pilot house, thus allowing interior access to the light. An aftermast had a sail that permitted the ship to remain on station more easily. *No. 101*'s first assignment was Cape Charles, Va., at the entrance to the Chesapeake Bay. In 1925 the Bureau of Lighthouses moved the black-hulled vessel to the Overfalls station, off the Delaware Bay breakwater, where it served for 26 years, after which it was made the relief lightship for the Nantucket station. The following year the Coast Guard moved the vessel to the Stonehorse Shoal, Mass., station at the entrance to Nantucket Sound and later sent it to the Cross Rip station, also in Nantucket Sound, for a short period.

The Coast Guard decommissioned the now red-hulled lightship in 1960 and for a time used it as a museum ship in Portsmouth, when it had "Portsmouth" painted on its sides. Some time later the Coast Guard turned over the vessel to Portsmouth to become part of the city's museum system. The vessel was altered somewhat over the years: in the early 1930s standard 375-millimeter lenses were installed on each mast; at the same time the pilot house and adjoining captain's cabin were remodeled; and in 1935 the Bureau of Lighthouses installed a diaphone fog signal to replace the original whistle. Resting in a concrete cradle located on the downtown waterfront, the lightship, beautifully displayed, is open to the public on a daily basis. NHL. [City of Portsmouth]

Left: New Point Comfort lighthouse in 1928. Below: *Lightship Portsmouth,* when it was assigned to the Overfalls station off the coast of Delaware.

SMITH ISLAND

■ **Cape Charles Lighthouse**
By boat to Smith Island
1828, 1864, 1895

The first lighthouse on this site, which marks the north side of the entrance to the Chesapeake Bay, was erected in 1828 and was 55 feet tall. The 1851 lighthouse investigation reported that the light was "very inferior," and in 1856 Congress authorized a new lighthouse. In 1858 work was begun on the tower but proceeded slowly, and by 1862 the tower was only 83 feet tall. That year, Confederates completely destroyed the 1828 light. In 1864 Congress authorized $20,000 to finish the second tower. Completed on May 7, 1864, erosion soon proved a threat to the 150-foot lighthouse; by 1883 the shoreline was within 300 feet of the tower and was moving closer at the rate of 30 feet a year. The Lighthouse Board's attempts to halt the erosion by building jetties proved futile. In 1889 a gale washed away part of the jetty, and at one point the tower and the two keepers' dwellings were surrounded by water.

Congress appropriated $150,000 for a new tower, and work on the new 191-foot steel pyramidal skeleton tower was completed in December 1894. A new first-order lens was mounted in the lantern and lighted on August 14, 1895. The tower was later painted black and white — the lantern and watchroom black, and the remainder white. The Coast Guard installed aerobeacons in the lantern and automated the light in 1963. The first-order lens was taken down and given to the Mariners Museum in Newport News, Va., where it is on display. [U.S. Coast Guard]

VIRGINIA BEACH

■ **Cape Henry Lighthouse**
Fort Story
Off U.S. 60
John McComb, Jr.
1792, 1881

Two Cape Henry lighthouses have been built, and both towers survive. During the colonial period Virginia planned to put a lighthouse at the southern point of the entrance to the Chesapeake Bay, and in 1774 the contractor went so far as to lay a foundation and ship thousands of tons of stones to the site for the tower. But the next year the colony encountered financial problems, and before they could be resolved, the Revolution precluded further work. After the war, there was little immediate interest in resuming the lighthouse project. In 1789 the state of Virginia offered the federal government two acres of land if it would build a lighthouse at Cape Henry. In 1790 Congress authorized the lighthouse, and the following year John McComb, Jr., who was later to build the Montauk Point lighthouse in New York, began work on the tower. He was able to use some of the stones collected for the first attempt but found that most had become buried so deep in the sand that it was not economically feasible to dig them out. McComb obtained additional sandstone and in 1792 completed the 90-foot octagonal tower, the first lighthouse started and finished by the federal government. In October of that year the keeper exhibited the light in the new tower for the first time. The lantern of the light tower was fitted with 18 Argand lamps, each with a 21-inch reflector. The lighthouse investigators of 1851 considered Cape Henry "one of the best reflector lights on the coast." In 1857 the Lighthouse Board had a Fresnel lens mounted in the lantern and at that time lined the tower with brick. As was their practice, the Confederates damaged the light and put it out of service during the Civil War. By 1863 the Union forces had it back in operation to facilitate their use of the Chesapeake Bay.

In 1870 large cracks began to appear in the tower. An examination convinced the Lighthouse Board that the tower was "in danger of being thrown down by some heavy gale," and it recommended building a new tower. Not until 1875 did Congress appropriate $75,000 for the work. Four years passed before the board entered into a contract to construct the new tower, and after two years and $50,000 more, on the evening of December 15, 1881, the keeper first lighted the lamp of the new first-order Fresnel lens, whose light was 164 feet above the water. The octagonal pyramidal tower is 163 feet tall and is described in the Coast Guard's *Light List* as having the "upper and lower half of each face alternately black and white." The station was equipped with a keeper's dwelling and fog signal that was updated over the years; most recently it was a diaphone. The light is still active.

The original tower, about 350 feet away, still stands, despite its weakened condition, and is the centerpiece of a plot set aside by the Association for the Preservation of Virginia Antiquities to commemorate the first landing of English settlers on Virginia soil. Both towers are within the bounds of Fort Story, which is open to the public. NHL. [Association for the Preservation of Virginia Antiquities (1792 tower). U.S. Coast Guard (1881 tower)]

Cape Henry light towers. The earlier octagonal tower in the foreground is topped by a bird-cage lantern. The later tower bears distinctive markings to make it a daymark.

SOUTHEAST

Sand Key lighthouse off Key
West, Fla., a screwpile light
that has guided ships through
the waters of the Florida
Keys for well over a century.

■ ■ ■ ■ ■ ■ ■ ■ FLORIDA ■ ■ ■ ■ ■ ■ ■ ■

CAPE CANAVERAL

■ **Cape Canaveral**
Lighthouse
Kennedy Space Center
U.S. 1 to Route 405 and
Space Center Museum
1848, 1868, 1894

The first lighthouse here, a 65-foot tower, was reported by the Lighthouse Board in 1852 to be a "very inefficient one." The light had been erected to guard ships against the shoals in the vicinity, but ships had to draw close to see the light and thus risked the danger of running onto the shoals. "This is one of the prominent points on the coast," wrote the board, "requiring the most powerful sea-coast lights to facilitate the navigator." Just before the Civil War began, the board sent workers to the site to put up a new 145-foot iron-plated tower, but it was not completed until after the war, on May 10, 1868. Five years later the board had the tower painted with alternate bands of black and white, a scheme similar to that of the Bodie Island light tower.

The lighthouse served well until sea erosion threatened it, beginning in the 1880s. Attempts to halt the erosion proved unsuccessful, and in 1893–94 the Lighthouse Board had the tower taken apart and reerected 1 1/3 miles west of the old site. The keeper relighted it on July 25, 1894, its first-order lens shining a light 137 feet above sea level. For a period of time in the 1960s and 1970s, this lighthouse was known as the Cape Kennedy light. Today, the Cape Canaveral light is automated and still active, although the ancillary buildings of the light station are in ruins. The lighthouse is on the bus tour given at the Kennedy Space Center. [U.S. Coast Guard]

Cape Canaveral lighthouse. All that remains intact of this light station is the tower.

Deactivated light atop Fort
Jefferson. The iron-plated
tower was the second lighthouse constructed at this site.

DRY TORTUGAS

The first lighthouse in the Dry Tortugas was placed on
Bush Key (now Garden Key), one of this group of seven
islands 70 miles west of Key West. The lighthouse keeper
and his family led a lonely life until 1846, when the Army
began building at the site a large fortification to be named
Fort Jefferson. It turned out to be the largest masonry fort
the United States had ever constructed (but never
completed). The fort went up around the lighthouse, and
for more than 10 years the light tower remained on the
fort's parade. The Lighthouse Board in 1852 considered
this a "very important light, especially to those navigators bound to and from the Gulf of Mexico." In 1858 the
board created a new Dry Tortugas light at Loggerhead
Key (see next entry) and reduced the old tower to a
harbor light, fitting the lantern with a fourth-order lens.

In 1876 the board built a new Fort Jefferson light 93 feet
away, a hexagonal iron tower 37 feet high at the top of a
staircase in the fort's walls, where it remained lighted
until 1912, about the time the fort was closed. The old
tower was taken down to below grade level. The metal
lighthouse from 1876 still rests on the staircase and is in
good condition. The foundations of the old light and
keeper's house can also be seen. Access to Fort Jefferson
National Monument from Key West is by a three- to four-
hour private boat ride or a half-hour seaplane flight. NR.
[National Park Service]

This lighthouse, a 157-foot conical brick tower with a
second-order lens, replaced Fort Jefferson as the main
Dry Tortugas light. The Lighthouse Board later had the
tower's upper half painted black and the lower half white.
In 1873 a hurricane so rattled the tower that the board,
fearful that the structure could not withstand another
such assault, asked Congress for money to erect a new

■ **Fort Jefferson Lighthouse**
Fort Jefferson
National Monument
By boat or plane
from Key West
1825, 1876

■ **Loggerhead Key
Lighthouse**
5 miles west of Fort Jefferson
1858

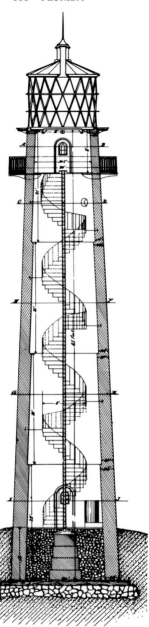

Above: Jupiter Inlet light with a helical lantern. Top right: Loggerhead Key light tower, which guards the Florida reefs at the entrance to the Gulf of Mexico. Center right: Amelia Island light near Fernandina Beach. Below right: St. Johns River lighthouse, a conical tower now surrounded by a naval station.

tower. While waiting for the appropriation, the board had the old tower repaired and the top nine feet rebuilt. Congress appropriated the money for the new tower, but before work could begin another hurricane swept across the Dry Tortugas. The repaired tower withstood the storm so well that the board decided not to build a new one. The tower is still active and well within view of Fort Jefferson. Camping by private boaters is permitted at the site. [U.S. Coast Guard]

FERNANDINA BEACH

Erected about two miles from the north end of Amelia Island, on the south side of the entrance to the St. Marys River, the border between Georgia and Florida, this 64-foot white conical tower has changed little over the years. The lantern was first fitted with 14 lamps, each having a 15-inch reflector. The light chandelier rotated, thus emitting a flashing white light with a red sector warning of the shoals in Nassau Sound. The 1852 report on lighthouses recommended that the tower be raised "and in other respects improved" to make it a coastal light. The tower was not altered, but a third-order lens, whose light is 104 feet above sea level, was later installed in the lantern. Still active, the lighthouse is now automated. [U.S. Coast Guard]

■ **Amelia Island Lighthouse**
Lighthouse Circle
Off Atlantic Avenue at
North 20th Street
Interstate 95 to Route 200
1839

JACKSONVILLE

Beginning in 1830 several light towers were built on this site east of Jacksonville and succumbed to erosion before the existing one was erected and lighted on January 1, 1859. During its active years it guided ships into the St. Johns River, which flows south through Jacksonville. The 66-foot conical red brick lighthouse had a third-order lens that emitted a fixed white light. For a time during the Civil War the light was out of service — darkened, according to a report of the time, by the last keeper, who shot out the lens so that the light could not be of use to federal gunboats. In 1887 the Lighthouse Board raised the tower 15 feet to 81 feet. The light served until January 15, 1929, when it was replaced by a yellow-hulled lightship positioned 6½ miles east of the old light tower. The tower has survived and is located on the grounds of the Naval station. It is open to the public on weekends. NR. [U.S. Navy]

■ **St. Johns River Lighthouse**
Mayport Naval Station
Route 105
1830, 1859

JUPITER ISLAND

Work began on this lighthouse about 15 miles north of Palm Beach in 1856, but heat, insects and other factors interfered, with the result that the light was not operational until July 10, 1860. The 105-foot brick tower on the north side of Jupiter Inlet was fitted with a first-order lens whose light was 146 feet above sea level. About a year after its lighting, the Confederates put it out. Relighted after the war, the lighthouse has continued to perform its dual function of warning vessels about the shoals in the

■ **Jupiter Inlet Lighthouse**
Coast Guard Station
U.S. 1 to Jupiter Drive
Lt. George G. Meade
1860

area and serving as a seacoast light. In 1938 a severe hurricane struck this section of the coast, knocking out the lighthouse's recently installed electricity. The keeper was ill, and, concerned that ships in the storm needed the light, his teen-aged son mounted the tower and through the night turned the lens by hand. The light has been automated, and its original first-order lens is still in place. The tower is painted a bright red. The Loxahatchee Historical Society has a small museum in the oil house at the tower's base. It is open only on Sundays from 12 to 2:30 p.m. NR. [U.S. Coast Guard]

KEY BISCAYNE

■ **Cape Florida Lighthouse**
Bill Baggs Cape Florida State Recreation Area
South end of Key Biscayne
Rickenbacker Causeway off U.S. 1
1825, 1855

Situated on Cape Florida at the north entrance to Biscayne Bay, this lighthouse station is the oldest in Florida. The original tower was 65 feet tall and purportedly had solid brick walls, two feet thick at the top and five feet thick at the bottom. Some years after its construction the local customs collector found that the contractor who had built the tower had defrauded the government—the walls were hollow.

In July 1836, during the Seminole War, when the area was under threat of attack, the lighthouse endured a siege by Indians. The keeper and his wife had gone to Key West, leaving the assistant keeper and a black servant to tend the light. The Indians nearly surprised the two, but they hastily fled to the light tower and slammed shut the heavy wood door. The keeper had a musket, some shot and powder in the tower and was able to hold off the Seminoles for awhile. But the balls from the Indians' muskets had punctured holes in the oil cans in the tower, and little streams of oil poured from the cans, soaking the defenders. Unable to get into the tower, the attackers set the wood door on fire, and in time the flaming portal started a fire in the tower. The besieged pair climbed the wood stairway to the lantern and sought refuge there, but the fire pursued them, turning the lantern into an oven and igniting the assistant keeper's oil-soaked clothing. The flames forced the two men from the lantern onto the outside walkway. The light keeper took a keg of powder he had brought from below and threw it into the stairwell, thinking to blow up the tower and himself, but the resultant explosion only shook the tower a little. The keeper's black companion died of bullet wounds shortly thereafter. The pain of his wounds and the heat caused the keeper again to consider suicide but a little later the stairway inside fell away and a cooling breeze sprang up to ease his physical torment through the night. When morning came, the Indians were gone, but he could not get down from his refuge. In the afternoon sailors from two Navy boats found him, lowered him to the ground and took him to a military hospital, where he eventually recovered.

Ten years passed before the lighthouse was repaired and reactivated. Ship captains regarded it as having a poor light and reported that the light's insufficiency had caused several preventable wrecks. In 1855 the Light-

Cape Florida lighthouse, oldest of Florida's lighthouses, shown in a historic photograph. The keeper's dwelling is now a museum.

house Board raised the tower so that the focal plane of the light was 100 feet above sea level and at the same time installed a Fresnel lens in the lantern to better mark "a prominent point on a most dangerous coast." The light was extinguished by southern forces during the Civil War and was not activated until 1866. Twelve years later Cape Florida's light was superceded by the new pile lighthouse on Fowey Rocks, a reef light that can be seen from the nearby beach.

The Cape Florida tower continued to serve as a daymark. In 1966 it became part of the Bill Baggs Cape Florida State Recreation Area, where it still stands, regarded as south Florida's oldest standing structure. A museum has been established in the keeper's house. In 1978, 100 years after the light had been extinguished, the Coast Guard relighted the brick tower. It displays a white light that exhibits a flash at equal intervals. NR. [Florida Department of Natural Resources]

KEY LARGO

Reef lighthouses are an adaptation to a particular condition: tall and spiderlike, they are built off shore and are not accessible. Although each is different in appearance from the others, reef lighthouses do have important common features. They are all of pile construction, either straight or screwpile; they have open members, offering little surface against which waves can crash; all have a lantern, a structure for living and working and a shaft that connects the two; and today they are all automated.

The oldest of these lighthouses is the one at Carysfort Reef near the north end of the Florida Keys. It was designed by I. W. P. Lewis, archcritic of his uncle, Winslow Lewis, who for years seemed to have a lock on lighthouse construction and installation of lights. Most of the construction of this lighthouse was supervised by Lt. George G. Meade, later to command the Union forces at Gettysburg. During his early career, Meade built a number of lighthouses, including several on the Florida reefs and on the Mid-Atlantic coast as well as the brick

■ **Carysfort Reef Lighthouse**
Northeast of Key Largo
I. W. P. Lewis,
Lt. George G. Meade
1852

Carysfort Reef light, a screwpile lighthouse off Key Largo, near the north end of the Florida Keys.

tower at Jupiter Inlet, Fla. He also developed for use in Fresnel lenses a lamp that bears his name. The Carysfort light, a screwpile structure, replaced a lightship, which proved unsatisfactory in these waters. Lighted in 1852, the lantern was at first fitted with lamps and reflectors. In 1855 the Lighthouse Board installed a first-order Fresnel lens whose light was 100 feet above sea level. The light was automated in 1960. It is still active but now has a third-order lens. The reef is accessible only by private boat. NR. [U.S. Coast Guard]

KEY WEST

■ **Key West Lighthouse**
936 Whitehead Street
1825, 1846

The first Key West lighthouse was a 65-foot masonry tower built on Whiteheads Point. A severe hurricane in 1846 toppled this light tower and killed the keeper's family. Because it was an important light, warning navigators of a most dangerous and treacherous area, the Treasury lost little time in getting a new light tower built. The 60-foot tower served for 50 years before the Lighthouse Board increased its height. The *Light List* later showed the tower to be 86 feet tall, with the focal plane of the light 91 feet above sea level. Eventually, the light from the third-order lens became less and less effective, mainly because the coast was accreting, a condition that prompted the Coast Guard to discontinue the light in 1969. The Key West Art and Historical Society, which had been operating a military museum in the 1887 keeper's quarters, asked that the tower be turned over to it for interpretation. Following a $217,000 restoration, the tower was reopened in early 1989 to launch the lighthouse bicentennial. The next project is the keeper's house. [Monroe County]

■ **Sand Key Lighthouse**
9 miles southeast of
Key West
I. W. P. Lewis,
Lt. George G. Meade (1853)
1827, 1853

The Sand Key light has always been an important one, guiding ships through the dangerous waters of the Florida Keys. The first lighthouse on the key, a stone tower with a keeper's house nearby, was constructed and lighted in 1827. Over the years hurricanes swept the area, damaging the structures. One hurricane demolished the keeper's residence and washed away part of the island. Repairs were made, and a seawall was built on the island to keep the sand from washing away. In 1846 a terrible hurricane struck the area, leaving death and destruction in its wake. Victims included the keeper and her children, all of whom had sought refuge in the masonry tower, as well as the tower itself. The Treasury immediately purchased a lightship and assigned it to the station until a new lighthouse could be placed on the island. I. W. P. Lewis designed a screwpile lighthouse and supervised placement of the iron piles. When Lt. George G. Meade finished work on the Carysfort light in 1852, he supervised the building of the Sand Key lighthouse. The keeper lighted the first-order lens on July 20, 1853. Hurricanes continued to batter the area but did little damage to the lighthouse. In 1865 a hurricane washed away the island and left the lighthouse standing in water.

The light remained active throughout the Civil War, most likely because of the presence of the Navy at Key West. Automated in 1941, the lighthouse continues in operation and has attracted many visitors through the years, although it is not open; the island, easily accessible by boat from Key West, is a popular picnic spot and bird-watching area. Because of the richness and diversity of the sea and bird life, the island is now a protected area. NR. [U.S. Fish and Wildlife Service]

Far left: Sand Key light, left standing in water by a hurricane in 1865. Left: Hillsboro Inlet light, an iron skeleton tower.

POMPANO BEACH

Located between Boca Raton and Fort Lauderdale on the north side of Hillsboro Inlet, this octagonal pyramidal iron skeleton tower has a metal cylinder housing the stairs and is 137 feet tall. Its second-order lens, with a focal point 136 feet above sea level, emitted a light measuring 5.5-million candlepower. The lower third of the structure is painted white, while the upper two-thirds is black. The light, now automated, serves both as a coastal aid and as a guide to the inlet. Although the lighthouse is not open to the public at present, visits to the station are allowed with prior permission of the Coast Guard. NR. [U.S. Coast Guard]

■ **Hillsboro Inlet Lighthouse**
Atlantic Boulevard
Off Interstate 95 to
Route A1A north
1907

PONCE INLET

■ **Ponce de Leon (Mosquito) Inlet Lighthouse**
4931 South Peninsula Drive
1835, 1887

Located south of Daytona Beach, the first light tower at Ponce de Leon Inlet, known as Mosquito Inlet until 1927, was constructed in 1835. A lack of oil, however, prevented the keeper from exhibiting the light. Later that year a storm washed away the sand from around the foundation of the tower. Because of the Seminole War, no remedial action was taken to save the tower, and it soon toppled over without ever having shown its light. In the 1870s the Lighthouse Board noted that of the 95 miles between the St. Augustine and Cape Canaveral lighthouses, 60 miles was unlighted. The board recommended a lighthouse for the inlet, and in 1882 Congress appropriated the requisite funds. In 1884 construction began with the landing of materials on the shore near the site. While helping with the landing, the lighthouse district engineer drowned. Work moved slowly, but finally, in the fall of 1887, the keeper displayed the light from the 168-foot red brick conical tower.

An aerobeacon was installed at the Coast Guard station in 1970 as the new Ponce de Leon Inlet light. The old light station was then turned over to the town of Ponce Inlet, which in turn made arrangements for the Ponce de Leon Inlet Lighthouse Preservation Association to restore the site as a museum. A decade after getting rid of the old station, however, the Coast Guard realized that its new and lower light would be obscured by a condominium development and made arrangements to reestablish the light on the old tower. Today, visitors can climb the tower and visit the ancillary buildings of the light station. One has been refurnished in the style of the 1890s, another is a museum containing the original lens and other lighthouse artifacts, and another is a museum of the sea. NR. [Town of Ponce Inlet]

ST. AUGUSTINE

■ **St. Augustine Lighthouse**
Anastasia Island
Off Route A1A
1824, 1874

Shortly after the United States's acquisition of Florida in 1821, the fifth auditor of the Treasury turned his attention to St. Augustine, the leading port of the territory, and had a tower built whose light was 73 feet above sea level. At best, this light was only a harbor light marking the entrance to St. Augustine, a status confirmed in 1855 when the Lighthouse Board had a small, fourth-order lens placed in the tower. The board, however, believed that a seacoast light was required at this site. During the Civil War the Confederates put out the light, and not until 1867 was it relighted. Soon afterward erosion began to threaten the old tower (which finally toppled in 1880).

In 1870 the board recommended that the light be relocated and a seacoast light be erected. With some difficulty, it acquired five acres about a half mile from the old tower, and in 1872 work began on the new tower. After the foundation had been laid and the tower walls had risen a few feet, erosion began to threaten the old tower. The crew became alarmed and began building jetties of brush and coquina. The jetties held back the erosion, and

work resumed on the new tower. On October 15, 1874, the keeper exhibited the light in the 161-foot tower for the first time. The focal plane of the light of the first-order lens was 161 feet above sea level. The tower was a duplicate of the lighthouses being built on the Outer Banks of North Carolina — tall conical brick towers. To make the tower a better daymark, the Lighthouse Board had the tower painted with spiral black-and-white bands, as had been done on the Cape Hatteras, N.C., tower. The Coast Guard automated the tower in 1955. The light is still active, with its first-order lens in place.

Above left: Ponce de Leon Inlet light station, whose ancillary buildings have been preserved as museums. Above right: St. Augustine lighthouse from the 1874 *Annual Report* of the Lighthouse Board.

The Junior Service League of St. Augustine took on the task of restoring the brick double keepers' quarters, which had been burned by vandals. After eight years of fund raising and restoration work, the league recently opened the building to the public. It has exhibits, refurnished rooms, a small theater and a bookstore. The light station is open seven days a week from 10 a.m. to 5 p.m. NR. [U.S. Coast Guard. St. John's County]

■ ■ ■ ■ ■ ■ ■ GEORGIA ■ ■ ■ ■ ■ ■ ■

DARIEN

The first lighthouse at this site was basically a harbor light, guiding vessels into Doboy Sound north of St. Simons Island. Built by Winslow Lewis, it was lighted with 15 lamps, each with a 15-inch reflector. In 1852 the Lighthouse Board report recommended that this light be made into a coastal light, ranking it in about the middle of those lights recommended for first-order lens. The board

■ **Sapelo Island Lighthouse**
Sapelo Island National
Estuarian Sanctuary
Off U.S. 17
Winslow Lewis (1820)
1820, 1905

Sapelo Island light station near Darien in 1932, showing the original 1820 light tower. The skeleton tower no longer exists.

must have changed its mind within a few years, for the tower received only a fourth-order lens. Confederates damaged the tower during the Civil War, and in 1868 the board repaired it. The light continued to serve until an 1898 hurricane, then it was replaced in 1905 with a square pyramidal steel tower 103 feet tall. The light from its third-order lens was 100 feet above high water. The second lighthouse served as late as 1933, after which the Bureau of Lighthouses deactivated and dismantled it and moved it away. The 1820 light, still here, has fallen into disrepair. It is now part of a sanctuary administered by the state. Sapelo Island may be reached by boat, but the lighthouse is not accessible to visitors (although it is visible). [Georgia Department of Natural Resources]

ST. SIMONS

■ **St. Simons Island Lighthouse**
Southern tip of
St. Simons Island
101 12th Street
Charles B. Cluskey (1872)
1810, 1872

This early light station near Brunswick, according to the Coast Guard's *Light List*, served to mark the entrance to St. Simons Sound. During the Civil War, the Confederates destroyed the tower. After the war the Lighthouse Board decided to erect a new one, a 100-foot conical white tower attached to a brick keeper's dwelling. Sickness plagued the construction crew, and not until September 1, 1872, did it finish the work. The light came from a third-order lens whose focal plane was 104 feet above the sea. The light tower, now automated, is still active. The Coastal Georgia Historical Society has a museum in the keeper's dwelling, and both it and the light are open year round except on Mondays. NR. [U.S. Coast Guard. Leased to Coastal Georgia Historical Society]

St. Simons Island lighthouse, completed after the Civil War to replace a tower destroyed during the war.

Tybee Island lighthouse with the remains of Fort Scriven in the background.

SAVANNAH

■ Tybee Island Lighthouse
Tybee Island
30 Meddin Street
Off U.S. 80
1736, 1742, 1771–73, 1867

Shortly after bringing the colonists to Georgia in 1733, Gen. James Oglethorpe directed that a tower be built on Tybee Island to mark the entrance to the Savannah River, which led to the new settlement of Savannah. This daymark, a 90-foot wood tower, was not completed until 1736. It lasted only until 1741, when it was toppled by a storm. The following year workers put up a similar tower, which may have had a light in its later years.

Because the tower had become threatened by erosion, the colony built a new brick tower in 1771–73, which may have been in service before the Revolution. At the time the federal government received it in 1791, the tower was active, apparently lighted with spermacetti candles. Later, the 100-foot octagonal brick tower was fitted with lamps, each having a 16-inch reflector. In 1852 the Lighthouse Board noted that this lighthouse was an important coastal light that also rendered great service to local users, and it recommended fitting the tower with a first-order lens. In 1857 the Lighthouse Board placed a second-order lens on the tower. Because of damage suffered during the Civil War, workers in 1866 began to mend the tower, tearing away the upper portion and rebuilding it. At that time they raised the tower to 145 feet and fitted it with a first-order lens whose light was now 144 feet above sea level. The keeper relighted it on October 1, 1867. Four years later cracks began to appear in the tower from the force of a gale. The Lighthouse Board recommended building a new tower, but Congress refused to approve the appropriation. Four years later another gale shook the tower, and an earthquake in 1886 caused more cracks and broke the lens. Congress still declined to appropriate money to rebuild the tower.

In the early part of this century the light served as a rear range light, but now it operates alone, painted black on its upper two-thirds and white on the lower third. Today, the tower, which still stands, is a monument to the skill of the colonial workers and their 19th-century successors and to the wisdom — or parsimony — of Congress. The oldest active light station on the Southeast coast, it has been leased to a local historical group that opens the site daily to the public and has established a museum in the 1881 keeper's cottage. NR. [U.S. Coast Guard. Leased to Tybee Island Historical Society]

■ ■ ■ ■ ■ ■   NORTH CAROLINA   ■ ■ ■ ■ ■ ■

BEAUFORT

■ Cape Lookout Lighthouse
Cape Lookout National Seashore
By ferry from Harkers Island
1812, 1859

Cape Lookout, at the south end of the Core Banks, had long been considered a hazard to navigation. Indeed, because of shoals that extend some 10 miles out, one early mapmaker labeled it "Promontorium tremendum," which means roughly "horrible headland." The first lighthouse the government established here was described as being two towers: "the inside one is of brick — the outside one is a wooden framed building, boarded and shingled, and painted in red and white stripes horizontally." The light, 96 feet high and 104 feet above sea level, was not well regarded by navigators. As a result, the Lighthouse Board had the light tower fitted with a first-order lens in 1856.

Three years later the board erected a 150-foot brick tower whose light was 156 feet above sea level, activated November 1, 1859. At the beginning of the Civil War, southern troops vandalized the lens, putting it out of operation. In 1863 the Lighthouse Board relighted the tower, using a third-order lens. Four years later the original first-order lens was repaired and reinstalled in the lantern. In 1873 the light tower was painted its distinctive black-and-white diamond pattern to make it a better daymark. In 1950 the Coast Guard automated the light, which is still active. The light tower, now in need of repair, is one of the principal historic structures in the Cape Lookout National Seashore. The tower is closed to visitors; however, the National Park Service has rehabilitated the keeper's quarters and made it into a visitor center. NR. [U.S. Coast Guard. National Park Service]

BUXTON

■ Cape Hatteras Lighthouse
Cape Hatteras National Seashore
North of Cape Hatteras Point
Henry Dearborn (1803)
1803, 1853, 1870

Located on the Outer Banks, about in the middle of the stretch of coast that came to be known as the "Graveyard of the Atlantic," this lighthouse was regarded in the 19th century as the most important light on the East Coast. Its principal purpose has been to warn coastal traffic about the dangerous and shallow Diamond Shoals, which extend for more than eight miles from the cape. The first tower had a stone foundation with a brick octagonal tower built by Henry Dearborn, a Revolutionary war officer, physician, congressman, secretary of war and ambassador to Portugal. It was an unsatisfactory light, however — the light from its Argand lamps and parabolic reflectors was 95 feet above sea level and frequently obscured by haze — and ship captains often complained about it. In 1851 the committee investigating the condi-

Above: Cape Hatteras lighthouse after a rare snowfall in 1988. This tower is the tallest brick lighthouse in the country. Left: 1870 sketch by George B. Nicholson of the first light tower at Cape Hatteras, showing the original tower with the 1853 addition.

tion of the country's lighthouse system recommended that this lighthouse be the first one fitted with a first-order Fresnel lens and that, for the light to be seen better at a distance, the tower be raised to 150 feet. Within two years the new Lighthouse Board implemented both recommendations, and the focal plane of the light was reported to be 140 feet in 1870. With the onset of the Civil War, the Confederates put the Cape Hatteras lighthouse out of operation by removing the lens from its lantern, but by June 1862 the Union forces had it back in service.

At the end of the war the Lighthouse Board noted that the tower was beyond repair and urged that a new tower be built. Congress appropriated the necessary funds in 1867, and the workers, with Dexter Stetson as the foreman, began putting up the new tower in 1868. On September 17, 1870, the keeper exhibited the light for the first time. Fearing that the old tower would topple over at any time, the district engineer set off a charge in it, following which "this old landmark was spread out on the beach, a mass of ruins." The new conical brick tower was 193 feet tall measured to the top of the lantern's ventilator ball. It was and still is the tallest in America. The focal plane of the light of its first-order lens was 191 feet above sea level. Ancillary buildings included a brick single keeper's dwelling and a board-and-batten double keepers' dwelling. To make the tower a better daymark, the Lighthouse Board had it painted with black-and-white spiral bands in 1873. Erosion has been a threat to the new tower off and on through the years. Although many techniques were tried, no preventive measures were effective against the sea's movement. In 1936 the Bureau of Lighthouses built a skeleton tower a mile from the 1870 light and moved the light to that point. At the same time the bureau gave the tower to the National Park Service for inclusion in the Cape Hatteras National Seashore. By 1950 the erosion abated, and the Coast Guard made arrangements with the National Park Service to reexhibit the light in the tower.

Erosion once again threatens the light tower, more seriously than ever. It is likely that the lighthouse, now a beloved landmark, will be moved as an extreme solution to save it (see the Epilogue). Meanwhile, the light station is still open to the public, although the tower, in need of repairs, is now closed to visitors. The single keeper's dwelling is being restored, and the park plans to refurnish it. The double keepers' dwelling has been converted into a museum dealing with the history of the lighthouse and also the U.S. Life Saving Service, which had a number of stations on the Outer Banks. The Cape Hatteras lighthouse is a popular and dramatic attraction at the Cape Hatteras National Seashore. It is a symbol not only of the park and the Outer Banks but also of the state of North Carolina. NR. [National Park Service]

COROLLA

■ **Currituck Beach Lighthouse**
Currituck Beach
U.S. 158 north of Kitty Hawk
1875

The present lighthouses at Cape Hatteras, Bodie Island and Currituck Beach were erected in that order between 1870 and 1875. As the workers finished one, they moved on to the next site. All three towers are majestic brick structures; the Cape Hatteras tower, 193 feet tall, is 30 feet higher than the others — but each is easy to find because these landmarks are at least 100 feet taller than anything else around. The spot chosen for the Currituck Beach light, northeast of Elizabeth City, was halfway (40 miles) between the lighthouses at Bodie Island and Cape Henry, Va. Many ships and lives had been lost on this dark stretch, so a light was vitally needed. The Currituck Beach light is a duplicate of the one at Bodie Island; it, too, had a workshop and watch room attached to the tower and was sited a considerable distance from the beach. In addition to the tower, a Queen Anne–style single keeper's house was constructed. A double keepers' quarters in a plainer style was also built. Unlike the other lighthouses on the Outer Banks, the Currituck light tower was left unpainted, and today its reddish brown brick distinguishes it from the others along the coast. The first-order lens, whose light is 158 feet above sea level, is still active.

A local preservation organization, the Outer Banks Conservationists of Manteo, N.C., has leased the grounds and structures, except the tower, from the Coast Guard and is restoring the buildings. The double keepers' dwelling appears to be in good condition, but the single keeper's house is deteriorating. The grounds are open to the public, and on certain days the restored double keepers' quarters is also. The tower is closed to the public. NR. [U.S. Coast Guard. Leased to Outer Banks Conservationists]

Currituck Beach light in 1893 with a workshop and watch room attached to the tower and the dwelling on the left.

OCRACOKE

The first lighthouse at Ocracoke Inlet was located on Shell Castle Island, just inside the inlet. It was built concurrently with the first Cape Hatteras lighthouse and was intended to guide vessels over the inlet bar at night. Built by Henry Dearborn, a former congressman and future secretary of war who also built the 1803 Cape Hatteras light, the old Shell Castle light served from 1803 until August 16, 1818, when lightning destroyed the tower and the dwelling. The Treasury had the lighthouse rebuilt in 1823 on the banks near the village of Ocracoke, an important shipping point. The 76-foot white conical masonry tower was an inlet aid, and in 1854 the Lighthouse Board installed a fourth-order lens in its lantern. The Confederates damaged the lens in 1861, so in 1864 the board installed another lens. Now automated, the light is 75 feet above the water and still active. It is one of the oldest lighthouses in North Carolina and one of the oldest active lights along the Southeast coast. The National Park Service has used aid from the Bicentennial Fund for rehabilitation work. NR. [U.S. Coast Guard]

■ **Ocracoke Lighthouse**
2 miles north of
Ocracoke Inlet
South of Cape Hatteras on
Route 12
By ferry from Cedar Island
off U.S. 70
Henry Dearborn (1803)
1803, 1823

OREGON INLET

■ **Bodie Island Lighthouse**
Cape Hatteras National
Seashore
2 miles north of Oregon Inlet
Route 12
Francis A. Gibbons (1848)
1848, 1859, 1872

Before the first Bodie Island light tower was put up in 1848, there was no light in the 80 miles between Cape Hatteras, N.C., and Cape Henry, Va., at the entrance to the Chesapeake Bay. Its principal purpose was to help vessels following the southbound inshore current shape a course to round Cape Hatteras without getting into the northbound Gulf Stream. The first light tower was a 54-foot brick structure built by Francis A. Gibbons, who became a prominent builder of lighthouses on the West Coast. Construction of the lighthouse was under the supervision of a former customs collector who knew nothing about construction. In violation of an order from the Treasury's fifth auditor, he did not have piles driven to support the structure, and within 10 years the tower was beyond repair. In 1859 the Lighthouse Board constructed a second light, this one 80 feet tall with the brick tower built on a sturdy foundation of driven piles and stone. The light of the third-order lens was 86 feet above the ground. Two years later the Confederates set off explosives in the lighthouse, leaving it in ruins.

After the war, at the urging of ship masters and insurance officials, the Lighthouse Board erected a third lighthouse at the site, a 163-foot conical brick tower that began service on October 1, 1872. The light of the first-order lens atop the tower was 156 feet above sea level. To make it a distinctive daymark, the tower was painted with wide black-and-white horizontal bands. Shortly after its lighting, a flock of birds, probably attracted by

Bodie Island light, the third tower at this site, now part of the Cape Hatteras National Seashore.

the light, flew into the lantern, breaking panes of glass in the lantern and seriously damaging the lens. The district engineer then rigged a heavy wire netting around the outside of the lantern to prevent another such incident.

The light has been automated for several decades, and its first-order lens is still in place. The Coast Guard has turned over the grounds and all the light station buildings except the tower to the National Park Service to be incorporated into the Cape Hatteras National Seashore. The Park Service has preserved the structures, including the double keepers' dwelling, which now houses a small museum and a bookstore. The light station is open to the public daily. [U.S. Coast Guard. National Park Service]

SOUTHPORT

Shortly after work began on the Cape Henry, Va., lighthouse at the entrance to the Chesapeake Bay, navigators urged the federal government to complete a lighthouse at Cape Fear on Bald Head begun earlier and needed to guide ships into the Cape Fear River toward Wilmington, N.C. Money was appropriated, and in 1796 the Cape Fear lighthouse first showed its light. In 1818 a new octagonal brick tower, whose light was 110 feet above sea level, was built. In the 1851 lighthouse investigation it was reported as not being effective as a seacoast light. Although the Lighthouse Board was concerned about getting vessels safely past the Frying Pan Shoals off Cape Fear and wanted to raise the tower, all it could do was

■ **Bald Head (Cape Fear) Lighthouse**
Smith Island
By ferry from Southport
1796, 1818

Bald Head light, an octagonal brick tower no longer in use. It is the oldest light tower in the state.

install a third-order lens on the old structure. In 1861 the Confederates closed down the lighthouse, and five years later it was decommissioned by the Lighthouse Board, superceded by the screwpile lighthouse being built at Federal Point. In 1879, however, the board discontinued the latter light and reactivated the Bald Head light station, placing a fourth-order lens on the tower, emphasizing its role as a harbor light. In 1903 the Lighthouse Board erected on Smith Island a skeleton tower with a first-order lens to serve as a coast light and whose light was 159 feet above sea level. At that time this new station officially became the Cape Fear lighthouse, and the old station was called Bald Head.

The Bald Head light station remained active until 1935, when the Bureau of Lighthouses deactivated it. In 1963 the government sold the lighthouse to a private owner, who later sold it to the Carolina Cape Fear Corporation. Subsequently, the Old Baldy Foundation came into being to raise funds to restore the lighthouse and create a museum here, and has since matched a rehabilitation grant from the Bicentennial Fund. The oldest lighthouse in the state, it is open to the public. NR. [Carolina Cape Fear Corporation. Old Baldy Foundation]

■ ■ ■ ■ ■ ■ PUERTO RICO ■ ■ ■ ■ ■ ■

AQUADILLA

■ Punta Borinquen Lighthouse
1.3 miles northeast of Point Borinquen
Off Route 107 to Hansen Road
1889, 1920

When the Lighthouse Board inherited Puerto Rico's lighthouses in 1900, it took over administration of 13 lights built by the Spanish as well as an out-of-condition buoy system. At Point Borinquen, located at the northwest corner of Puerto Rico, the Spanish had erected a 40-foot light tower with a fourth-order lens. This light was low and against a bluff. In addition, part of the light was obscured by a stand of trees. With the increase of Panama Canal traffic, a better landfall light was needed. In 1920 the Bureau of Lighthouses built another tower on top of the bluff and equipped it with a third-order lens. This gray cylindrical tower was 60 feet tall, but its light was 292 feet above sea level. In 1947 a first-order lens was installed because of the increased importance of this light as a landfall. The light, which is automated and still active, also serves as a guide along the coast. NR. [U.S. Coast Guard]

ARECIBO

■ Arecibo Lighthouse
Port Arecibo
1898

Built by the U.S. military government on the east side of the entrance to Port Arecibo, situated along the island's north-central coast, this was the last of the major lights built in Puerto Rico. The 46-foot hexagonal white tower, attached to the flat-roof dwelling, holds a third-order lens, whose light is 120 feet above sea level. The light tower and the dwelling survive, and the flashing white light can be seen for 16 miles. NR. [U.S. Coast Guard]

Left: Punta Borinquen light tower. The lantern is a metal cage surrounding aerobeacons. Below: Arecibo light station, the last of the major Puerto Rican lighthouses, in 1959.

CULEBRITA ISLAND

This 43-foot stone-colored cylindrical tower rising from a flat-roof dwelling was built by the Spanish on this island located between Puerto Rico and St. Thomas, V.I., on the west side of the Virgin Passage. Because the lighthouse was situated on the highest point on the island, the light of its fourth-order lens was 305 feet above sea level. Later equipped with a 3½-order lens, the light could be seen for 19 miles. Now automated, the lighthouse is still active although its visibility has been reduced to 13 miles. The dwelling has been trimmed in red, probably to make it a more distinctive daymark. NR. [U.S. Coast Guard]

■ Isla Culebrita Lighthouse
Summit of Culebrita Island
1885

Above: Isla Culebrita light station about 1900, off the northeast coast of Puerto Rico. Right: Cabo San Juan light station on the north coast in 1959. The lighthouse has never been rebuilt.

FAJARDO

■ **Cabo San Juan Lighthouse**
Cape San Juan
Route 3
1880

To guide vessels along the north and east coasts of Puerto Rico, Spain established a lighthouse at Cape San Juan near the island's northeast corner. A 45-foot cylindrical tower attached to the front of the keeper's dwelling, it was originally equipped with a third-order lens. Later, this was changed to a larger, first-order lens and subsequently to a fourth-order lens. The lighthouse was solidly constructed and has continued in service. Placed on the highest point of the cape, the light is 260 feet above sea level and can be seen for 26 miles. To make the tower a better daymark, a black band has been painted around the base of the white tower. Now automated, the light is still active. NR. [U.S. Coast Guard]

SAN JUAN

The Spanish built a traditional conical masonry light tower on the fortification at El Morro, at the entrance to San Juan Harbor near the island's north coast. Adm. William T. Sampson's bombardment of the fort in 1898 badly damaged the tower, but the military government repaired the tower in 1899 to try to get the light back into operation. These repairs were not effective, however, and in 1907–08 the Lighthouse Board built another light on the site. A ponderous square brick tower with rounded corners and a castellated wall with miniature sentinel towers at the corners, this 51-foot lighthouse was fitted with a third-order lens. The focal plane of the light, which is now automated, is 118 feet above sea level. El Morro is part of the San Juan National Historic Site, which embraces all the fortifications of San Juan, one of the last remaining fortified cities in the New World. The fortification is open daily to the public, and visitors can get a closeup view of the light tower but cannot go inside. NR. [U.S. Coast Guard]

■ **Puerto San Juan Lighthouse**
El Morro
San Juan National Historic Site
1853, 1908

Puerto San Juan light tower atop El Morro, the old Spanish fortification now part of the San Juan National Historic Site.

■ ■ ■ ■ ■ ■   SOUTH CAROLINA   ■ ■ ■ ■ ■ ■

BEAUFORT

Shortly before the Civil War, the Lighthouse Board erected a lighthouse on Hunting Island, located about halfway between Charleston and Savannah. It is uncertain what happened to the lighthouse, but by the end of the Civil War it was not standing. After the war the board selected a new site about a mile from the end of the island and built a new 128-foot cast-iron light tower that held a second-order Fresnel lens, which the keeper lighted on July 1, 1875. Within three years the keepers could see the effects of sea erosion — the lighthouse was just 440 feet from the ocean's edge. The Lighthouse Board built jetties and revetments to impede shore erosion, but these were ineffective. By 1887 the water was within 60 feet of the dwelling and 152 feet of the tower. When the water came

■ **Hunting Island Lighthouse**
Hunting Island State Park
U.S. 21
1859, 1875, 1889

Hunting Island light tower and keeper's dwelling near Beaufort, probably before the tower was removed to another site safely distant from an encroaching ocean.

another 20 feet closer, the board decided to move the tower. It was dismantled and reassembled 1⅓ miles from the old site. On October 3, 1889, the keeper relighted the rebuilt tower. The Bureau of Lighthouses deactivated the light in 1933 and used buoys instead. In good condition today, the tower is in Hunting Island State Park. [State of South Carolina]

CHARLESTON

■ Old Charleston (Morris Island) Lighthouse
Charleston Harbor
Morris Island
1767, 1876

By the end of the Revolution, only two lighthouses could be found south of the Delaware Bay: this old Charleston light from 1767 and the one at Tybee Island, Ga. Navigational aids were relatively sparse in the southern colonies, perhaps because there were fewer ship owners and thus neither shipping interests nor merchants were as influential as their northern counterparts in agitating for lighthouses.

Located at the entrance to Charleston Harbor, the first light here was an octagonal conical masonry tower 102 feet tall with a revolving light 125 feet above sea level. It became the new federal government's responsibility in 1790. In 1851 the lighthouse investigators recommended that this important light have a first-order lens and a fixed light, as it was used as a range light by ship captains to align with another light in crossing the bar. The Lighthouse Board installed one in 1857, and it began service on January 1, 1858. At the beginning of the Civil War, southern troops destroyed the lantern and lens, and at some time during the war the tower itself was demolished, perhaps by Confederates or during the battle for Battery Wagner, also located on Morris Island.

In 1874 the board began construction of a new light

tower near the site of the old one. It was built on piles, some driven 50 feet into the ground, on which was laid a grillage of 12-inch-square timbers. On this framework was poured a concrete foundation, eight feet thick, and on this base the builders erected a 161-foot masonry tower. The light of the first-order lens, which shone for the first time on October 1, 1876, was 155 feet above sea level. At some point before 1885, most likely about the time of construction, the tower was painted with black-and-white bands like the one at Bodie Island, N.C. Damaged by a hurricane and later by an earthquake, the lighthouse continued to function until the early 1960s, when erosion began to wear away the surrounding land. Replaced by the new Charleston lighthouse in 1962, the light at Morris Island is now in private ownership, rising from the water as if cast adrift, for the island has eroded completely from around the light's foundation. NR. [Privately owned]

Below left: Old Charleston light station in 1885. Erosion claimed the dwelling, and the light tower is now surrounded by water. Below right: New Charleston light tower, the only U.S. lighthouse equipped with an elevator and the last traditional, or tended, light station built.

When Morris Island began to erode, the Coast Guard concluded that the light had to be replaced and decided to erect another lighthouse on Sullivans Island on the north side of the Charleston Harbor entrance. The last traditional-style lighthouse to be built in the United States, it is also the only light tower with an elevator. The tall masonry structure, clad in aluminum, is triangular rather than round and rises 163 feet. Its 28-million candlepower light, once the most powerful in the Western Hemisphere, has been reduced to about 1.2 million. [U.S. Coast Guard]

■ **New Charleston Lighthouse**
Coast Guard Station
South side of
Sullivans Island
Coleman Boulevard
Off U.S. 17 to Route 703
1962

Georgetown lighthouse, which serves as a harbor light. The station is one of the oldest in the region and has had three lights.

GEORGETOWN

■ **Georgetown Lighthouse**
North Island
Off U.S. 17
By boat from Georgetown
1801, 1812, 1867

This light station, one of the earliest in the Southeast, was erected on North Island at the entrance to Winyah Bay. The light tower was rebuilt in 1812 and again in 1867. It was never more than a harbor light; the last tower, which is 87 feet tall and painted white, never had a light more powerful than a fourth-order lens. Now automated, the light is still active. The Coast Guard has leased the station to the South Carolina Department of Youth Services for a rehabilitation center. Access to the island is by private boat from Georgetown. NR. [U.S. Coast Guard. Leased to State of South Carolina]

McCLELLANVILLE

■ **Cape Romain Lighthouse**
Cape Romain National
Wildlife Refuge
Off U.S. 17 and 701
By boat from McClellanville
1827, 1858

The first Cape Romain lighthouse, a 65-foot tower, was built on Raccoon Key, about 10 miles southwest of the entrance to the Santee River. Its principal purpose was to guide ships past the dangerous shoals in the vicinity and keep southbound ships out of the Gulf Stream. This light, according to the 1852 lighthouse report, was no better than a fourth-order lens.

Cape Romain light, noted for many years as the leaning lighthouse, because its foundation began to sink after it was built.

The Lighthouse Board later recommended that the tower be replaced by a taller one with better lighting. Congress authorized such a light, and a new 150-foot octagonal pyramidal tower, now fitted with a first-order lens, was built near the old tower. (The *Light List* later indicated that the new tower was 161 feet tall.) The keeper exhibited the light on January 1, 1858. The Confederates put the light out of operation in 1861, and not until 1866 did the Lighthouse Board get it back into use. To make the light a better daymark, the board had its lower half painted white and the faces of the upper half painted alternately black and white. In the 1870s cracks began to appear in the tower. The district engineer's examination revealed that the tower was almost two feet out of plumb, and the lens had to be set level. The tower continued to settle and slipped more out of plumb, and again the lens had to be adjusted. The light continued to serve until 1947, when the Coast Guard replaced the tower with lighted buoys and reduced it to a daymark. Today, both towers are in the Cape Romain National Wildlife Refuge and they have received support from the Bicentennial Fund for rehabilitation. Access to the island is by private or charter boat from town. NR. [U.S. Coast Guard. U.S. Fish and Wildlife Service]

GULF OF MEXICO

Lydia Ann lighthouse, Port Aransas, Tex. The 1857 tower has a wire screen to protect the lens from birds and is topped by a ventilator ball and lightning rod. The lighthouse is surrounded by rich shrimp-breeding marshes that attract a wide variety of birds.

■ ■ ■ ■ ■ ■   ALABAMA   ■ ■ ■ ■ ■ ■

MOBILE

■ **Middle Bay Lighthouse**
Mobile Bay
1885

Mobile Bay's only full-scale screwpile lighthouse began service on December 1, 1885. Like many screwpile structures in the Chesapeake Bay, this one, located in midbay, has a hexagonal dwelling with a tower rising from the peak of its pyramidal roof. The dwelling was painted white, the piles red, the shutters green and the lantern black. Near the end of construction the piles settled 7½ feet into the mud. All the piles sank almost evenly so that no dislocation occurred and to the eye the structure appeared level. To prevent possible further settling, the workers drove a dozen creosote-treated wood piles next to the iron framework and bolted it to the piles, which they then cut off at water level. No further settling took place. In 1905 the Lighthouse Board removed the lantern and lens from the lighthouse and erected an iron post in the center of the lantern platform with "two lens-lantern lights 10 feet apart." The structure was not otherwise altered. In 1967 the Coast Guard decommissioned the lighthouse and planned to tear it down, but local protest was so vehement that the Coast Guard changed its mind. In 1974 the Mobile Historic Development Foundation spearheaded restoration of the old lighthouse, and more detailed work was undertaken in 1984 under the leadership of the Middle Bay Light Centennial Commission. The lighthouse still serves as a daymark and is a special favorite of boaters. NR. [Alabama Historical Commission]

Middle Bay light, a screwpile lighthouse located literally in the middle of Mobile Bay that is a popular attraction for boaters.

■ **Mobile Point Lighthouse**
Fort Morgan State Historic Site
Route 180
West of Gulf Shores
1822, 1873, 1966

The first lighthouse here, a 55-foot conical brick tower, was established as a harbor light on the east side of the entrance to Mobile Bay at Mobile Point, where Fort Morgan is now located. In 1835 Winslow Lewis changed this fixed light to a flashing one. Complaints came from shipping interests and ship captains because the light

Above: Mobile Point light station with the remains of Fort Morgan in the middle ground. The 1873 skeleton tower is on the left. Far left: Illustration from *Frank Leslie's Illustrated Newspaper* of the first lighthouse at Mobile Point showing damage suffered during the Civil War. Left: Mobile Point's 1873 light tower, which now lies on its side.

looked like the Pensacola light in Florida just 40 miles away. The Lighthouse Board in 1852, noting this similarity and the possibility of confusion to navigators, recommended that "the characteristic distinction of one of them should be changed." In 1858 the board placed a small, fourth-order lens in the lantern of the Mobile Point lighthouse, confirming its status as a harbor light. During the Civil War, because it was at Fort Morgan, the light tower was riddled by shots and shells from the guns of Union forces. It was damaged beyond repair, so in 1864 on the southwest bastion of the fort the Lighthouse Board established a temporary light with a sixth-order lens. Finally, in 1873 the board erected a 35-foot iron skeleton tower on the bastion and installed a fourth-order lens in the lantern. The focal plane of the light was 49 feet above sea level. This tower, which now lies on its side near its original location, was replaced in 1966 by a tall steel skeleton tower whose flashing white light is 125 feet above sea level. NHL district. [Alabama Historical Commission. U.S. Coast Guard]

■ **Sand Island Lighthouse**
Sand Island
3 miles southwest of Fort Morgan State Historic Site
1838, 1859, 1873

Alabama's only coastal light is on Sand Island, located on the west side of the main channel into Mobile Bay and three miles from the Mobile Point light. The Treasury first placed a 55-foot light tower on the island in 1838 to mark the approach to the entrance to Mobile Bay. In 1852 the Lighthouse Board recommended that a seacoast light be built in this area, either at Mobile Point or on Sand Island. The board resolved its uncertainty and in 1859 erected a new tower on Sand Island, fitting it with a large, first-order lens. The tower did not survive the Civil War, for southern troops destroyed it. The board installed a temporary light in 1864 on a wood tower and made plans to construct a new tower. In September 1873 the keeper lighted the second-order lens in the 132-foot brick conical tower, whose light is 131 feet above sea level.

The lighthouse soon began a long-running battle with erosion. By 1882 the remains of the old tower stood in the water, and the board began building jetties and bulkheads and placed riprap at the new tower's base to halt the water's action. These endeavors only slowed the natural processes, and in the 1890s the dwelling had to be moved. Then the erosion process reversed, attacking from another side. Congress became alarmed enough to appropriate money to be used, when necessary, to move the tower. In 1906 a storm destroyed the assistant keeper's house, killing him and his wife. At this time the tower's entrance, a stairway from the keeper's dwelling, was moved from the south to the north side and raised 30 feet. Meanwhile, erosion continued, and in 1914 the tower stood in water, but, again, the pattern of erosion changed.

Sand Island light on an island that was once 400 acres. Riprap, or blocks of stone, now secures the island.

The Coast Guard automated the light in 1947 and deactivated the station in 1971. Two years later the keeper's dwelling burned. Today, the tower stands alone on the island, once 400 acres in size and now just a little larger than the base of the light tower. Riprap surrounding the tower holds the island together, but ultimately the sea will claim the tower. Although the tower is not open, the lens is in the Fort Morgan museum. NR. [U.S. Coast Guard]

■ ■ ■ ■ ■ ■ FLORIDA ■ ■ ■ ■ ■ ■

APALACHICOLA

Stephen Pleasonton, fifth auditor of the Treasury, ordered construction of the first lighthouse on St. George Island, on the Gulf side of Apalachicola Bay. A white conical structure, the tower was 72 feet tall. In 1847 the lighthouse had to be rebuilt. Four years later a wind toppled this tower, and the following year a new tower was built and lighted. During the Civil War the Confederates damaged the lighthouse but not so seriously that it could not be repaired. It went back into service and remains active, surrounded by Cape St. George State Park. The light is accessible only by water. NR. [U.S. Coast Guard]

■ **Cape St. George Lighthouse**
Southwest point of Cape St. George Island
Cape St. George State Park
1833, 1847, 1852

Cape St. George light. A ground cable for lightning runs up the conical 74-foot tower. The light's focal plane is 72 feet above sea level.

In 1837 a lighthouse on this site west of Apalachicola was considered a useless expenditure, but the discovery of shoals off Cape San Blas changed Congress's mind, and it appropriated the funds for one, completed in 1847. Four years later a storm toppled the tower. Rebuilt in 1856, the tower was in service only a few months when another storm "totally destroyed" it; the Lighthouse Board reported that "a lagoon now occupies the site of the lighthouse." The board had a new tower erected in 1859, but southern forces inflicted extensive damage to it and put it out of use. It was not repaired until July 1865.

■ **Cape San Blas Lighthouse**
Route 30 south of Port St. Joe
1847, 1856, 1859, 1885

Cape San Blas light west of Apalachicola, an unusual skeleton tower because the cylinder surrounding the stairway begins above the ground, probably because of a concern with flooding.

In 1869 the light station began a 50-year battle with erosion. In 1875, when the Gulf waters came within 150 feet of the tower, the Lighthouse Board became alarmed enough to ask Congress for money to fight the creeping danger, but no action was taken. In 1878 the Gulf washed the base of the light tower and then receded; with no funds for a proper jetty, the board took no action. In 1880 the sea once again lapped against the tower. The board tried to slow the erosion with brush mattresses, but the sea quickly pounded them to shreds, and the light tower stood in water. With no appropriation on the horizon, the Lighthouse Board had the lens removed from the tower—not a minute too soon. On July 3, 1882, the tower stood in eight feet of water; with the sea pounding against it, it began to tilt, crack and then fell over. The Lighthouse Board soon asked Congress for funds to put up a skeleton tower. The money was appropriated, and on June 30, 1885, the keeper lighted the third-order lens in the 96-foot square pyramidal skeleton tower, located more than 400 yards from the shore. This tower had only two years of peace: between 1887 and 1890 the Gulf waters came within 144 feet. Fearful for the tower's safety, the board asked for and received money in 1890 to move it. Acquisition of land proved difficult, and the board instituted condemnation proceedings in 1894. In October of that year a storm struck the area, putting out the light, wrecking the two keepers' dwellings and leaving the tower standing in water. The light was immediately reexhibited. Two years later the board began moving the light station to Black's Island in St. Joseph Bay, but when the move was about half completed, the board changed its mind, reestablished the light in the abandoned skeleton tower and relighted it in September 1897. In 1903 the board received money to put up a new tower at a new location, but the shore had begun to rebuild so the board decided to leave the tower where it was. The tower was to have one last scare: in 1916 the sea once again threatened the site, and in 1919 the Bureau of Lighthouses moved the Cape San Blas light tower a quarter mile north to its present site. It is now automated. NR. [U.S. Coast Guard]

BOCA GRANDE

This lighthouse west of Fort Myers was established by the Lighthouse Board "to mark the entrance to this harbor and to enable vessels to avoid the shoals on both sides of the outer portion of Gasparilla and Lacosta Islands." The board also reported that there would be an increase in traffic because "Punta Gorda a town at the head of Charlotte Harbor is the southern terminus of the Florida Southern Railroad, and . . . lines of steamers are to be established with this railroad." Lighted on December 31, 1890, the structure was originally known as the Gasparilla Island lighthouse. It is a square dwelling with a pyramidal roof and a square light tower rising through its center; a verandah runs around three sides of the structure. The dwelling rests on iron piles, allowing high waters to pass through without disturbing the foundation. Atop the tower is a black lantern that contained first a 3½-order then a fourth-order lens; its white light, varied by a red flash, was 44 feet above mean low water. A smaller square assistant keeper's dwelling was built at the same time. The Coast Guard decommissioned the light station in 1967. It lay idle until 1972, when local residents, disturbed by the vandalization of the structure, successfully petitioned to have the old lighthouse transferred to the county. Later, the Gasparilla Island Conservation and Improvement Association undertook the restoration of the structure. With the permission of the Coast Guard, the association relighted the old fourth-order lens on November 21, 1986. The lighthouse is now back on the *Light List.* Plans call for the old structure to house a maritime museum. NR. [Lee County]

■ **Port Boca Grande (Gasparilla Island) Lighthouse**
South end of Gasparilla Island
Route 771 south of Placida
1890

Below left: Port Boca Grande light station. The dwellings are typical of the Gulf Coast with wrap-around verandahs and pile foundations. Below: Crooked River light, a pyramid-shaped skeleton tower.

CARRABELLE

The loss of a lighthouse on nearby Dog Island and the growth in the area's lumber trade increased demand for a lighthouse on the mainland to serve the deep-water port formed by the Crooked River. Congress appropriated funds in 1889, but because of problems concerning purchase of the land for the light station, construction was not completed until 1895. The keeper lighted the light

■ **Crooked River Lighthouse**
Off U.S. 319 southwest
1895

of the new lighthouse on October 28. The structure was a type popular in the late 19th century — a square pyramidal skeleton tower with a metal cylinder for the stairs. The tower is 103 feet tall, and the focal plane of the fourth-order lens, which emits a flashing white light, is 115 feet above sea level. Still active, the light tower is painted dark red on its upper half and white below. NR. [U.S. Coast Guard]

CEDAR KEY

■ **Cedar Keys Lighthouse**
Seahorse Key
Cedar Keys National Wildlife Refuge
1854

Erected on Seahorse Key, this lighthouse, a white tower on a dwelling, began service on August 1, 1854. Its fourth-order lens issued a fixed white light with a three-second flash every 60 seconds, whose focal plane was 75 feet above mean low water. During the Civil War, the Confederates extinguished the light. Relighted after the war, it continued to serve until 1915, when the Bureau of Lighthouses deactivated it. The light station later was transferred to the U.S. Department of Agriculture and, in 1936, to the Fish and Wildlife Service of the U.S. Department of the Interior to become part of Cedar Keys National Wildlife Refuge. Today, the University of Florida uses the site for a marine laboratory, and some of the old light station buildings house students who come to the lab. [U.S. Fish and Wildlife Service]

PENSACOLA

■ **Pensacola Lighthouse**
Naval Air Station
Route 292 south
1825, 1859

Pensacola was the first site selected for a lighthouse on Florida's west coast. With Congress's authorization, Stephen Pleasonton of the Treasury built one at the south entrance to Pensacola Bay. The focal plane of the light was 80 feet above sea level. A lighthouse inspector in 1837 recognized that the light should be higher and recommended replacing it with one on a more raised site. The Lighthouse Board's 1852 report said that the light was "deficient in power, being fitted with only ten lamps and sixteen inch reflectors." The board was also disturbed by the fact that the light was a flashing one, like the Mobile Point light just 40 miles away. Because Pensacola was a major naval base, the board recommended that the port have "a first-class sea coast light." Two years after the report, the commandant of the naval station urged that the light tower be raised 20 to 25 feet. In 1858 the Lighthouse Board erected a new 171-foot conical brick tower on the north side of the bay entrance, and on January 1, 1859, the flashing white light shone for the first time, with the focal plane of the first-order lens 191 feet above sea level.

During the Civil War southern troops bombarded the light tower and put the light out of operation. The Lighthouse Board placed it back in service in 1863, using a fourth-order lens, which it replaced in 1869 with a first-order lens. Years later, the residual effects of the bombardment surfaced when cracks appeared in the tower, requiring repointing. No further problems occurred, and the lighthouse has continued in service, its automated light visible 27 miles out to sea. To make it a good daymark, the upper two-thirds of the tower is painted black and the lower third white. To visit the lighthouse, contact the guard at the entrance to the naval air station. NR. [U.S. Coast Guard. U.S. Navy]

ST. MARKS

Stephen Pleasonton, the Treasury's fifth auditor, let the contract for the first St. Marks lighthouse to Winslow Lewis. Lewis in turn subcontracted the job in 1828 to two builders who constructed such a poor lighthouse — the walls were hollow rather than solid as called for in the contract — that the local customs collector refused to accept the work. Another contract was awarded to rebuild the tower. This work was satisfactory, and the masonry tower went into service in 1831. Nine years later, erosion threatened the lighthouse, and Pleasonton ordered it moved. The same person who had constructed the tower took it down and reerected it. During the Seminole War, the keeper, concerned about an Indian attack, asked Pleasonton for a guard to protect the lighthouse. Pleasonton denied the request. The keeper then asked that a boat be assigned to the station so that he and his family could escape should the Indians attack. Pleasonton denied this request also. Fortunately, no attack occurred. The Confederates attempted to destroy the lighthouse during the Civil War and blew a large hole in the base of the structure, causing structural damage.

After the war the Lighthouse Board had the tower reconstructed, and the keeper relighted it on January 8, 1867. This 82-foot white conical tower, located south of Tallahassee on the east side of the entrance to the St. Marks River, has survived and today, automated, is the rear St. Marks range light. A generator in the base of the tower is ready if the electric power fails. A Coast Guard auxiliary unit has just leased the light station, except for the tower, and is converting the site into a base for rescue operations in the area. The surviving keeper's quarters is being adapted for this use. Visitors may walk around the grounds. NR. [U.S. Coast Guard]

■ **St. Marks (Rear Range) Lighthouse**
St. Marks National Wildlife Refuge
Route 59 off U.S. 98 at Newport
1831, c. 1840, 1867

St. Marks lighthouse, with a work building attached. Out back is a water tank.

ST. PETERSBURG

■ **Egmont Key Lighthouse**
North end of Egmont Key
Across from Fort DeSoto
State Park
Off Route 693
Francis A. Gibbons
1848, 1858

Because of increased shipping activity in Tampa Bay, the Treasury's fifth auditor, Stephen Pleasonton, had a lighthouse established on Egmont Key at the entrance to Tampa Bay. The masonry lighthouse was built by Francis A. Gibbons, who was a few years later to undertake, with a partner, the building of the first lighthouses on the West Coast. Ten years after construction, the tower, whose foundation had become undermined by shifting sand, had to be replaced. The new masonry tower was 87 feet tall. For a time it served as a rear range light. Today, the light is automated and still active, although the Coast Guard has removed the lantern and placed an aerobeacon on top of the tower. Coast Guard personnel are still on the island but will depart when the Florida Department of Natural Resources licenses the site. The lighthouse can be seen from Fort DeSoto and is accessible by boat. [U.S. Coast Guard]

SANIBEL

■ **Sanibel Island Lighthouse**
Sanibel Point, east end of
Sanibel Island
Causeway on Route 867
J. N. "Ding" Darling National
Wildlife Refuge
1884

Sanibel Island light station,
consisting of a skeleton tower,
two Gulf Coast–style
dwellings equipped with
several water tanks and
work buildings.

Lighted on August 20, 1884, this lighthouse was established because the Lighthouse Board realized that increasing traffic on Florida's Gulf Coast demanded a light between Key West and Egmont Key to the north. At the time of construction, the ship transporting the iron materials to the site sank off the east end of the island, but the captain unloaded some of the material before the vessel went down. Facing delays in having replacement parts fashioned, the district engineer hired a diver to retrieve the missing parts of the lantern from the submerged ship. His ingenuity proved successful, for the diver retrieved all the pieces except for two small brackets. The 102-foot light tower is a square pyramidal skeleton structure with a cylinder enclosing a stairway. Its lantern housed a flashing third-order lens whose focal plane was 98 feet above sea level. The station also has

two keepers' dwellings, square cottages built on piles with pyramidal roofs and verandahs. The tower today is painted brown, and the light, now automated and equipped with a modern plastic lens, is still active. The town of Sanibel has a 10-year license to preserve and interpret the light station, and town employees occupy the keepers' dwellings. NR. [U.S. Coast Guard. U.S. Fish and Wildlife Service]

■ ■ ■ ■ ■ ■   LOUISIANA   ■ ■ ■ ■ ■ ■

BERWICK

The town of Berwick south of Morgan City on the Gulf is developing a lighthouse park on the banks of the Atchafalaya River, bringing to it several lighthouses inaccessible to most of the public and building a lighthouse museum. One of the first lighthouses identified for removal to the park is the Ship Shoal light. The lighthouse, originally located off the coast of Louisiana between the Timbalier and Atchafalaya bays, is similar to the Florida reef lighthouses. The 125-foot brown tower rested on screwpile legs in 15 feet of water, its lantern holding a second-order lens. Automated in the 1950s, it was deactivated some time before 1970. After the Coast Guard retired the light, the tower continued to serve as a daymark. [Town of Berwick]

■ Ship Shoal Lighthouse
Old Spanish Trail Ferry Crossing
Off U.S. 90
1859

Ship Shoal lighthouse on its original site, a reef light stabilized by screwpile construction.

The second lighthouse selected for Berwick's lighthouse park is a square pyramidal tower sheathed in iron plates with a lantern containing a fourth-order lens, which went into service on September 1, 1858, in the Atchafalaya Bay. Adjacent to the tower was a rectangular structure that probably served as the living quarters; on top of this building was the fog bell apparatus. This assemblage of structures was mounted on the spindly legs of a pile

■ Southwest Reef Lighthouse
Old Spanish Trail Ferry Crossing
Off U.S. 90
1858

framework. The tower was lower until 1872, when it was raised on another set of framework legs. The light was decommissioned in 1916, when the Point au Fer Reef lighthouse on the eastern side of the bay came into service. [Town of Berwick]

MADISONVILLE

■ Tchefuncte River Rear Range Light
North shore of Lake Ponchartrain
2 miles south of Madisonville
1838, 1857

Below: Tchefuncte River rear range light station with bell tower and residence. Below right: Chandeleur Island light, with a stairway cylinder beginning above ground.

Erected where the Tchefuncte River empties into Lake Ponchartrain north of New Orleans, the first light here was replaced in 1857 and was described in the *Light List* as a 34-foot conical white brick tower with a light 38 feet above lake level. In 1867 the tower had to be repaired, probably because of damage incurred during the Civil War. At that time the lantern from the Cat Island lighthouse in Mississippi was installed on the tower, which was relighted in 1868. For the next 20 years the light station led an uneventful life. On August 19–20, 1888, a hurricane passed through and left nothing standing but the tower and the keeper's dwelling. Repairs were made to the light station. The tower, now with a black stripe and a light 49 feet above lake level, has functioned as a rear range light since 1903. The light is automated and has a 250-millimeter plastic lens. NR. [U.S. Coast Guard]

NEW ORLEANS

■ Chandeleur Island Lighthouse
North end of Chandeleur Island
Breton National Wildlife Refuge
1848, 1856, 1896

The first lighthouse to mark this crescent-shaped series of islands east of New Orleans, forming the outer boundary of Chandeleur Sound to the north and Breton Sound to the south, was placed on the southern end of Chandeleur Island and went into service in 1848. It lasted only six years. In 1856 another brick lighthouse, this one on the northern end of the island, displayed the light from its fourth-order lens. The keeper's dwelling was built on piles. Abandoned by the Confederates at the beginning of the Civil War, the lighthouse was quickly put back in service by federal forces to help their blockading squadron. The light and tower continued in operation until October 1893, when a storm swept the area and washed the sand from the lighthouse's foundation, tilting it dangerously out of plumb.

Congress then voted funds to replace the light tower. This time the Lighthouse Board in 1896 erected a square pyramidal iron skeleton tower, 61 feet tall, with a cylinder in the center enclosing the stairs. Although iron skeleton light towers are common in the United States, this one is different in that the cylinder containing the stairs does not go all the way to the ground. A tall center pole, or leg, supports this cylinder, access to which is via a stairway to the first level, where the entrance is located. At the time of construction the light was upgraded with the installation of a third-order lens whose focal plane was 99 feet above sea level. Still in service, the tower is painted brown, the lantern black. NR. [U.S. Coast Guard]

The New Canal was dug in the 1830s to connect downtown New Orleans with Lake Ponchartrain, and in 1838 a lighthouse was built at the entrance to the canal. The tower was beyond repair by 1854, so in 1855 the Lighthouse Board placed a wood tower holding a fifth-order lens on the hipped-roof keeper's dwelling. This structure survived until 1890, when the board discontinued the lighthouse, replacing it with a light on a pole in front of the lighthouse. On the following day the board sold the dwelling and tower at public auction. In 1901 the board built a new iron-pile dwelling, a square two-story structure with verandahs; the pyramidal roof had a square tower rising from the center. The light was 52 feet above the water. This structure survives and still supports an active light, now a 190-millimeter plastic lens. NR. [U.S. Coast Guard]

■ **New Canal Lighthouse**
West End Boulevard and Lakeshore Drive
1838, 1855, 1901

New Canal light, the last of three lights on this site to guide traffic into the canal connecting New Orleans with Lake Ponchartrain.

PONCHATOULA

This lighthouse was needed to guide ships into Pass Manchac, which connects Lake Maurepas and Lake Ponchartrain. The first lighthouse here, a brick tower, went into service in 1837 and had to be rebuilt in 1846. The third lighthouse was lighted in February 1859; unlike

■ **Pass Manchac Lighthouse**
West shore of Lake Ponchartrain
North side of Pass Manchac
1837, 1846, 1859, c. 1867

Pass Manchac light station near Ponchatoula in 1914. Today, only the tower exists, with water covering its base.

the previous two, it was a tower on top of a dwelling, with a light 45 feet above lake level. This tower was severely damaged during the Civil War, and a fourth lighthouse apparently was built, because the postwar structure, a 35-foot cylindrical brick tower painted white and attached to the dwelling, does not match the description of the prewar structure. The last date shown in the *Light List,* however, is 1859, indicating that the 1859 tower was reconstructed rather than replaced. In 1952 the Coast Guard tore down the dwelling and left the tower standing. When the light was automated, its Fresnel lens was replaced by a 250-millimeter plastic lens. Now deactivated, the tower remains upright with a few feet of water covering its base; only the dwelling's foundations are visible. NR. [U.S. Coast Guard]

SABINE PASS

■ **Sabine Pass Lighthouse**
Louisiana Point
Lighthouse Bayou
Off Route 87
1856

Positioned at Louisiana Point, on the east side of the mouth of the Sabine River, this octagonal light guides vessels bound for Port Arthur, Tex., into the pass. The Confederates put the third-order Fresnel lens out of operation during the Civil War, but the Lighthouse Board

Sabine Pass light before the hurricane that destroyed much of the station. As the "rocket ship" light, this lighthouse is a unique design in the United States.

repaired it and placed it back in service in 1865. In October 1886 a severe hurricane destroyed the station except for the light tower, whose design doubtless contributed to its stability. The 81-foot tower is supported by six buttresses at the base that give it immense stability and the appearance of a rocket ship. Later restored, the station was decommissioned in 1952 and some years later turned over to Louisiana for a state park. The state subsequently gave back the site to the federal government, and the General Services Administration eventually sold it to a private citizen. Unfortunately, a fire destroyed all the structures at the site except for the light tower and a brick storage shed. Plans for the site are uncertain. It is accessible only by private boat but can be clearly seen from the Texas side of the pass at the town of Sabine. NR. [Privately owned]

■ ■ ■ ■ ■ ■   MISSISSIPPI   ■ ■ ■ ■ ■ ■

BILOXI

This conical cast-iron tower, 61 feet tall, is the best-known and most prominent of Mississippi's lighthouses. In 1867 erosion of the bank caused the tower to tip two feet out of plumb, but workers corrected that condition by digging out the other side and letting the tower settle back to level. The tower was painted black in 1867, supposedly as a sign of mourning for President Lincoln, but in actuality to make it a better daymark. Painted black, however, the tower was even more difficult to see against its background of dark green trees. The tower was later painted white. Maria Younghans served as keeper of this lighthouse for 51 years, retiring in 1918 with, the Lighthouse Service said, "a perfectly clear record and the highest approval of her services." The lighthouse now is part of a city park and is open to the public from May through Labor Day. The light is still exhibited but as a private aid to navigation. Repairs are being made through a Bicentennial Fund grant. NR. [City of Biloxi]

■ **Biloxi Lighthouse**
Median strip of U.S. 90 at Porter Street
1848

Biloxi lighthouse in the early 1900s. The cast-iron tower now is in a city park.

PASCAGOULA

■ **Round Island Lighthouse**
Round Island
1833, 1859

This light station was established to guard ships against the shoals off Round Island. After the 50-foot white brick conical tower was discontinued in 1944, the Coast Guard maintained it as a daymark until 1954. During at least part of its active years, this tower was equipped with a fourth-order lens, the focal plane of which was 44 feet above the water. The 1859 keeper's dwelling, a typical Gulf Coast–style square structure with a verandah built on piles, was destroyed by a fire in 1954. The tower now belongs to the city of Pascagoula, which plans to restore and relight it. NR. [City of Pascagoula]

Round Island light station when it was active and still had its keeper's house.

■ ■ ■ ■ ■ ■ ■   TEXAS   ■ ■ ■ ■ ■ ■ ■

MATAGORDA

■ **Matagorda Lighthouse**
Matagorda Island State Park
West side of Pass Cavallo at
entrance to Matagorda Bay
1852, 1873

Shortly after Texas entered the Union, the value of Matagorda Bay as a port was recognized, so Congress appropriated funds to build a lighthouse at its entrance. In 1852 workers completed the light station and the iron tower began service. With the onset of the Civil War the Confederates attempted to destroy the lighthouse by dynamiting the foundation. They succeeded in partially throwing it over, and that fact, in addition to the threat of sea erosion, prompted the Lighthouse Board in 1867 to take down the tower and put the iron plates in storage. Later, the board had new plates cast to replace the damaged ones and then reerected the tower on the west

Matagorda light station, 1950. The tower was painted black to serve as a daymark. Three water tanks flank the cottage-style dwelling on one side.

side of Pass Cavallo at the entrance to Matagorda Bay. The keeper exhibited the light of the reconstructed 90-foot conical lighthouse on September 1, 1873. In 1886 a storm swept the coast and destroyed all the buildings at the light station except the tower and the keeper's dwelling, rocking the tower so hard that a segment of the lens was jarred out and smashed to pieces on the tower deck. The tower required considerable repair, and the dwelling had to be rebuilt. For a number of years the light tower has been painted black. Still active and maintained by the Coast Guard, the lighthouse is within Matagorda Island State Park, located northeast of Corpus Christi, and accessible by boat. NR. [U.S. Coast Guard]

PORT ARANSAS

Near Corpus Christi, south of Matagorda Island, this lighthouse guided ships along the coast and through the Aransas Pass into Corpus Christi Bay. After some debate over what type of navigational aid to put on the site — a lightship, screwpile structure or masonry tower — the Lighthouse Board decided on an octagonal brick tower with a wood keeper's dwelling to be built inside the bay on Harbor Island. Work began in 1855, but the light tower did not display the light from its fourth-order lens until two years later. Badly damaged during the Civil War, the tower's top 20 feet had to be rebuilt. During these repairs that Texas phenomenon, a "blue norther," struck the area. The Lighthouse Board reported that "the cold was so intense that fish, thrown ashore by the hundreds, were frozen, and birds of all sorts sought refuge in the tower and camp of the workmen, where they perished in large number." In 1867 repairs were completed and the tower was relighted.

■ **Lydia Ann (Aransas Pass) Lighthouse**
Harbor Island
Northwest of Aransas Pass
1857

Over the years several more structures were added to the station: a hollow-tile double keepers' quarters in stucco with a pyramidal roof, wood assistant keeper's quarters, oil house, wood radio shack, dock, wood cisterns and raised walkways. Because the site is emerging land and is usually completely or partially covered with water, all these structures, except the tower and oil house, were built on piles. The raised walkways were mandatory for the same reason. As time passed, nature worked against the station. The Aransas Pass was inching southward, with the result that the light's location was no longer suitable for guiding ships into the harbor. Moreover, advancing technology and automation caught up with the light station. In 1952 the Coast Guard closed it and moved the light to a skeleton tower at its station on the south side of the Aransas Pass.

The Coast Guard declared the old site surplus, and in 1970 the General Services Administration sold it to the highest bidder. The present owner, who purchased it from the original owners, has gone to considerable expense to put the historic station into a good state of repair. With the exception of the missing oil house, which was destroyed by a hurricane in 1970, the station is complete. The owner obtained a 300-millimeter lens,

Lydia Ann light station near the Aransas Pass, 1946. From left to right the structures are a radio beacon, now gone, principal dwelling, radio shack, double keepers' and assistant keeper's dwellings, light tower and oil house, which is also gone.

similar to one used at the station during repairs in 1944, and relighted the tower on July 4, 1988. The fixed white light can be seen seven miles. Because it cannot use its original name—when the Coast Guard moved the light in 1954 it retained the name — the old lighthouse is now known as the Lydia Ann light, after the channel that runs in front. The old light tower has since returned to duty, recognized now by the Coast Guard as an official aid to navigation. It is the only staffed light station on the Gulf Coast, for the owner has hired two keepers to tend the light, maintain the structures and restore the buildings. It is not open to public visitation, but the station can be viewed from the Lydia Ann Channel. NR. [Privately owned]

PORT BOLIVAR

■ **Point Bolivar Lighthouse**
Route 87, ⅓ mile west of
Route 2612
1852, 1865, 1873

The first lighthouse on this site north of Galveston went into service at about the time the Lighthouse Board was taking over the country's aids to navigation. The tower, made of iron, remained here until the Civil War, when the board had it taken apart and put in storage. At the end of the war the board erected a temporary light at this point, which remained in operation until November 19, 1873, when the keeper shone the light of the new 117-foot brick-lined iron tower. A sturdy structure, it withstood the famous 1900 hurricane that devastated Galveston. During the storm 125 people sought refuge in the tower. Fifteen years later another memorable hurricane with 125-mile-per-hour winds lashed the tower. It survived, as did the 50 people who took shelter here. The Bureau of Lighthouses discontinued the tower in 1933 and ultimately sold it. The old light station is in private hands, and its dwellings, one on each side of the tower, serve as summer residences. NR. [Privately owned]

PORT ISABEL

■ **Point Isabel Lighthouse**
Point Isabel Lighthouse State
Historic Site
Route 100
1853

On the northern end of Brazos Island at the site of Gen. Zachary Taylor's encampment during the war with Mexico, the Lighthouse Board built a brick conical lighthouse whose light was 82 feet above sea level. The light marked the Brazos Santiago Pass, the entrance to

Port Isabel, which is north of Brownsville. Southern troops took it out of operation during the Civil War, but in 1866 the Lighthouse Board repaired and relighted the tower. It remained in operation until 1888, when the board decided that a light was no longer needed at that site.

About this time the board realized that it did not own the site of the lighthouse; General Taylor had simply appropriated it for a camp and depot without buying the land. The rightful owners reclaimed the land and took possession of the light tower and the other buildings of the light station. The board began to reconsider the value of the light and determined that one was indeed needed at Point Isabel. The owners offered to sell the land and buildings for $8,000, which the board thought was a fair price, and Congress appropriated the money. But the Justice Department, unhappy with this solution, began condemnation proceedings, which dragged on for four more years. The owners finally settled for $6,000, and the light tower was relighted on July 15, 1895. The light station remained in operation for 10 years, when the Lighthouse Board again discontinued it. It then lay idle for more than 20 years. In 1927 the Bureau of Light-houses sold it to the highest bidder for $2,760. It eventually came into the hands of Mr. and Mrs. Lon C. Hill, who donated it to the state of Texas, which designated it a state historical park two years later. The old tower is in remarkably good condition. NR. [State of Texas]

Below left: Point Bolivar light, a well-built tower that has survived two devastating hurricanes. Below: Point Isabel light, now part of a state historical park.

GREAT LAKES

Duluth South Breakwater Inner lighthouse, Duluth, Minn., c. 1906, a steel skeleton tower topped by a lantern and watch room. The French lens was manufactured in 1896. A cylinder encloses the stairway to the lantern.

■ ■ ■ ■ ■ ■ ■ ■ **ILLINOIS** ■ ■ ■ ■ ■ ■ ■ ■

CHICAGO

**■ Chicago Harbor
Lighthouse**
South end of
north breakwater
1832, 1893

Chicago Harbor has had several lighthouses since its first one was built in 1832. The current Chicago Harbor lighthouse was originally located at the entrance to the Chicago River and lighted in 1893. Its red-and-white paneled third-order Fresnel lens had initially been intended for the new Point Loma lighthouse in San Diego. The lens, an exceptionally fine one and the winner of several awards, was on display at the 1893 World's Columbian Exposition in Chicago when the Lighthouse Board assigned another one to the Point Loma station. The board decided to hold the lens for the Chicago Harbor lighthouse, then being built. With the completion of this light in 1893, workers moved the lens to the new tower. The white conical steel-plated lighthouse is brick lined and on each side has a hipped-roof structure; one contains the fog signal, and the other is a boat house. The Chicago Harbor lighthouse remained at its mainland site until 1919, when the Bureau of Lighthouses moved the structure to the south end of the north breakwater, putting the focal plane of its light at 82 feet above the mean lower lake level. The light is still active. NR. [U.S. Coast Guard]

EVANSTON

■ Grosse Point Lighthouse
2535 Sheridan Road
1873

The Lighthouse Board had the Grosse Point lighthouse erected in 1873 to serve as a primary coastal light for Lake Michigan and gave it a second-order Fresnel lens whose focal plane was 121 feet above lake level. The light was a fixed white one with a red flash every three minutes. The red flash was obtained by the rotation of a panel of red glass around the outside of the lens; a clockwork system, energized by a falling weight, powered the rotating panel. The station consisted of a 110-foot light tower, made of brick but now encased in four inches of concrete, connected by an enclosed brick passageway to a two-story double keepers' dwelling made of yellow brick. Two other brick structures, used as barns for fog signaling equipment, were built on each side of the pathway leading from the tower toward the lake shore. The Bureau of Lighthouses automated the light in 1935 and turned over most of the buildings and grounds to the city of Evanston. In 1941 the Coast Guard decommissioned the light tower and transferred it, with its lantern and second-order lens, to the city. Relighted in 1946, the tower is now maintained as a private aid to navigation principally of value to small boats.

This lighthouse today is located adjacent to Northwestern University in a district of stately old homes and occupies a lot that stretches to the beach, just as the other houses in the vicinity do. The light tower and dwelling are impressive, and the grounds, with their tall trees, lend a romantic touch. The buildings of the light station have been restored, most recently with assistance from the Bicentennial Fund, and are maintained in good condi-

Left: Chicago Harbor light, whose tower was moved from the mainland to this breakwater. Below: Grosse Point light in Evanston, whose light once could be seen for 21 miles.

tion. The tower has been painted yellow to match the brick of the dwelling, and the lantern and gallery are red, as are the Italianate braces supporting the lantern. One of the fog signal buildings is now used as a nature center and the other as a maritime museum; both are open to the public only on weekends. The grounds are open daily. [City of Evanston. Evanston Environmental Association]

■ ■ ■ ■ ■ ■ ■ ■ **INDIANA** ■ ■ ■ ■ ■ ■ ■ ■

MICHIGAN CITY

■ **Michigan City Lighthouse**
Washington Park
Heisman Harbor Road
1837, 1858

In 1858 the Lighthouse Board replaced the first light-house on this site with a two-story, gable-roof brick dwelling with a square tower resting on one end of the roof. For 46 years this lighthouse guided ships into the harbor off Lake Michigan. The Lighthouse Board then determined that Michigan City also needed a fog signal, to be placed at the end of the east pier, and decided that the light should be moved to the same point. In the fall of 1904 the new station with a fog signal went into service at the end of the recently extended east pier (see next entry). The old brick dwelling was remodeled and enlarged and made into a residence for two keepers. Two rooms were added to the north end of the structure, the tower was removed from the roof (its fifth-order lens had been moved to the new lighthouse), a circular porch with a balcony above was placed at the entrance, the second floor was given wood siding, and the fenestration was redesigned. This structure continued to serve as the keeper's residence until 1940. Michigan City acquired the house after the Coast Guard closed it in 1960 and leased it to the Michigan City Historical Society, which restored it to its post–1904 appearance. In 1973 the society replicated the tower and lantern and placed it back on the roof of the dwelling. The lighthouse is open from noon to 4 p.m. during the summer. NR. [City of Michigan City]

■ **Michigan City East Pier Lighthouse**
Washington Park
End of Franklin Street
1904

Michigan City's east pier is only a short way from the old 1858 lighthouse, but the pier extends a considerable distance. This light, first exhibited on October 20, 1904, is located at the end of the pier. A brick building enclosed by metal plates with an octagonal tower rising from the center of its pyramidal roof, its design is not uncommon in the Great Lakes area. The fence blocking off the pier and the adjacent waterfront Coast Guard property

prohibits visitors, but the lighthouse, now automated, can be viewed from the head of the pier just outside the fence. At present, the catwalk to the lighthouse needs repairs. The city wants the Coast Guard to make these repairs, because the catwalk is an integral part of the historic pier light. The Coast Guard does not have further use for the catwalk and thus says that the catwalk is too expensive to maintain. NR. [U.S. Coast Guard]

■ ■ ■ ■ ■ ■   MICHIGAN   ■ ■ ■ ■ ■ ■

ALCONA

To guide ships around this point of land protruding into Lake Huron, this 68-foot conical brick tower was built, holding a lens whose light was 69 feet above lake level. In 1887 the Lighthouse Board replaced the original lens with a 3½-order lens. The keeper's dwelling, which is attached to the tower by a short brick passageway, is a two-story brick structure with a shed built on its rear. All these structures are painted white. Today, the light is automated and still active. The Coast Guard has leased the site to the Alcona County Historical Society, which has established a museum here. NR. [U.S. Coast Guard. Leased to Alcona County Historical Society]

■ **Sturgeon Point Lighthouse**
U.S. 23 south to Lakeshore Drive, then to Point Road
1870

Sturgeon Point light, a conical brick tower constructed on land donated by its first keeper, Perley Silverthorn.

BEAVER ISLAND

■ **Beaver Island Lighthouse**
South end of Beaver Island
East Side Drive,
between Nicksau's and
Appleby's Points
By ferry from Charlevoix
1852, 1858

Beaver Island light, with its
10-sided steel lantern and
keeper's dwelling built in
1866.

This Lake Michigan lighthouse northwest of Charlevoix was designed to mark the western approach to the Mackinac Straits. The first lighthouse built here lasted only six years and was replaced in 1858. The new station included a 46-foot cylindrical yellow brick light tower with a lantern and an 1866 two-story yellow brick dwelling with a short passageway connecting it to the tower, plus a fog signal building. The tower served until some time after 1970, when the Coast Guard deactivated the light and removed the lens. In 1975 the Charlevoix Public School District acquired the old light station and turned it into an environmental and vocational education center. Surviving structures at the site include the tower, dwelling and fog signal building. NR. [Charlevoix Public School District]

■ **St. James (Beaver Island Harbor) Lighthouse**
North side of
harbor entrance
By ferry from Charlevoix
1856, 1870

At the north end of Beaver Island the Lighthouse Board established a light to guide vessels into this harbor of refuge. To better serve the mariners, the board replaced the original tower with a taller one in 1870 and fitted it with a fourth-order lantern and lens. The 41-foot cylindrical tower exhibits a red light and is the only structure of the light station that has survived. The light, now automated, is still active. [U.S. Coast Guard]

Above: St. James light, on Beaver Island, where all that remains is the tower. Left: Big Bay Point light, a massive brick structure consisting of a crenelled tower and double keepers' dwelling with 18 rooms.

BIG BAY

Established to light a dark stretch along the northern coast of the Upper Peninsula on Lake Superior, this lighthouse was placed at the point where a number of vessels had come to grief. A square brick tower crowned by a watch room and lantern with a third-order lens, it is attached to the lake side of a two-story brick dwelling that was the double keepers' quarters. A brick fog signal house, two brick privies and a brick oil house have survived along with later buildings that served as garages. The light was automated in 1941, and after moving the light to a steel skeleton tower in 1961, the Coast Guard sold the light station to a private party who used it as a home. In 1986 the owner sold the house to another person who has converted the old dwelling into a bed-and-breakfast inn. [Privately owned]

■ **Big Bay Point Lighthouse**
Big Bay Point
Lighthouse Road, 3 miles
northeast of Big Bay
1896

BRIMLEY

The Point Iroquis lighthouse steered vessels past the rocks off Point Iroquois and the reefs off Gros Cap in Canada and into the St. Marys River near Sault Ste. Marie. The river is the only waterway connecting Lake Superior with the other Great Lakes. In 1855 the St. Marys Falls Canal (Soo Locks) opened to enable ships

■ **Point Iroquois Lighthouse**
Iroquois Point
Hiawatha National Forest
Off Lake Shore Drive
1855, 1871

Point Iroquois light station near Brimley, replaced by buoys in 1962. The light guided ships from Lake Superior to the St. Marys Falls Ship Canal (Soo Locks).

carrying copper and iron ore from the ranges of Lake Superior to transport their cargoes to the steel plants in the lower lakes. To aid the ore carriers entering the St. Marys River, the Lighthouse Board in 1855 built a simple wood lighthouse and installed a small, sixth-order lens. This structure served until 1871, when the Lighthouse Board replaced it with a conical brick tower, 65 feet tall to the top of the ventilator ball on the lantern. The tower is connected by a short enclosed passageway to the two-story brick keeper's residence. In 1884 a fog signal was placed at the station; four years later it was replaced with a fog whistle. Barns, an oil house, a boathouse and a wharf were added later, as was a 1902 addition to the keeper's dwelling that provided quarters for an assistant keeper.

The lighthouse served until 1962, when the Coast Guard decommissioned it, relying on buoys to guide ships past the dangerous rocks. In 1965 the Coast Guard turned over the light station to the Forest Service as an addition to the Hiawatha National Forest. The Bay Mills–Brimley Historical Research Society recently stabilized the old structure with help from the Bicentennial Fund and placed exhibits in it. It is open to the public. NR. [U.S. Forest Service. Leased to Bay Mills–Brimley Historical Research Society]

COPPER HARBOR

■ Copper Harbor Lighthouse
East of harbor entrance
Fort Wilkins State Park
Off U.S. 41
1849, 1867

Located near the eastern end of the Keweenaw Peninsula, at the tip of Michigan's Upper Peninsula, the Copper Harbor light went into service on Lake Superior in 1849, just five years after the discovery of a rich copper vein near here. The station had a stone tower and a separate dwelling, and in 1856 the tower received a Fresnel lens. The Lighthouse Board moved the light 100 feet closer to the water in 1867, when it had a new lighthouse built. The square masonry tower was on one end of the yellow brick dwelling. The light remained active until 1883, when the Lighthouse Board discontinued it. Reactivated five years later, the light has continued to serve through the years,

marking the entrance to Copper Harbor, although not on the same site, for in 1933 the Bureau of Lighthouses took the old tower out of service and moved the light to a skeleton tower placed nearby. The old lighthouse is now part of Fort Wilkins State Park and has been converted into a maritime museum. [Michigan Department of Natural Resources]

Copper Harbor light, located in an area whose early history included explorations for copper.

■ **Manitou Island Lighthouse**
Off Keweenaw Peninsula
East of Copper Harbor
1850, 1861

A lighthouse was established on Manitou Island, located off the tip of the Keweenaw Peninsula east of Copper Harbor, to guide ships to and around the peninsula, particularly vessels entering Lake Superior through Whitefish Bay. The first lighthouse was lighted on the island in 1850. In 1861 it was replaced by a 60-foot iron skeleton tower with a cylinder enclosing the spiral stairway. It and the one at Whitefish Point reportedly are the oldest skeletal lighthouses on the Great Lakes, and both are early examples of this type built in the United States. This light tower's third-order lens, now automated, is still active. The keeper's wood dwelling at the station apparently dates to the construction of the present tower. NR. [U.S. Coast Guard]

EAGLE HARBOR

An Eagle Harbor lighthouse first went into service on Lake Superior in 1851, equipped with Argand lamps and parabolic reflectors, which were replaced by a fourth-order Fresnel lens in 1857. By 1868 the Lighthouse Board thought that the buildings were in poor condition and requested money to rebuild them. Congress acquiesced, and in 1871 the new tower and dwelling were completed. The 44-foot brick octagonal tower held a fourth-order lens whose light was 60 feet above the lake. The tower was attached to the 1½-story dwelling. In 1895 the Lighthouse Board added a fog signal to the station and 34 years later a radio beacon. In 1968 aerobeacons replaced the lens, and 12 years later the station was automated. The Coast Guard leased the dwelling and grounds to the Keweenaw County Historical Society, which has opened

■ **Eagle Harbor Lighthouse**
West end of harbor
Off Route 26
1851, 1871

Eagle Harbor light station. The octagonal brick light tower's walls are 12 inches thick.

the site and dwelling to the public and established a museum in the keeper's house. Today, the dwelling and tower survive, as do a brick oil house, fog signal building and two wood dwellings brought to the station after World War II. The light is still active. [U.S. Coast Guard. Leased to Keweenaw County Historical Society]

ESCANABA

■ **Escanaba (Sand Point)**
Lighthouse
Sand Point
Ludington Park
U.S. 2 and 41
1868

Established at Sand Point to guard vessels against the point and the nearby shoals, this lighthouse served until 1939. By that time dredging and filling had so altered the bay and harbor that the tower's fixed red light, 44 feet above lake level, was no longer of much help to navigators. The square brick light tower attached to an end of the one-story brick house served from then until 1985 as quarters for Coast Guard personnel. During this period the Coast Guard altered the structure substantially. The roof of the dwelling was raised to make it a two-story structure, and the tower's lantern and upper 10 feet were removed. In addition, the Coast Guard covered the tower and dwelling in aluminum siding and made interior changes to both structures.

When the Coast Guard no longer needed the lighthouse, the Delta County Historical Society became concerned and started negotiations in 1985 to obtain permission to restore the lighthouse to its original condition. Granted a 30-year license the next year, the society immediately began working with a local architect to resurrect the old light. A fund-raising campaign obtained corporate and grass-roots donations as well as substantial grants from the state of Michigan. Restoration began in 1987, and by the fall of 1988 the lighthouse was back to its original appearance, with the dwelling reduced and the tower raised to their original heights. The society is working with the Coast Guard to secure a lantern for the tower, so that the old lighthouse, inside and out, will look the way it did when it was an active aid to navigation. [U.S. Coast Guard. Leased to Delta County Historical Society]

FRANKFORT

Point Betsie, the turning point for vessels going both north and south, was regarded as one of the most important points on the eastern shore of Lake Michigan. In 1858 the Lighthouse Board erected a short conical brick tower and dwelling on a rise just back from the shore and topped the tower with a fourth-order lantern and lens. The tower, whose height including the lantern is 37 feet, is connected to the dwelling, which was enlarged to its present size in 1894. Beach erosion has been a serious problem for the lighthouse; major steps were taken as early as 1890 to halt it. The tower's base has been reinforced with a concrete revetment, jetties have been added, and a large concrete apron runs from the lighthouse to near the lake's edge. The lighthouse was automated in 1983 but is still active, with its fourth-order lens still in place. The site is now used as housing for Coast Guard personnel. [U.S. Coast Guard]

■ **Point Betsie Lighthouse**
Off Route 22 north to west end of Point Betsie Road
1858

Point Betsie light, the last lighthouse maintained by a keeper on Lake Michigan's eastern shore.

GRAND MARAIS

Until 1910 this lighthouse was known as the Big Sable light station. Located on the northern coast of Michigan's Upper Peninsula, it is not to be confused with the Big Sable light station later erected on the Lower Peninsula's Lake Michigan shore. The Au Sable lighthouse was established to fill in a dark space between Whitefish Point and Grand Island, a distance of some 80 miles. This area, infamous for shipwrecks, had acquired the sobriquet "Graveyard Coast." The brick tower was 87 feet tall, but its land elevation put the focal plane of the light at 107 feet above lake level. A third-order Fresnel lens emitted a steady white light. An enclosed short brick passageway connected the tower to the brick keeper's dwelling. The tower was painted white to make it a more distinct daymark against the woods. This isolated light station, 12 miles from the nearest town, could be reached by boat or wagon and a three-mile hike over a rough trail.

In 1909 the Lighthouse Board authorized major alterations and additions to the station. The original keeper's house was enlarged to create a home for two assistant keepers, and a new keeper's dwelling, brick privy and cistern were installed. Other changes occurred to the

■ **Au Sable (Big Sable) Lighthouse**
Au Sable Point, west of Grand Marais
Pictured Rocks National Lakeshore
Off Route H58
1874

Au Sable light station near Grand Marais, which includes a fog signal building, tower and keeper's and assistant keeper's dwellings.

station from time to time, including a brick oil house in 1895, fog signal in 1897, stone retaining wall (which has subsequently virtually disappeared) in 1906, iron oil house in 1915 and two-car garage in 1954. In 1958 the Coast Guard automated the Au Sable lighthouse and 10 years later transferred all the grounds and buildings, except the light tower, to the National Park Service for inclusion in the Pictured Rocks National Lakeshore. The Coast Guard also transferred the third-order lens to the Park Service for display at the visitors center. [U.S. Coast Guard. National Park Service]

■ **Grand Marais Harbor Range Lights**
Pier in harbor
Off Routes 77 and H58
1895–98

Grand Marais Harbor on Lake Superior is the only deep-water harbor between Whitefish Bay and Munising. Each of the pyramidal skeleton range lights here supports a lantern and light, below which is the enclosed steel-sided watch room. The outer light, 34 feet tall, was erected in 1895, and the inner light, 47 feet tall, was put up three years later. The lights are still active. [U.S. Coast Guard]

GULLIVER

Seul Choix ("only choice") was the name given to this point by French explorers, who found it to be one of the few harbors of refuge along this section of Lake Michigan on the southern shore of the Upper Peninsula. Although authorized to place a light here in 1886, the Lighthouse Board did not do so until 1892. The newly constructed tower was found to be unsatisfactory and had to be rebuilt. By 1895 the station had all its structures. The conical brick tower, 78 feet, 9 inches tall, held a third-order Fresnel lens whose focal plane was 80 feet above lake level. The tower, painted white, is connected by an enclosed brick passageway to the red brick dwelling, whose stone foundation matches and is the same height as the ashlar foundation of the tower. This residence, a two-story gable-roof structure with bowed wood gable ends, was expanded in 1925 with a one-story brick addition. A barn, workshop and oil house complete the complex. The Coast Guard replaced the third-order lens with an aerobeacon and automated the light and later turned over the station to the state of Michigan, which has opened the grounds to the public. The dwelling is occupied, and it, as well as all other structures, are closed to visitors. NR. [Michigan Department of Natural Resources]

■ **Seul Choix Point Lighthouse**
Seul Choix Point
U.S. 2 to end of Route 431
1892–95

Seul Choix Point light, now outfitted with an aerobeacon. Because of a number of problems, nine years elapsed between the time the station was funded and when it began operation.

HART

Like its older sister on Lake Michigan's eastern shore to the north at Big Sable Point in Ludington, this lighthouse is a brick conical tower 107 feet tall. At the time of construction, the site was not accessible by land, and all materials had to be landed on the beach and moved to the site, a not uncommon procedure in building lighthouses in the 19th century. The light of the third-order lens of the Little Sable tower winked on in the spring of 1874. A short

■ **Little Sable Lighthouse**
Silver Lake State Park
Off U.S. 31 west
to Route B15
1874

Little Sable light today, showing the tower stripped of its whitewash, and in 1914, with the brick keeper's dwelling.

enclosed passageway attached the tower to a brick dwelling. The tower was painted white to distinguish it from the Big Sable lighthouse, which had wide black-and-white bands. The Coast Guard electrified the lighthouse and in 1954 automated it. Later, it tore down all the structures at the light station except the tower, which remains active. The whitewash has virtually disappeared from the tower, revealing its red brick construction. Today, the lighthouse overlooks a bathing beach in Silver Lake State Park. NR. [U.S. Coast Guard]

HOLLAND

■ **Holland Harbor South Pierhead Lighthouse**
Holland Harbor
Off Interstate 196 and
U.S. 31, west of Holland off
South Shore Drive
1872, 1907, 1936

The 1907 light station here, designed to guide ships into Lake Macatawa off Lake Michigan, consisted of a keeper's residence with a steel skeleton light tower holding a sixth-order lens, which replaced a wood lighthouse from 1872. In 1936 the skeleton tower was removed and the light placed on a tower built on one of the twin gables of the keeper's quarters. The dwelling was then encased in steel plates, which were painted red. The gable roof of the lighthouse reflects the heavy Dutch settlement so preva-

Holland Harbor South Pierhead light on a twin-gabled residence. The building is covered with steel plates painted red.

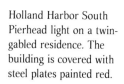

lent in the area. The light today primarily guides pleasure boats into the channel leading to the lake, which is bordered on both sides by public bathing beaches. The lens was removed in 1936 and given to the Netherlands Museum in the town of Holland. NR. [U.S. Coast Guard]

ISLE ROYALE

The search for copper ore in the Great Lakes increased in the 1850s, and one focus of this exploration was Isle Royale, an island at the most northern point in the Upper Peninsula. To provide safe passage for vessels going to the mines located on the southern side of the island, this lighthouse at the entrance to Siskiwit Bay was authorized by Congress. It is one of several significant lighthouses on or near Isle Royale, which is now a national park whose boundaries include one of the lights.

This red sandstone lighthouse with a fourth-order fixed lens was lighted on September 20, 1875. White-washed to be a better daymark, the tower was attached to the red sandstone keeper's house by a short red sandstone enclosed passageway. The tower is 61 feet tall, and the focal plane of its light is 70 feet above lake level. The Coast Guard automated the light in 1941. Today, the tower emits a flashing white light that can be seen 16 miles. Isle Royale can be reached in the summer months by ferries that run from Houghton and Copper Harbor. NR. [U.S. Coast Guard]

■ **Isle Royale Lighthouse**
Menagerie Island
Southeast side of Isle Royale
By ferry from Houghton and
Copper Harbor
1875

Below left: Isle Royale light station before it was automated. Below: Passage Island light, the northern-most American lighthouse on the Great Lakes.

This octagonal rubblestone light tower went up on Passage Island's southwestern point to mark the channel between the island and Isle Royale and to aid vessels in getting past these islands. The tower was built into a corner of the 1½-story residence, also made of rubblestone. At 44 feet tall, the tower raised the focal plane of the fixed red light of the fourth-order lens to 78 feet above lake level. The lens has been electrified and automated and can be seen for 25 miles. NR. [U.S. Coast Guard]

■ **Passage Island Lighthouse**
Passage Island
Off northeast tip
of Isle Royale
1882

■ **Rock Harbor Lighthouse**
Isle Royale National Park
Northeast side of Isle Royale
By ferry from Houghton and
Copper Harbor
1855

Because of the rocks and shoals in the area, Congress authorized a lighthouse at this northeastern point to assist vessels in entering Rock Harbor and to handle the increased traffic expected to result from the opening of the new locks at Sault Ste. Marie. The lighthouse was built and lighted in the same year that the new locks opened. When the mining explorers ceased their activity, the Lighthouse Board closed the lighthouse in 1859, but after mining activity in the area resumed, Congress authorized the relighting of the tower in 1874. When mining stopped in 1878, the lighthouse closed permanently the next year. Used off and on by summer campers and occasional fishers, the stone dwelling and attached conical brick tower, 50 feet tall, has survived. The lighthouse became a part of Isle Royale National Park when Congress established the park in 1931. The National Park Service has begun restoring the lighthouse, particularly to stabilize the tower, which began to lean in the 1950s. NR. [National Park Service]

■ **Rock of Ages Lighthouse**
Off southwest end
of Isle Royale
1908

Heavy shipping traffic on the northern shore of Lake Superior necessitated the building of a powerful lighthouse as an aid to safe navigation. Rock of Ages, at the southwestern end of Isle Royale, was selected as the site because this traffic often sailed in the lee of the island. Although the Lighthouse Board initially requested the lighthouse in 1895, money to begin work on the structure was not appropriated until 12 years later. In 1907 the builder blasted out the rock island so that a steel caisson 30 feet high and 50 feet wide could be placed on it and filled with concrete to act as a foundation for the lighthouse. The foundation and much of the tower were

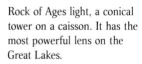

Rock of Ages light, a conical tower on a caisson. It has the most powerful lens on the Great Lakes.

completed that year, and the tower went into service the next year. At that time the board placed a temporary third-order lens on the conical, steel-plated tower that rises 130 feet above the ground. In 1910 the permanent second-order flashing lens arrived, and the keeper exhibited it on September 15.

The light and fog signal served well through the years, but they could not prevent all shipwrecks in the vicinity. One notable wreck occurred in 1933, when the U.S.S. *George M. Cox* ran aground in a low fog. With the assistance of the light keepers, the 125 passengers and crew of the vessel were taken ashore to the lighthouse, where they spent the night, most of them sitting on the tower's spiral stairway. Rescue vessels transported the survivors to the mainland the next day. Rated at 700,000 candlepower, this lighthouse emits the most powerful light on the Great Lakes. The base and lantern are painted black and the tower white. The lighthouse was automated in 1977, and in 1985 the second-order lens was moved to Isle Royale National Park for display at the Windigo Ranger Station. NR. [U.S. Coast Guard]

LELAND

South Manitou Island, a source of fuel for steamers that burned wood, also had a natural harbor that could be a place of refuge in time of storms. The need for a lighthouse on the island to guide ships into the harbor and also through the much-traveled Manitou Passage was recognized early, and in 1839 the first one was built. The tower was replaced with a 35-foot tower in 1858, but it, too, proved inadequate. In 1871 the keeper lighted the lamp in a third-order lens on a new 104-foot brick conical tower. The focal plane of the light was 100 feet above the lake. In addition to the tower, the station consisted of a two-story gabled dwelling, fog signal building, other outbuildings and a long passageway that connected the tower and 1858 residence. The light remained active until the Coast Guard decommissioned the station in 1958.

In 1970, when Congress authorized the Sleeping Bear Dunes National Lakeshore, the legislation included South Manitou Island and the lighthouse in its boundaries. Restoration work has been done on the light station structures. The site is open to visitors; public access is by ferry from the mainland at Leland from May through mid-October. A lighthouse built on nearby North Manitou Island has not survived, but its lens, an interesting square or cube-shaped type, is on display in the Sleeping Bear Dunes National Lakeshore visitors center in Empire. NR. [National Park Service]

■ **South Manitou Island Lighthouse**
Sleeping Bear Dunes National Lakeshore
Near National Park Service Ranger Station
By ferry from Leland
1839, 1858, 1871

LUDINGTON

In 1865 the Lighthouse Board recognized that the last important point on Michigan's western shore that remained unlighted was Big Sable, then called Grande Point au Sable. At this point coasting southbound vessels went farther out into Lake Michigan and returning ships

■ **Big Sable Point Lighthouse**
Ludington State Park
Route 116
1867

Big Sable Point light in Ludington, whose brickwork is completely encased with concrete covered with steel plates. In the foreground is the fog signal building.

drew closer to the shore, so that a light was needed to show navigators where to change course. The Lighthouse Board had a 107-foot conical brick tower built here and topped it with a third-order lens. An enclosed passageway connected the tower and the dwelling. The brick in the tower deteriorated severely, and between 1900 and 1905 the board had the tower completely encased in iron plates and cement poured between the brick and the plates. To make the tower a good daymark, the keepers painted the lantern and the middle third of the tower black and the upper and lower sections white. The light is still active and is now part of Ludington State Park. The Coast Guard has leased the site to an organization that plans to open a visitors center here. NR. [U.S. Coast Guard. Leased to Foundation for Behavioral Research]

MACKINAW CITY

■ **Old Mackinac Point Lighthouse**
Michilimackinac State Park
Southeast side of the base
of the Mackinac Bridge
Off Interstate 75
1892

This lighthouse grew out of a foghorn station placed at this point in 1890 to serve traffic in the waters of the Mackinac Straits, which connect Lake Michigan and Lake Huron. Two years later a light went into operation here, just below the Upper Peninsula. This light was of particular use to local water-borne traffic, such as ferries traveling to Mackinac Island and St. Ignace across the straits from Mackinaw City. The cylindrical light tower, 40 feet tall, is attached to the two-story dwelling. Design

Old Mackinac Point light station, showing its distinctively Romanesque design influence.

elements in the structure suggest a fort or castle; perhaps the designer was picking up on the style of nearby Fort Michilimackinac, which was built by the French. The lighthouse remained in operation until 1957, when the bridge across the straits opened; from then on boats tended to rely on the lights of the bridge to guide them. Since 1960 the lighthouse has been owned by the Mackinac Island State Park Commission, which has established a maritime museum in the structure. The lighthouse and the old fort form a 27-acre historical park on the water's edge. NR. [Mackinac Island State Park Commission]

MARQUETTE

The discovery of iron ore deposits spurred the establishment of a lighthouse at Marquette, located on Lake Superior. Within 13 years it was in poor condition and was replaced. A new 40-foot square masonry tower was built on one end of the dwelling, which in 1906 had a second story added to it. The light from the tower's fourth-order lens was 77 feet above lake level. Still active, the lens has been replaced by an aerobeacon and automated. NR. [U.S. Coast Guard]

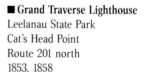

■ **Marquette Harbor Lighthouse**
North point of harbor
Coast Guard Station
Off U.S. 41 to Lake Street
1853, 1866

NORTHPORT

Erected on Cat's Head Point to mark the entrance to Grand Traverse Bay off Lake Michigan, this lighthouse was established to guide shipping into the bay. In 1858 the first lighthouse was replaced by a square brick tower built into a square brick two-story dwelling. The light came from a fourth-order Fresnel lens. The Coast Guard decommissioned it in 1972 and moved the light to a steel skeleton tower built nearby. The land and buildings were leased to the state to become part of Leelanau State Park. The lighthouse is operated by the Grand Traverse Lighthouse Foundation, which has opened it to the public. NR. [U.S. Coast Guard. Leased to State of Michigan]

■ **Grand Traverse Lighthouse**
Leelanau State Park
Cat's Head Point
Route 201 north
1853, 1858

Grand Traverse light station, no longer in use. A skeleton tower with an aerobeacon remains on the beach in the right background.

PORT AUSTIN

■ **Point aux Barques
Lighthouse**
Lighthouse Road
Off U.S. 25
1848, 1857

Situated on the eastern side of Saginaw Bay, the Point aux Barques lighthouse guided ships into the bay. The lighthouse had to be rebuilt in 1857, and an 89-foot conical brick tower attached to a 1½-story brick dwelling was constructed. The light from its Fresnel lens was 90 feet above lake level. A second dwelling was added in 1908. The light has been automated, and the tower's flashing white light, rated at 1-million candlepower, has a nominal range of 30 miles, according to the latest *Light List,* but an actual range of 18 miles because of the earth's curvature. The tower is painted white. Huron County acquired the property, except for the tower, in 1958 and has since created a park on the site. The third-order lens from the lighthouse is now on display in the Grice Museum in Port Austin. NR. [U.S. Coast Guard. Huron County]

PORT HURON

■ **Fort Gratiot Lighthouse**
Head of St. Clair River
Lighthouse Park
Omar and Garfield Streets
1825, 1829

Port Huron, on the Michigan-Ontario border, was established in 1686, when the French built a fort on the site. Americans settled here in 1790, and in time the St. Clair River became an important manufacturing area. In 1825 the Treasury's fifth auditor established a lighthouse near Fort Gratiot. A storm destroyed the lighthouse three years later, and in 1829 the lighthouse was rebuilt. In 1861 the light tower was raised 20 feet, and 14 years later the double keepers' dwelling was completed. Automated in 1933, the light is still active. The conical brick light tower is 82 feet tall, and the focal plane of its light is 86 feet above lake level. Considered the oldest light tower still standing in Michigan, it is now part of Lighthouse Park in Port Huron. NR. [U.S. Coast Guard. City of Port Huron]

■ **Lightship Huron
(No. 103; WLV-526)**
Adjacent to Pine Grove Park
1921

Constructed in 1918–20 by the Consolidated Shipbuilding Company of Morris Heights, N.Y., and commissioned in 1921, this 340-ton lightship is 97 feet long with a beam of 24 feet and a draft of 9 feet. The vessel's mushroom anchor weighed 5,000 pounds. Its first assignment was as the relief lightship in Lake Michigan's Lighthouse District 12, where it remained on duty for 14 years. The Bureau of Lighthouses then assigned it for several years to Gray's Reef, Mich., off the east coast of Lake Michigan. It spent one season at Manitou Shoals on northern Lake Michigan, and then in 1935 the Bureau of Lighthouses assigned it to Corsica Shoals, a station off Port Huron that saw its first lightship in 1893. *No. 103,* with the word *Huron* in large block letters on its side, remained at these shoals until it was decommissioned in 1970, the last lightship on the Great Lakes. In 1949 it was modernized in a shipyard in Toledo: diesel engines replaced the steam one, and radar, a radio beacon and a fog signal were added. After 1945, when the Coast Guard made red the standard color for all lightship hulls, *Lightship No. 103* was the only black lightship in the Coast Guard. Reportedly, it was painted that color because it was on the port side of the channel and black was the designated

Top: Point Aux Barques light in Port Austin, marking the turning point from Lake Huron into Saginaw Bay. Above: Fort Gratiot light in Port Huron, the second tower on this site, automated in 1933. Left: *Lightship Huron* on duty at night.

Top: Port Sanilac light, an
octagonal tower topped by
an octagonal lantern
complete with a Fresnel lens
from France. Above: Old
Presque Isle light, whose
tower is a combination of
stone and brick. Right: 1871
Presque Isle light, which
replaced the old Presque Isle
light. The exterior brick has
been replaced with white
brick to avoid repainting.

color for buoys on that side. In 1971 the Coast Guard turned over the lightship to the city of Port Huron, where it had spent the winter months for 35 years, and docked it permanently on the St. Clair River adjacent to Pine Grove Park. Visitors to the park can see the lightship from the grounds. [City of Port Huron]

PORT SANILAC

This white octagonal brick light tower is 59 feet tall, and the focal plane of the light from its fourth-order lens is 69 feet above lake level, making it visible for 16 miles. The light is still active, guiding vessels along this section of the Lake Huron shore. Since the light was automated, the dwelling has no longer been needed and is now in private hands. [U.S. Coast Guard. Privately owned]

■ **Port Sanilac Lighthouse**
Lake Street
Off Routes 25 and 46
1886

PRESQUE ISLE

Presque Isle, the best harbor of refuge on Lake Huron between Port Huron and Michilimackinac, was used increasingly by vessels in the early 19th century. In the late 1830s Congress appropriated funds for a lighthouse here, and in 1840 a 30-foot conical stone tower with a separate stone dwelling went into service. The light was active until 1871, when a new and taller light tower a mile away was built and activated (see next entry). The old light tower was eventually sold; today, it is privately owned but is open to the public during summer months. It houses antiques of the Great Lakes, including items on the area's maritime history. NR. [Privately owned]

■ **Old Presque Isle Lighthouse**
5295 Grand Lake Road
(Route 405 north)
1840

Put up to replace the old Presque Isle lighthouse on the same peninsula, this white conical brick tower, 109 feet tall, was fitted with a third-order Fresnel lens, which is still in the lantern. The focal plane of the light is 123 feet above Lake Huron. The tower is attached to a 1½-story dwelling by a short brick enclosed passageway typical of light stations of the Great Lakes. Still active, the lighthouse is surrounded by a 100-acre park. The keeper's house is being developed as a museum by the Presque Isle Lighthouse Historical Society. [U.S. Coast Guard. Leased to Presque Isle Lighthouse Historical Society]

■ **Presque Isle Lighthouse**
4500 Grand Lake Road
(Route 405 north)
1871

ROGERS CITY

In the 1890s the Lighthouse Board requested a coastal lighthouse to light the dark middle portion of the 50-mile-long coast between Presque Isle and Cheboygan on Lake Huron. Congress in time appropriated the money, and on May 1, 1897, the keeper put the Forty Mile Point lighthouse into service. Attached to a red brick double keepers' dwelling, the 53-foot square brick tower is painted white. A fourth-order lens had a flashing white light 66 feet above lake level. Still active, the light station includes a fog signal building, oil house and two brick privies. The lighthouse is now part of Presque Isle County Park. NR. [U.S. Coast Guard. Leased to Town of Rogers City]

■ **Forty Mile Point Lighthouse**
Presque Isle County Park
Off U.S. 23
1897

ST. HELENA ISLAND

■ **St. Helena Island Lighthouse**
Southeast end of
St. Helena Island
By boat from St. Ignace
1873

In an isolated spot in the Straits of Mackinac, St. Helena's white conical brick tower is 71 feet tall and is attached to one end of the 1 ½-story gabled brick keeper's dwelling by a covered way. Originally equipped with a 3½-order lens, the tower now has a modern plastic lens whose light is 71 feet above lake level. The light was automated in 1922. Unattended for two decades, the dwelling deteriorated severely and was victimized by vandals. Recently, the Great Lakes Lighthouse Keepers Association has taken a special interest in the old residence and has leased the house and grounds from the Coast Guard. The organization received money to rehabilitate the dwelling, covered way, oil house and privy from the Bicentennial Fund, whose grant was matched with donated labor. The keeper's house now is furnished with period pieces. The association is developing plans to adapt the site perhaps as an education center. Access to the island from the mainland is by boat; the nearest launch site on the mainland is at St. Ignace. [U.S. Coast Guard. Leased to Great Lakes Lighthouse Keepers Association]

ST. IGNACE

■ **Round Island Lighthouse**
Between Mackinac and
Bois Blanc Islands
Hiawatha National Forest
By boat from St. Ignace
1895

Round Island is located in the Straits of Mackinac between Mackinac and Bois Blanc islands. To avoid the shoals near the island, vessels from Lake Huron originally traveled the longer way around it to get through the straits. Congress thus authorized a lighthouse for Round Island, and in 1895 the keeper lighted the lens in the lantern of the square brick light tower built on a corner of a 2½-story dwelling. The light was automated in 1924, at which time the complement of the light station was reduced from three keepers to one. In 1947 the Coast Guard discontinued the station and 11 years later turned it over to the Forest Service for inclusion in the Hiawatha National Forest. The lighthouse has subsequently been restored, and today boats visit the small island. The Friends of Round Island Lighthouse and the Mackinac Island Historical Society have worked with the Forest Service in raising funds for the lighthouse. NR. [U.S. Forest Service]

Round Island lighthouse, focus of an intense restoration campaign. The light once guided vessels around dangerous shoals in the channel between Mackinac Island and Round Island.

SKANEE

In the late 1860s the Lighthouse Board became aware of the increasing traffic on the Keweenaw Peninsula, particularly between Marquette and Keweenaw Bay on Lake Superior. Two island groups on the route — Granite Island and the Huron Islands — posed a serious danger. The Huron Islands, the board said, "are a constant source of anxiety to the navigators, wrecks having frequently occurred at this point." On West Huron Island, the board erected a 39-foot granite tower attached to a granite dwelling. The light, 197 feet above lake level, was automated in 1972 and is still active. NR. [U.S. Coast Guard]

■ **Huron Island Lighthouse**
West Huron Island
East of Point Abbaye
1868

Huron Island light station, built on a high granite outcropping.

SOUTH ROCKWOOD

The main purpose of this lighthouse, located at the entrance to the Detroit River on Lake Erie, was to prevent vessels from grounding on Bar Point, a dangerous shoal projecting from the Canadian shore. A prefabricated wood crib filled with cement was transported out to the site and then sunk, and a granite pier was built around it.

■ **Detroit River Lighthouse**
Off Interstate 75
1885

Detroit River lighthouse, a cast-iron tower attached to a fog signal structure. The complex evokes an anchored vessel.

A problem of uneven settling was soon resolved. On this base was constructed a 49-foot cast-iron tower with an attached building to house the fog signal apparatus. The pier was built with pointed ends, apparently in anticipation of vessels running into it. Indeed, over the years on several occasions ships and tows have bounced off the structure. The light and the fog signal are still active. [U.S. Coast Guard]

STONINGTON

■ **Peninsula Point Lighthouse**
Hiawatha National Forest
Route 513 south
1866

This lighthouse guided ships past the shoals of Peninsula Point on Lake Michigan and into the Little Bay de Noc, with its several commercial centers. The 40-foot square light tower was at one time attached to the 1½-story keeper's house. The Bureau of Lighthouses deactivated the light in 1936 and the following year transferred it to the Forest Service. In 1959 the dwelling burned, so all that is left today is the tower. Located in the Hiawatha National Forest, the lighthouse is open, and visitors may climb the spiral stairway to the lantern. [U.S. Forest Service]

Above: Peninsula Point light tower. Right: Tawas Point lighthouse.

TAWAS CITY

■ **Tawas Point Lighthouse**
Tawas Point State Park
End of Tawas Point Road
Off U.S. 23
1853, 1876

Five years after the lighting of Port Austin's Point aux Barques lighthouse, a lighthouse went into service on Tawas Point on the opposite side of the entrance to Saginaw Bay on Lake Huron. The point of land built up steadily, and in less than 20 years the lighthouse was more than a mile from the lake. With the light so far away from the shore, the Lighthouse Board received funds from Congress to erect a new lighthouse at the point. Lighted in the spring of 1876, the tower was 68 feet tall, with the focal plane of the light of its fourth-order lens 70 feet above lake level. The conical white light tower is connected to the 1½-story red brick keeper's quarters by a short passageway. The light, now in Tawas Point State Park, is automated and still active. NR. [U.S. Coast Guard]

TRAVERSE CITY

At the tip of the thin peninsula that divides Grand Traverse Bay north of Traverse City, the Lighthouse Board constructed a small wood lighthouse to guide vessels into the bay. The site is located on the 45th parallel, halfway between the equator and the North Pole. Although Congress agreed to fund the lighthouse as early as 1859, it was not completed until 1870, after the Civil War. The square wood tower rises from the roof of the clapboard dwelling. Today, the lighthouse is the centerpiece of Lighthouse Park, administered by Peninsula Township. Although visitors may walk around the structure, the lighthouse is the residence of a township employee and is closed to the public. [Peninsula Township]

■ **Old Mission Point Lighthouse**
Old Mission Peninsula
Lighthouse Park
Route 37 north
1870

WHITEFISH POINT

Whitefish Point, a protrusion of land on Lake Superior's Whitefish Bay, has long been known as the "Graveyard of the Lakes." It is a dangerous coast because of the numerous shoals in the area, which is northwest of Sault Ste. Marie. The U.S.S. *Edmund Fitzgerald* went down here in 1875, giving rise to a popular ballad. Recognizing the need for an aid to navigation here, the Treasury's fifth auditor authorized a masonry lighthouse for this point. It went into service in the fall of 1848 and served until 1861, when the Lighthouse Board replaced it with an 80-foot white cylindrical metal tower supported by a steel skeletal framework. The Coast Guard automated the lighthouse in 1970 and subsequently leased the dwelling to the Great Lakes Shipwreck Historical Society for use as a maritime museum. Over the years the museum has developed a fine reputation. The light is still active. NR. [U.S. Coast Guard. Leased to Great Lakes Shipwreck Historical Society]

■ **Whitefish Point Lighthouse**
Whitefish Road
North of Paradise
1848, 1861

Whitefish Point light station, with the skeleton tower, two keepers' dwellings and Moderne-style fog signal building.

WHITEHALL

■ **White River Lighthouse**
6199 Murray Road
Off U.S. 31
1875

Now the home of the Great Lakes Marine Museum, the White River lighthouse is an octagonal brick tower attached to the corner of a 1½-story keeper's dwelling. The tower had a fourth-order Fresnel lens that today is on display in the museum. Located at the mouth of the White River, this lighthouse served as a guide to the river until 1941, when it was decommissioned. Fruitland Township acquired it in 1966 and created the museum, which is open daily from June to August and on weekends from May to October. [Fruitland Township]

■ ■ ■ ■ ■ ■ ■ MINNESOTA ■ ■ ■ ■ ■ ■ ■

DULUTH

■ **Duluth South Breakwater Inner Lighthouse**
Inner end of breakwater
Off Lake Avenue south
1889, 1901

Like its 1889 predecessor, this lighthouse ranged with the outer breakwater light. A steel skeleton tower 67 feet tall, it has a cylinder that holds the stairway leading to the lantern. A round watch room is just below the lantern. The tower has a fourth-order Fresnel lens that gives off a flashing white light, still active, whose focal plane is 68 feet above Lake Superior. NR. [U.S. Coast Guard]

GRAND MARAIS

■ **Grand Marais Lighthouse**
End of east breakwater
Off U.S. 61
1885, 1922

Above: Duluth South Breakwater Inner light, with its fourth-order lens. Above right: Grand Marais light, another steel skeleton tower on a breakwater.

Located near the state's northeastern tip, this four-legged steel skeleton tower, which replaced the original lighthouse, is similar in appearance to the Chequemegon Point light in the Apostle Islands of Wisconsin. Square in shape, the pyramidal tower supports a lantern that contains a fifth-order Fresnel lens whose light guided ships into and out of the harbor on Lake Superior. Below the lantern is a square watch room. The structure, located at the end of the breakwater, is 34 feet tall; the focal plane of the light, still active, is 38 feet above lake level and can be seen 16 miles. The 1896 keeper's quarters also survives as a museum and the headquarters of the Cook County Historical Society, which received Bicentennial Fund support for its restoration. NR. [U.S. Coast Guard. Licensed to Cook County Historical Society]

TWO HARBORS

Blessed with a spectacular view, this lighthouse northeast of Duluth is one of the most picturesque on the Great Lakes. The need for a lighthouse and fog signal at Split Rock was made apparent by increased shipping traffic, particularly ore carriers, and by subsequent shipwrecks on the northern shore of Lake Superior. Also a factor, noted the Lighthouse Board, was "the unusual magnetic attractions and the impossibility of getting reliable soundings in the neighborhood [that] make navigation difficult in thick weather." The site selected for the light station was a promontory rising 130 feet above the edge of Lake Superior. Construction, which began in 1909, was not easy because the site required a derrick to lift more than 300 tons of building materials to the top of the rock from lighters floating below. By the end of the working season in November, three dwellings, storage buildings, a fog signal building and an oil house were almost completed, and the light tower had its framing of steel girders in place. Work resumed the following spring, and on August 10, 1910, the keeper lighted the second-order bivalve, or clamshell, lens, and for the next 60 years it served the ships of this portion of Lake Superior. The station, then and now, consisted of three two-story, three-

■ **Split Rock Lighthouse**
Split Rock State Park
Off U.S. 61, 20 miles
northeast of Two Harbors
1910

Split Rock light station, one of the most picturesque on the Great Lakes. The station, now the centerpiece of a state park, includes a tower, fog signal building, three barns, oil storage structure and three keepers' dwellings.

bedroom keepers' dwellings, the tower, oil house, fog signal building, barns and other outbuildings.

The Coast Guard decommissioned it in 1969 and turned over the light station to the state of Minnesota in 1975. The state established a 100-acre park with the light station as the centerpiece. The Minnesota Historical Society restored the station to its pre-1924 appearance, partly with the help of a Bicentennial Fund grant, and built a visitors center nearby that has exhibits and audiovisual programs telling the story of this light station. Guided tours of the site are available during the summer. The historical society has done an excellent job with the restoration and has a well-run, well-interpreted site. NR. [State of Minnesota]

■ **Two Harbors Lighthouse**
Off U.S. 61
1892

A square red brick tower attached to a larger square two-story red brick dwelling, this 50-foot lighthouse on Agate and Burlington bays went into service in 1892. Its fourth-order lens guided iron ore carriers to Two Harbors, where they were loaded with ore. The carriers then transported the ore to the furnaces of U.S. Steel. Although greatly reduced from its halcyon days, this activity is still an important part of the economy of Two Harbors, evidenced by the huge ore docks in the harbor and ore carriers usually seen here during the period of the year Lake Superior is free of ice. The Coast Guard replaced the original Fresnel lens with aerobeacons in 1970. This automated light, 78 feet above lake level, continues to assist ships in this area. The Lake County Historical Society is developing plans to interpret the property and has used Bicentennial Fund money to clean and repoint the masonry. NR. [U.S. Coast Guard]

Two Harbors light station. The massive brick tower attached to the keeper's dwelling supports an octagonal cast-iron lantern. The light continues to direct vessels transporting iron ore.

■ ■ ■ ■ ■ ■ ■ NEW YORK ■ ■ ■ ■ ■ ■ ■

BARCELONA

Twenty miles southwest of Dunkirk, N.Y., situated on a bluff near the shoreline of Lake Erie, is this conical fieldstone tower attached to a fieldstone dwelling, one of the earliest lighthouses on the Great Lakes. At the time the tower was built, it was named the Portland Harbor lighthouse. Its first keeper was Joshua Lane, described as being "a superannuated clergyman, having numerous female dependents." Two years after completion, the tower was lighted with 11 lamps and 14-inch reflectors fueled with "natural carburetted hydrogen gas" piped from a source that the settlers called a "burning spring." A group of local people dug out the area of the seeping gas and erected "a cone of solid mason work, so tight as to contain the gas," and with wood pipes conducted the gas to the lighthouse. A special lighting system of pipes had to be devised: attached to each pipe with a flame was a reflector, and there were two tiers of burners, six on the upper tier and seven on the lower tier. One writer said that "when viewed from the lake at night, the whole tower represented one complete, constant and unwavering blaze." Another observer said, "As a light for a lighthouse it exceeds, both in quantity and brilliancy, anything of the kind I ever saw." The gas gave out in 1838, and the light keeper had to revert to lamps using oil. The gas did return, but it was not wholly satisfactory, for water collected in the pipes, impeding the flow of gas. Oil lamps had to be kept on hand for use when the gas failed.

In 1859, when it discovered that Barcelona did not have a harbor, the Lighthouse Board discontinued the light. In 1872 it sold the lighthouse and dwelling to the highest bidder. Today, the tower is in relatively good condition, and the keeper's dwelling is a private residence. NR. [Privately owned]

■ **Barcelona Lighthouse**
Route 5
1829

Barcelona lighthouse, a conical fieldstone tower attached to a fieldstone keeper's dwelling. No longer in use, the lantern and light have been removed. A wood frame now defines where the lantern was once.

BUFFALO

■ Buffalo Breakwater South End Lighthouse
21 Columbia Street
1903

This bottle-shaped pierhead light, one of two once located in Buffalo Harbor, marked the north side of the main entrance to the harbor. Constructed of boiler plate, this 29-foot beacon was placed on a concrete foundation on the breakwater. The sixth-order lens, which exhibited a fixed red light, had a domed roof that was removed about 1960, when the lens also was removed and the modern green plastic lens was installed. Tending the beacon was the responsibility of the keeper of the main Buffalo light. When the Coast Guard no longer wanted it, the breakwater light was relocated to town — a move that is likely to result in its loss of National Register status but that saved the light. A similar beacon was installed in 1903 at the south entrance to the harbor on the breakwater and was known as the South Buffalo North Side light; this light has been moved to the entrance of the Dunkirk lighthouse (see subsequent entry). NR. [U.S. Coast Guard]

■ Buffalo Lighthouse
Coast Guard Station
1819, 1833

The first Buffalo lighthouse was lighted in the same year as the first one at Presque Isle, Pa. (now the Erie Land light), thus making them the first official lighthouses on the Great Lakes. Within six years some in the maritime community complained that this light on Lake Erie was often difficult to see. In the late 1820s work began on a new stone tower, but the effort apparently went slowly. According to the date on the lintel over the doorway, the structure was not completed until 1833, and records in the National Archives indicate that the tower may have been lighted at an even later date. In 1852 the Lighthouse

Buffalo light, an unusual octagonal stone tower, c. 1905.

Board recognized the importance of this light and recommended that it be fitted with a third-order lens, which was installed four years later. At that time the height of the tower was raised three feet, to 60 feet, putting the focal plane of the fixed light at 76 feet above lake level.

Over the years the harbor and the city grew, and this growth had its effect on the lighthouse. In 1905 the light tower received a new lens that gave off a flashing light so that it could be distinguished from the city lights. In addition, harbor improvements and the construction of a new breakwater required additional lights in different arrangements. In 1914, with the rebuilding of the breakwater lighthouse, the Bureau of Lighthouses decommissioned the old stone tower, and its third-order lens was moved to the new lighthouse. When this lighthouse, by then known as the North Breakwater light, was torn down in 1961, the Coast Guard gave the lens to the Buffalo and Erie County Historical Society.

The stone tower survived, but in time it needed repairs. In 1985 the Buffalo Lighthouse Association was formed to make structural repairs, restore the light tower and interpret the site to the public. Today, the tower can be viewed from the Erie Basin Marina across the Buffalo River from the Coast Guard station. Meanwhile, the association is developing plans to create access to the old light tower, now one of the oldest on the Great Lakes, landscape the site and open it to the public. NR. [U.S. Coast Guard. Leased to Buffalo Lighthouse Association]

CAPE VINCENT

Within a few years of the development of navigational aids for the Great Lakes, the federal government began placing similar aids to guide ships into and through the St. Lawrence River. One of these was a lighthouse at the Lake Ontario entrance to the river. Located at Tibbetts Point, the 59-foot conical tower survived until 1854, when the Lighthouse Board had it rebuilt and its tower fitted with a fourth-order Fresnel lens whose flashing

■ **Tibbetts Point Lighthouse**
Tibbetts Point Road
1827, 1854

Tibbetts Point light station, now a youth hostel.

white light was 69 feet above lake level. In 1896 the station received a whistle fog signal. The lighthouse has survived and is still active. The Coast Guard automated the light in 1981 and three years later leased the keeper's quarters to American Youth Hostels for use as a hostel. In March 1988 the Tibbetts Point Lighthouse Historical Society came into being with the mission of "restoring and preserving the Tibbetts Point Lighthouse and its buildings, as an educational and historic entity." NR. [U.S. Coast Guard. Leased to American Youth Hostels]

DUNKIRK

■ **Dunkirk (Point Gratiot) Lighthouse**
Lighthouse Drive
Off Route 5 west and
Sycamore Road
1829, 1875

Situated at Point Gratiot on a bluff overlooking Lake Erie southwest of Buffalo, the Dunkirk lighthouse guided ships along this section of the lake's shore and, in conjunction with a pierhead light, into the city's harbor. The first lighthouse on this site served for 45 years, when engineers determined that the structure was in poor condition. In 1875 the Lighthouse Board replaced it with the present tower and dwelling. The square brick tower initially was round but shortly after construction was squared, according to local tradition, to blend better with the angular dwelling. The circular lantern atop the tower houses a third-order Fresnel lens. The focal plane of this fixed light is 82 feet above lake level. The light is still active and can be seen for approximately 17 miles. The tower, the upper two-thirds of which is painted white, is connected by an enclosed short brick passageway to the brick two-story dwelling. A substantial and commodious structure, High Victorian Gothic in style, the dwelling has a steeply pitched roof, expected in an area where there is heavy snow. Leased by a veterans organization from the Coast Guard, the lighthouse is open to the public. The dwelling's first floor contains exhibits related to the lighthouse's history, and the second floor is devoted to displays of the various military services, including the Coast Guard. A metal oil house is near the dwelling. A bottle-shaped pier light, similar to a Chianti bottle, marks the entrance to the lighthouse grounds. It originally was the South Buffalo North Side light. NR. [U.S. Coast Guard. Leased to Chatauqua County Armed Forces Memorial Park Corporation]

Dunkirk light station's large dwelling with Stick Style details and attached tower. The tower originally was cylindrical, as evidenced by the circular gallery around the lantern, but was converted to a rectangular shape to complement the dwelling.

OSWEGO

The first Oswego lighthouse, located on the east side of the Oswego River off Lake Ontario, consisted of a stone tower and a small stone keeper's dwelling, typical of residences built at Lake Ontario lighthouses in the 1820s and 1830s. The lighthouse served until 1836, when another was erected on the west pier. The *New Coast Pilot for the Lakes* described this lighthouse in 1896 as an octagonal gray tower with an oil room attached. It had a third-order lens that exhibited a fixed white light visible for more than 15 miles. When the pier was extended, a beacon was put at its end, but the lighthouse was left in service and was not taken down until 1930. In the early 1930s a new stone breakwater was laid, at the end of which was a new lighthouse built on a concrete pier. Over the basement sunk in the pier was placed a white metal one-story dwelling with a red pyramidal roof. Attached to the lake side of the dwelling is a white square metal light tower that holds a lantern with a red roof and a red fourth-order rotating lens, colored by red panels on the glazing of the lantern. The standby, or emergency, light, a modern red plastic lens, rests on the railing of the lantern's gallery, or walkway. Antennas for the radio beacon complete the station. A boat accident in 1942 killed several Coast Guard personnel during the changing of keepers and thus speeded automation of the light. The light is still active and was due for a recent renovation. The 1822 keeper's dwelling of Oswego's first lighthouse survives, although enlarged, and is a short distance outside the walls of old Fort Ontario. It is used today as the residence of the director of the historic fort. [U.S. Coast Guard]

■ **Oswego West Pierhead Lighthouse**
End of west pier
Off U.S. 104
1822, 1836, 1934

Oswego West Pierhead light, the third lighthouse built for this harbor. Radio towers are on the left.

PULASKI

This lighthouse went into service in what is now the village of Selkirk at the mouth of the Salmon River on Lake Ontario amid high hopes for rapid development in the area. Unfortunately, the area, northeast of Oswego, did not develop as anticipated, mainly because of the failure to attract a railroad and the silting of the river mouth. Consequently, the Lighthouse Board took the light out of service in 1859. The lighthouse, which survives, is a 2½-story fieldstone dwelling with a gable roof, on the peak of which is perched the lantern. The original lantern, a type commonly used before the introduction of Fresnel lenses, also survives. The old-style lanterns were usually inadequate for Fresnel lenses, which the Lighthouse Board in the 1850s ordered installed in all active lighthouses. These old lanterns thus were removed and replaced with the new lanterns, and most did not survive. Because the Selkirk lighthouse went out of service in the early stages of refitting the nation's lighthouses with the new French lenses, the lantern was never replaced and appears to be one of perhaps six left today in the country. Until recently this lantern retained much of its original glass, but a concussion caused by an explosion at the nearby marina destroyed

■ **Selkirk Lighthouse**
Lake Road west
Off Route 3
1838

most of the old panes; the remainder of the lantern is still intact. Because the lighthouse has been in private hands for more than 90 years, some alterations have been made to it. An aluminum-sided addition with a porch was placed on the rear of the dwelling in 1973, the windows have been replaced, and the interior has been altered somewhat to accommodate modern demands of its occupants. Although the lighthouse is not open to the public at this time, it can be seen from the road. In addition, the present owner, who has not yet determined how he will use the lighthouse, is generous in showing it to students of pharology. NR. [Privately owned]

ROCHESTER

■ **Genesee Lighthouse**
Charlotte
70 Lighthouse Street
Lakeshore Drive to Lake
Avenue, then north to
lighthouse behind Holy
Sepulcher Catholic Church
1822

Now the second oldest lighthouse on the Great Lakes, this 40-foot limestone light tower in an octagonal pyramidal shape was erected on the edge of the bluff overlooking the mouth of the Genesee River off Lake Ontario. At the same time a 20-by-34-foot one-story dwelling, also of limestone, was built nearby. The lantern on the tower was fitted with 10 Argand lamps, each with a reflector. This light served until 1853, when repairs were made. The old wood stairs in the tower were replaced with an iron circular stairway, and the tower was fitted with a new lantern and a fourth-order Fresnel lens. A decade later a new 2½-story brick dwelling was built within a few feet of the tower and the old dwelling torn down. Probably at that time an enclosed passageway connecting the tower and the dwelling was constructed; it was removed years later. In 1881 the Lighthouse Board ordered the light discontinued and had the old lens moved to the newly built iron beacon on the west pier. The dwelling continued to be used by personnel of the Lighthouse Service.

The old light tower, boarded up, remained standing. In the mid-1960s the federal government threatened to tear it down, but a local uprising, led by students at Charlotte High School, forced assurances from the Coast Guard that the lighthouse would not be touched. In 1982, when the Coast Guard had no more use for the dwelling, it offered to lease both it and the tower to the Charlotte Community Association. In September of that year, at a

Genesee light, the second oldest on the Great Lakes. It was at first fitted with Argand lamps. The residence is the second for the site.

ceremony on the grounds of the old light station, the Coast Guard formally turned over the property to the care of the association. Later, the Charlotte-Genesee Lighthouse Historical Society evolved and now has the responsibility of preserving the structures and interpreting the lighthouse through talks and exhibits in the keeper's dwelling. The grounds are open to the public daily, but the tower and dwelling are open only on weekends and at other times by special arrangement. The site has changed considerably over the years because of the filling in of the river and the lake. NR. [U.S. Coast Guard. Leased to Charlotte Community Association]

ROCK ISLAND

One of six lighthouses put up along the St. Lawrence River to guide traffic to and from Lake Ontario through the waterway, the Rock Island station is the best preserved, as all of its structures still survive. For the most part these structures date from 1882, when they were built to replace the first light station. The 40-foot limestone light tower, built on a concrete foundation a few feet from the island, is connected to the island by a stone and concrete walkway. In its active days its lantern held a sixth-order lens. A two-story Shingle Style dwelling, clapboard boathouse and carpenter shop, and metal-sided generator house make up the station. A small stone structure, now identified as a paint locker, may originally have been the oil house. Now part of the River Parks unit of the Thousand Islands State Park Commission, the island near the Canadian border is open to the public. No public boat transportation is available, but private boats may stop here and visitors may walk around the grounds and climb the light tower. The River Parks staff maintains the structures, but a group of summer residents has taken an interest in the old station and contributed to its upkeep. NR. [State of New York]

■ **Rock Island Lighthouse**
Thousand Islands State Park
Interstate 81
1 mile west of Thousand
Islands Bridge
1847, 1882

Rock Island light station
along the St. Lawrence River.

SODUS POINT

The lighthouse that the Treasury's fifth auditor had built at this site on Lake Ontario was a conical masonry tower 40 feet tall. The keeper's dwelling, also of masonry, was similar in design to the first one at the Genesee light in Rochester and the first at Oswego. By 1868 the tower and dwelling were in need of extensive repairs. Congress appropriated money to build a new tower and dwelling.

■ **Sodus Point Lighthouse**
End of Ontario Street
Off Route 14
1825, 1871

Sodus Point lighthouse, a limestone tower and dwelling with a wood addition.

Work began in 1870 and was completed in June of the following year. The square limestone tower, 45 feet tall, was attached to a two-story residence, also made of limestone. The tower had a fourth-order Fresnel lens. At the time of construction of the new lighthouse, a permanent beacon was installed at the end of the nearby pier, which had been laid a few years earlier.

In 1901 the Lighthouse Board discontinued the light on the tower, believing that the pier light was adequate. The dwelling, which later received a wood addition, continued to be used by Lighthouse Service personnel until 1984. At that time the Coast Guard turned over the tower, dwelling, modern garage and grounds to the village of Sodus Point. The village, in turn, leased the property to the Sodus Bay Historical Society, which maintains the old lighthouse and has created a maritime museum on the first floor of the dwelling. The tower recently received a 3½-order lens. On weekends during the summer months, cultural events such as concerts are held on the grounds. The lighthouse and dwelling are open during the summer on weekends from 1 to 5 p.m. NR. [Village of Sodus Point. Leased to Sodus Bay Historical Society]

SOMERSET

■ **Thirty Mile Point Lighthouse**
Golden Hill State Park
Lower Lake Road
Off Route 18E
1876

Designed as a coastal light, this lighthouse is located on Lake Ontario at a point 30 miles east of the mouth of the Niagara River, northeast of Lockport and Niagara Falls and west of Rochester. The light tower is 54 feet tall, and the flashing white light from its third-order lens, 78 feet above lake level, was visible for 16 miles. The unpainted square tower, made of gray stone, is attached to the north side of a two-story dwelling with a basement, also made of gray stone. This lighthouse served until 1959, when the light was moved to a steel skeleton tower and automated. Both the tower and dwelling are now part of Golden Hill State Park. The lighthouse is open on weekends from 2 to 4 p.m. NR. [State of New York]

Above: Somerset's Thirty Mile Point light and dwelling, both constructed of stone. Here, the lens is draped with a protective covering. Left: Fort Niagara light tower and ground-level work room, both sturdy limestone examples of Romanesque architecture. The tower was raised in 1900 using brick.

YOUNGSTOWN

Since the earliest colonial days, the mouth of the Niagara River, which connects Lake Ontario and Lake Erie, has been an important harbor and base for shipping operations. Although neither the French nor the British felt the need to establish a lighthouse at this point, increased traffic during the Revolution necessitated that one be built. The first lighthouse lasted until the early years of the 19th century. In 1823 the Treasury's fifth auditor had a wood lighthouse constructed on the mess house of Fort Niagara. It served until after the Civil War, when the mess house was converted to officers' quarters. By this time the light tower was in poor condition, and the Lighthouse

■ **Fort Niagara Lighthouse**
Off Route 18F
c. 1780, 1823, 1872

Board decided to put up a new stone tower just outside the fort.

This octagonal gray limestone tower, about 50 feet tall, went into service in 1872. A small attached structure provided a work area for the light keepers, and a small iron edifice nearby served as an oil house. The board also had a keeper's quarters built just north of the light tower. In 1900 the Lighthouse Board raised the tower 11 feet to increase the visibility of the light from the lake and to provide a watch room. This buff-colored brick addition placed the occulting, or flashing, white light at 91 feet above lake level. The light is still active and is now automated. The Old Fort Niagara Association, which has leased the site from the Coast Guard, has opened it to visitors and operates a small museum. The historic light station is open daily from July to Labor Day from 10 a.m. to 4:30 p.m. and on weekends only in June. NR. [U.S. Coast Guard. Leased to Old Fort Niagara Association]

■ ■ ■ ■ ■ ■ ■ ■   OHIO   ■ ■ ■ ■ ■ ■ ■ ■

CLEVELAND

■ Cleveland West Pierhead Lighthouse
Entrance to
Cleveland Harbor
1910

Located on the east breakwater, this light was established to mark the entrance to Cleveland Harbor. It is a four-story conical brick tower sheathed in wood painted white. The tower, whose light from its fourth-order lens is 63 feet above lake level, contained living quarters for the keepers. To the rear of the tower is a steel-framed foghorn house erected in 1916; a covered passageway connects the two structures. The light tower is floodlighted from sunset to sunrise. The station also has a radio beacon. NR. [U.S. Coast Guard]

MARBLEHEAD

■ Marblehead Lighthouse
Bay Point
Route 163
1821

Overlooking the entrance to Sandusky Bay at Bay Point, this lighthouse is the oldest active one on the Great Lakes. At the time of construction the conical stone tower was 55 feet tall, but at some point the tower was raised 10 feet to accommodate an improved lighting system, because now it is 65 feet high. Equipped with a fourth-order lens, the tower is still active and automated, exhibiting a flashing green light. The Coast Guard has leased the keeper's quarters to the Ottawa County Historical Society for use as a museum. NR. [U.S. Coast Guard. Leased to Ottawa County Historical Society]

TOLEDO

■ Toledo Harbor Lighthouse
Off entrance to Toledo
Harbor and Maumee Bay
1904

The dredging of the channel to the Maumee River in 1897 made the Toledo Harbor accessible. To guide ships to the harbor entrance, the Lighthouse Board erected a lighthouse here. The Corps of Engineers designed a three-story square brick Romanesque structure with a light tower rising from its center. A one-story wing held the fog signal. The lighthouse was built on a stone-and-concrete

Left and below: Cleveland West Pierhead light with and without ice. High winds and low temperatures often contribute to such icy formations.

Marblehead light, the oldest active light tower on the Great Lakes.

Toledo Harbor light, a lighthouse with Romanesque arches built on a stone-and-concrete pier. Riprap protects the foundation from floating winter ice.

pier a few miles northeast of the harbor's entrance. The tower held a 3½-order Fresnel lens whose flashing red-and-white light was 72 feet above lake level. The Coast Guard automated the light in 1965, and it is still active. NR. [U.S. Coast Guard]

■ **West Sister Island Lighthouse**
Southwest end of West Sister Island
1848

Built to guide shipping traffic safely past the island, the West Sister Island light underwent a renovation in 1868 that included installation of an iron stairway and a new lantern. The limestone-and-brick conical tower, fitted with a fourth-order lens that emitted a fixed white light, was connected to the dwelling by an enclosed passageway. The Bureau of Lighthouses automated the light in 1937. During World War II the Army used the island for target practice, and about 1945 the keeper's dwelling was destroyed, although it is not clear if there is a connection between the two events. With the removal of its lantern, the tower has been decapitated, reducing its height to 55 feet. The light is still active, and today a 300-millimeter plastic lens on top of the tower sends forth a flashing white light. All other structures have disappeared. The island is now a national wildlife refuge. NR. [U.S. Coast Guard]

West Sister Island light, now equipped with a plastic lens without a lantern.

■ ■ ■ ■ ■ ■ PENNSYLVANIA ■ ■ ■ ■ ■ ■

ERIE

The original Presque Isle light station, on the peninsula in Lake Erie known as Presque Isle at the entrance to Erie Bay, was one of the first two on the Great Lakes. In 1867 the Lighthouse Board built a new lighthouse nearby to replace the 1819 light, which seems to have experienced settling problems. This new conical sandstone tower was erected on a 20-foot foundation of timbers, limestone, cement and coursed stone. It rose 41 feet, exclusive of the lantern, which is now missing. The tower is attached to a small structure of similar material that appears to be the passageway to the dwelling. In 1870 the name of this lighthouse was changed to the Erie light station, and it is now known as the Erie Land lighthouse. The lighthouse remained in operation until 1881, when the board discontinued it and sold the property. It later thought better of this action, perhaps because of public outcry, and repurchased the land and relighted the lighthouse in 1885. The light continued in operation for 12 years. Today, the light is a reminder of Erie's early days as an important port. A grant from the Bicentennial Fund aided the restoration of various structures here. NR. [City of Erie]

■ **Erie Land (Old Presque Isle) Lighthouse**
Lighthouse Park
Dunn Boulevard
1819, 1867

Erie Land light, a sandstone tower without its lantern, attached to a passageway to the lost keeper's dwelling. The tower is now part of a city park.

When it was built, this lighthouse on the Presque Isle Peninsula was officially named the Presque Isle light station. For this reason the name of the 1867 lighthouse in town, which had replaced the first Presque Isle light, was changed to the Erie (now Erie Land) light station. Work began on this lighthouse in 1872, but difficulties occurred in getting materials to the construction site. Finally, the

■ **Presque Isle Lighthouse**
Presque Isle State Park
Off Route 5A
1873

Presque Isle light station in 1934. The station, with its 68-foot tower, is very much the same today, although trees and brush are more overgrown.

light was exhibited on July 12, 1873. The light station consisted of a square brick tower attached to a two-story brick dwelling. A fourth-order Fresnel lens shone a fixed white light whose focal plane was 73 feet above lake level. Located on the outer, or lake, side of a loop road, the light is now automated, and the dwelling continues to serve as a residence. The property is enclosed by a fence, but the fenced area is small, and one can get close to the lighthouse without trespassing. A study of possible adaptive uses of the site was financed through the Bicentennial Fund. NR. [U.S. Coast Guard]

■ ■ ■ ■ ■ ■ ■   WISCONSIN   ■ ■ ■ ■ ■ ■ ■

APOSTLE ISLANDS

Within the boundaries of the Apostle Islands National Lakeshore is the largest and finest single collection of lighthouses in the country. The Apostle Islands, located in Lake Superior just off Bayfield, Wis., and east of Duluth and Two Harbors, Minn., were named by early French missionaries who thought that there were only 12 islands here; in actuality, there are 22. As this region developed its resources — iron ore, brownstone, lumber and agricultural products — shipping traffic carrying these commodities to market grew in the mid-19th century. The 1855 opening of the Soo Locks on the Michigan-Canada border facilitated the shipment of raw materials around Lake Superior to steel mills and other users. Bayfield, along with Ashland to the south, became an important point in this east-west trade. To get vessels past and safely through the Apostles, the government built lighthouses that ringed the outer edges of the island group. With the increase in traffic to Bayfield, two lighthouses — Raspberry Island and La Pointe, one on each side of the cluster — guided vessels to and from the port.

Each of the Apostle light stations is different, and each is remarkably complete with all its structures. While the lights functioned alone, as a collection they guarded ships against one large navigational hazard. All the lighthouses are open and accessible by excursion boats and water taxis from Bayfield from June to mid-August. Volunteers of the National Park Service's V.I.P. program live at the stations during the summer to interpret them to visitors.

One of two lighthouses on the elongated Long Island close to Bayfield, the Chequamegon Point light is at the opposite end from the La Pointe station (see subsequent entry). This square pyramidal skeleton tower, whose spindly legs support a square watch room just below the lantern, is 35 feet tall, and the focal plane of its light is 39 feet above lake level. It emits a flashing green light in summer and a white one in winter. The La Pointe light keeper also tended this one. [National Park Service]

■ **Chequamegon Point Lighthouse**
Long Island
1895

Chequamegon Point light, a square skeleton tower.

The last lighthouse to be placed in the Apostle Islands was authorized by Congress in 1888, but it failed to appropriate enough funds to build the light tower. The Lighthouse Board used some of its available money and built a temporary wood skeleton light tower, keeper's dwelling and fog signal building on Devil's Island in the northern part of the group. Lighted in 1891 this tower served for 10 years before the permanent light went on. Construction of the new tower, a 71-foot steel cylinder fabricated at the district depot, was begun in 1897 and completed in 1898. No lens was available, so the tower sat idle for three years before the Lighthouse Board could obtain a lens and ship it to the island. The new third-order Fresnel lens was installed and lighted in 1901. The tower has survived through the years but apparently with some changes in its support. Early photographs show the slender cylinder supported by fluted braces at the base, but today a simple steel skeleton framework surrounding the tower gives it additional support. The tower sends out a flashing red light, created by placing large red panes of plexiglass over the lantern glass, whose focal plane is 100 feet above lake level. In winter the red panes are taken down, and the light becomes a flashing white one. This light station remained staffed until 1978, when the Coast Guard automated the light, the last one in the Apostles to be automated. Today, the light station is complete, with

■ **Devil's Island Lighthouse**
Devil's Island
1891, 1901

Devil's Island light station in winter. In summer the lantern would be lined with red panels, as shown on the previous page, to distinguish this light from others in the area.

the tower, two original keepers' residences (including a two-story brick-and-shingle house for the assistant keeper from 1897), fog signal building, tool and storage structures and other outbuildings still standing. The remains of the island's tramway are plainly visible. NR. [U.S. Coast Guard. Leased to National Park Service]

■ **La Pointe Lighthouse**
Long Island
1858, 1895

La Pointe light station, with skeleton tower, keeper's dwelling and fog signal structure.

The first light in the Apostles apparently was originally planned for Madeline Island, but before construction the decision was made to put it on Long Island, across the channel from Madeline. When completed in 1857 the first Apostle Islands lighthouse was actually on Michigan Island, the island north of Madeline. The next year, in 1858, a lighthouse was built on Long Island, but records give no indication that government funds were used to build this lighthouse. In any event, a wood dwelling with a wood tower on it was in place at La Pointe in 1858. This lighthouse served until 1895, when the Lighthouse Board built a 51-foot pyramidal steel skeleton tower with a cylindrical shaft in the center containing the spiral stairway to the lantern, which had a fourth-order lens. In 1964 the

Coast Guard automated the lighthouse and replaced its lens with an aerobeacon emitting a flashing green light whose focal plane is 70 feet above lake level. The light is still active. NR. [U.S. Coast Guard]

Located on a plateau roughly 90 feet above the lake, this fascinating light station encompasses two lighthouses side by side, each reflecting a different era in lighthouse construction. The older one, and the oldest of the Apostle lights, is a masonry tower with a black lantern attached to a masonry dwelling. It fits the description of the lighthouse that was supposed to have been built on Long Island to the south the same year (see La Pointe light entry). Stuccoed and whitewashed, the tower and dwelling are reminiscent of lighthouses constructed in New England at that time. The dwelling has a gable roof with a single dormer on each side; a stone masonry lean-to is attached to the end. The lighthouse went out of service after a year but was reactivated in 1869. Its light, 129 feet above lake level, guided ships along the eastern side of the Apostle Islands until it was replaced in 1930 by the second Michigan Island lighthouse. The tower and the dwelling, along with a board-and-batten workshop and storeroom and an oak privy, compose the scene of a typical mid-19th-century light station. A large grant from the Bicentennial Fund recently helped solve some serious moisture problems here.

In 1929 the Bureau of Lighthouses began reerecting an older 102-foot pyramidal steel skeleton tower on Michigan Island to replace the masonry tower. A white cylindrical shaft for the spiral stairway rises out of a small structure at the tower's base. Oddly, this base bears a date of 1880, usually an indication of the year in which a structure was built. But this skeleton tower was moved in 1919 from Schooner Ledge in Maine, where it had been constructed in 1869. None of these dates seems to have any relationship to the 1880 date on the base, unless perhaps the base came from another, unrecorded, site. Fully reconstructed in 1930, the steel tower carried a third-order Fresnel lens whose light had a focal plane of 170 feet above lake level. Today, this lighthouse reflects several time periods, with added structures including a 1930 red brick two-story bungalow, brick oil and storage

■ Michigan Island Lighthouses
Michigan Island
1857, 1869

Above: Michigan Island skeleton light, the newer light tower complete with a small work room at its base. Left: Original stuccoed masonry tower and dwelling at Michigan Island.

house and white wood workshop (its second floor now converted into living quarters), plus a tramway that runs up the hillside from the dock to a turntable at the top and then past all the sheds and workshops of the island. The still-active light can be seen for a distance of 16 miles and remains under Coast Guard ownership. NR. [U.S. Coast Guard. National Park Service]

■ Outer Island Lighthouse
Outer Island
1874

With the increasing east-west shipping traffic around the Apostle Islands, a light was needed on Outer Island, at the northeastern tip of the cluster. After several years of urging by the Lighthouse Board, a light was finally built here and lighted in October 1874. The 80-foot conical tower has Italianate bracketing, a popular feature on brick towers of the Great Lakes. It was topped by a lantern containing a third-order lens that emitted a flashing white light, the focal plane of which was 130 feet above lake level. A short enclosed passageway connected the tower to the red brick dwelling. The station also included a wood fog signal house, brick oil house and brick privy. The fog signal was at first placed at the edge of the water but was moved to the upper level near the lighthouse the next year. The original fog signal was steam, but in 1925 a diaphone signal was installed. Electrification of the station in the 1930s permitted the light to operate automatically during the winter. The Coast Guard fully automated the station in 1961. The tower is whitewashed and its trim painted black. Its lantern now holds a small modern plastic lens with bull's-eyes and a strap holding about eight small bulbs; when a bulb burns out, another moves into place. With batteries and solar panels to help regenerate the bulbs, Coast Guard personnel need only inspect the light on an annual basis. The Coast Guard has retained ownership of the tower. NR. [U.S. Coast Guard. National Park Service]

Below: Outer Island light tower behind the dwelling. Solar panels are placed on both structures. Below right: Outer Island light station, showing the tramway up to the station and the fog signal building above the cliff.

At a site near the lake's edge and 40 feet above the water, the Lighthouse Board erected a two-story white clapboard dwelling here with a wood tower rising out of the gable roof. The focal plane of the light of the fifth-order lens was 40 feet above the ground. A red brick structure housing a steam whistle fog signal, later converted to a diaphone type, was added in 1902. With the addition of personnel to the station, the keeper's residence was enlarged to a double keepers' quarters, with the keeper having half and two assistants sharing the other half. Most of the outbuildings are board and batten and include a barn, workshop, tool house, oil house, boathouse and privies. A rail tramway rounded out the station. The Coast Guard automated the light in 1957 and moved it to a pole at the bluff's edge in front of the fog signal house. This 160-candlepower light can be seen seven miles. Today, the station is complete and well maintained by the staff at the Apostle Islands National Lakeshore. From photographs and other documentation, the staff has restored the grounds to their 1920s appearance, with ornamental and fruit trees, flowers and a vegetable garden. NR. [National Park Service]

■ Raspberry Island Lighthouse
Raspberry Island
1863

Below left: Raspberry Island light station, the most visited station in the Apostle Islands, with its double keepers' dwelling and tower, fog signal building, work and storage sheds, privies and a tramway. Below: Sand Island light, a brownstone lighthouse and dwelling.

Because the Raspberry Island light was not easily visible from shipping lanes and ship captains complained that there were not enough navigational aids on the Duluth–Soo Locks route, Congress authorized a lighthouse to be built on Sand Island at the western edge of the Apostle Islands. Constructed of local brownstone, this Gothic-style lighthouse has an octagonal tower attached to the dwelling at the northwest corner. The focal plane of the fourth-order lens was 52 feet above lake level. The keepers kept the lighthouse in operation until 1921, when the Bureau of Lighthouses installed an automatic acetylene light. In 1933, when the bureau moved the light to a steel skeleton tower, it decommissioned the lighthouse. The old structure has survived in remarkably good condition, and the interior as well as the exterior appear to be structurally sound. NR. [National Park Service]

■ Sand Island Lighthouse
Sand Island
1881

BAILEYS HARBOR

■ **Baileys Harbor Range Lights**
Ridges Wildlife Sanctuary
Ridges Drive
Off Route 57
1870

With the construction of these range lights, the Lighthouse Board discontinued the older, single Baileys Harbor lighthouse in the outer harbor. Located near the tip of the Wisconsin peninsula forming Green Bay to the west, the lights helped guide traffic on Lake Michigan. The range lights consisted of a small wood tower 21 feet tall that served as the front light and, 950 feet away, a 1½-story clapboard dwelling with a gabled tower that held the rear light and guided vessels into the harbor. The Bureau of Lighthouses automated the station in 1930, when electricity was introduced, and the Coast Guard discontinued the lights in the 1960s. Door County received the navigational aids and has leased the dwelling to the Ridges Wildlife Sanctuary for use as housing for seasonal employees. [Door County. Leased to Ridges Wildlife Sanctuary]

■ **Cana Island Lighthouse**
Route Q, 4 miles northeast
of Baileys Harbor
1870

Positioned between Baileys Harbor and North Bay of Lake Michigan, this light tower, 86 feet tall, was made of yellow brick, which in time began to erode. In 1901 the Lighthouse Board had the tower encased in metal plates and painted white. A short passageway connects the tower with the yellow brick dwelling, a 1½-story, gable-roof structure with a brick shed built onto its rear elevation. The light, visible for 17 miles, is now automated and still active. The Coast Guard has leased the old light station to the Door County Maritime Museum, which has carried out repairs with aid from the lighthouse fund and now opens it to the public from 10 a.m. to 5 p.m. during summer months. NR. [U.S. Coast Guard. Leased to Door County Maritime Museum]

EPHRAIM

■ **Chambers Island Lighthouse**
Northwest end of
Chambers Island
1868

This lighthouse was placed on Chambers Island, located in the middle of Green Bay east of Menominee, Mich., to guide ships into the west passage of the bay. The octagonal brick tower was built into one corner of the 1½-story gable-roof brick dwelling. The focal plane of the light was 68 feet above lake level. This lighthouse served until 1961, when the Coast Guard erected a skeleton tower nearby and moved the light to it. The new tower raised the light nearly 30 feet. Although the lighthouse has lain idle since 1961, it has survived, but all the ancillary structures are gone except for a privy and boathouse. The Coast Guard has leased the lighthouse to an adjacent property owner who uses the old structure as a summer residence. NR. [U.S. Coast Guard. Leased to private individual]

■ **Eagle Bluff Lighthouse**
Peninsula State Park
Off Route 42
1868

Erected to mark the east channel into Green Bay off Lake Michigan, this 43-foot brick light tower was built diagonally into the corner of the 1½-story brick keeper's dwelling. The focal plane of the light was 76 feet above lake level. In 1909 the Lighthouse Board automated the light, and today it is still active. In the early 1960s the Door County Historical Society restored the dwelling and converted it into a museum dealing with the history

Above left: Upper range light and keeper's quarters of Baileys Harbor range lights. Above: Lower range light at Baileys Harbor, which probably also served as a striking daymark. Left: Cana Island light, sheathed in metal plates to secure the brickwork. Below: Coast Guard supply vessel visiting the Chambers Island light station near Ephraim.

Eagle Bluff light station, c. 1914, now part of a state park near Ephraim.

of the lighthouse and maritime activity in the area. Rehabilitation work has been furthered with the help of a Bicentennial Fund grant. NR. [U.S. Coast Guard. Leased to Door County Historical Society]

GILLS ROCK

■ **Pilot Island Lighthouse**
Pilot Island
1850

Porte des Morts ("death's door"), as its name implies, was a dangerous passage with a long history of wrecked vessels that used it as a shortcut to Green Bay. To help shipping traffic get through this area, a lighthouse was erected in 1850 on Pilot Island, a small island in the passage at the tip of the Wisconsin peninsula jutting into Lake Michigan. The tower, whose light was 37 feet above lake level, was too short, and in 1858 the light was raised to 46 feet above lake level, a goal perhaps achieved by moving the lantern from an attached square tower to the roof of the dwelling. Today, the lighthouse is a two-story brick dwelling with a gable roof; the short light tower and lantern rest on one end of the roof. The lantern originally had a fourth-order lens, but now the light is automated and a plastic lens rises above the roof of the lantern. A new roof and masonry repairs were completed with help from a Bicentennial Fund grant, matched locally. NR. [U.S. Coast Guard]

Pilot Island light station, where the double keepers' dwelling also serves as the base for the lantern.

MILWAUKEE

To mark the entrance to the Milwaukee River, the Lighthouse Board first erected a brick lighthouse here. In time erosion threatened the structure, and the board replaced it with a 39-foot octagonal cast-iron tower. By the turn of the century tall trees had begun to obscure the light. To raise it, workers in 1912 began to put up a 35-foot octagonal steel structure beside the old tower. When it was finished, they lifted the old light tower onto the new structure. The work was not completed until 1913, but the light was moved to the raised tower and relighted in December 1912. The new tower totaled 74 feet in height, and the focal plane of the light from its fourth-order lens was 154 feet above lake level. The 2½-story frame double keepers' dwelling dates from 1855. NR. [U.S. Coast Guard]

■ **North Point Lighthouse**
Lake Park
Wahl Street at Terrace
1855, 1888, 1913

Left: North Point light, an unusual combination of two towers — a steel structure topped by an earlier cast-iron tower. Below: Original Racine Harbor lighthouse at right, with a life-saving station on the left.

RACINE

Built to guide traffic into Racine Harbor off Lake Michigan south of Milwaukee, this lighthouse was placed on a pier off shore, but as the years passed the land has built out to it. It served until 1903, when the Lighthouse Board moved the light to a steel skeleton tower nearby. At the same time the tower, attached to a brick dwelling, had its lantern removed and was capped with a pyramidal roof. Originally 1½ stories tall, the dwelling was remodeled in 1903 into a 2½-story structure. NR. [U.S. Coast Guard]

■ **Racine Harbor Lighthouse**
North pier at
harbor entrance
1866

■ Wind Point Lighthouse
Wind Point
Tower Circle
Off Lighthouse Drive
1880

Wind Point light station on a wash day.

The Lighthouse Board built this lighthouse to guide southbound vessels into Racine Harbor. The 108-foot brick light tower was attached to the 1½-story keeper's dwelling by a short passageway. The tower had a third-order lens whose flashing white light was 108 feet above lake level. The lens was replaced in later years by an aero-beacon. In 1900 the Lighthouse Board added a fog signal to the station. Today, the light is automated and still active. The tower is painted white, with the lantern, watch room and Italianate supports painted black. The tower is closed to the public, but visitors are permitted to walk around the grounds. NR. [U.S. Coast Guard]

STURGEON BAY

■ Sherwood Point Lighthouse
End of Sherwood Point Road
1883

The Lighthouse Board erected this lighthouse at Sherwood Point to mark the entrance to Sturgeon Bay, a prominent harbor off Green Bay. A square brick light tower, 35 feet tall, is attached to one end of the 1½-story brick dwelling. A fog signal structure was built near the tower. The focal plane of the light of the tower's fourth-order Fresnel lens is 61 feet above lake level. The Sherwood Point lighthouse was the last lighthouse on the Great Lakes to have a staff. NR. [U.S. Coast Guard]

■ Sturgeon Bay Canal Lighthouse
North side of Sturgeon Bay Canal entrance
Off Lake Forest Road
1899, 1903

The first lighthouse at this point was an experimental design: a metal cylinder that was stabilized by lattice buttresses anchored in a concrete foundation and that supported a watch room and the lantern. The tower could not take the stress of the strong, continuous winds, however, and had to be rebuilt in 1903. A steel skeleton framework was erected to support the watch room and lantern, and the concrete foundation anchoring the lattice buttresses was widened. The cylinder now supports only the metal stairs, not the watch room and lantern. The tower is 98 feet tall, and the focal plane of its third-order lens is 107 feet above lake level. The light is still active. NR. [U.S. Coast Guard]

Left: Sherwood Point light station on Sturgeon Bay, with its bell tower converted into a fog signal building. Below left: Sturgeon Bay Canal light, a metal cylinder with lattice buttresses. The skeleton framework was added to further stabilize the structure. Below: Rawley Point light, a 111-foot skeleton tower.

TWO RIVERS

The first lighthouse at this point on Lake Michigan north of Manitowoc went into service in 1853. It was replaced in 1874 by a square brick tower and large brick 2½-story keepers' dwelling. In 1894 a 111-foot white iron skeleton tower with a cylinder containing the spiral stairway replaced the second tower. Part of the tower, including its watch room and lantern, had been at the entrance to the Chicago River. The focal plane of the light of its original third-order lens was 113 feet above lake level. The Coast Guard has automated the light, and today the lantern is equipped with an aerobeacon that has a range of 28 miles. The light station also has a radio beacon. The tower is painted white, with its watch room and lantern trimmed in black. NR. [U.S. Coast Guard]

■ **Rawley Point Lighthouse**
Point Beach State Forest
1853, 1874, 1894

WEST

St. George lighthouse, off Crescent City, Calif., one of the most exposed lighthouses on the Pacific coast. It was also one of the most expensive lighthouses ever built because of difficulties presented by the stormy site.

■ ■ ■ ■ ■ ■ ■ ALASKA ■ ■ ■ ■ ■ ■ ■

ALEUTIAN ISLANDS

■ Cape Sarichef Lighthouse
Unimak Island
North end of Unimak Pass
1904, 1950

Located at the northern end of the Unimak Pass to guide ships through the Aleutians, this 35-foot octagonal lighthouse, rising from the center of the pyramidal roof in the octagonal fog signal building, had a fixed third-order lens whose light was 126 feet above sea level. Regarded as too isolated for a family station, only keepers were assigned here. The station had the usual range of ancillary buildings, including a derrick, which was standard equipment at Alaska lighthouses. Perhaps remembering the tidal wave that in December 1914 had climbed more than 100 feet up the side of the island to flood the pantry and kitchen of the keeper's dwelling, and alarmed by the damage done to the Scotch Cap light station by the tsunami in 1946, the Coast Guard in 1950 relocated the station and replaced the fog signal building and light tower with reinforced-concrete structures. Automated in 1979 and equipped with a 375-millimeter plastic lens, the light is 170 feet above sea level. [U.S. Coast Guard]

Right: Cape Sarichef's reinforced-concrete lighthouse, c. 1966, before it was replaced by a skeleton tower with a plastic lens. Below: Cape Sarichef light station, probably in the 1930s. A tramway on the right helped keepers transport materials.

■ Scotch Cap Lighthouse
Unimak Island
South end of Unimak Pass
1903, 1940, 1950

The Scotch Cap light station marked the south entrance to an important pass through the Aleutians, the crescent-shaped group of islands separating the Bering Sea and the Pacific Ocean. The octagonal light tower rose through the center of the pyramidal roof of the one-story octagonal wood fog signal building. The 35-foot tower was

equipped with a lantern and third-order lens whose light was 90 feet above sea level. Three dwellings, two oil houses, a barn and a boat house rounded out the station. Improvements were made over the years. A radio beacon was added in 1931, and in 1940 the fog signal building and light tower were reconstructed, this time of reinforced concrete. In the spring of 1946 a tidal wave engulfed the light station, sweeping the lighthouse and other structures into the ocean. Five Coast Guard personnel died in this disaster; another crew on a cliff above the light station witnessed the event. The lighthouse was replaced by a rectangular one-story building with a square light tower at one end. This new lighthouse, the dwelling and other structures were positioned at a higher site on the island. Automated in 1971, the light is still active. [U.S. Coast Guard]

Above left: Scotch Cap lighthouse before its destruction by a 1946 tidal wave. The architecture is typical of Coast Guard stations in the state. Above: The remains of the station after the tidal wave. A beacon acted as a temporary light until a new light station was built.

CORDOVA

While this lighthouse, located at the entrance to Prince William Sound, southeast of Valdez, was under construction, a small light cared for by one keeper was in operation at the site. The new octagonal light tower, topped by a lantern with a third-order lens, rose from the

■ **Cape Hinchinbrook Lighthouse**
Southwest end of Hinchinbrook Island
1910, 1934

First lighthouse at Cape Hinchinbrook, a tower rising from a fog signal building.

Present light at Cape Hinchinbrook, near Cordova at the entrance to Prince William Sound, 1950. Here, Arie Van Der Meer, Jr., of the Coast Guard points out sites to James S. Muzzy, officer of the *Northwind*, during a refueling visit.

center of a two-story octagonal fog signal building. The focal plane of the light was 235 feet above sea level. The fog signal building also contained quarters for four keepers. This structure lasted until the late 1920s, when earthquakes weakened its foundation. In 1934 the Bureau of Lighthouses rebuilt the lighthouse of reinforced concrete on a rock foundation nearby. It was automated in 1974 and is still active. [U.S. Coast Guard]

HAINES

■ **Eldred Rock Lighthouse**
Lynn Canal
1906

This octagonal tower rising from the center of a two-story octagonal fog signal building guided ships along the Lynn Canal to Haines and Skagway. The light tower is 56 feet tall, but the site raises the light to 91 feet above sea level. The lantern held a fourth-order lens. Never rebuilt, the lighthouse was automated in 1973. One of the oldest surviving lighthouses in the state, it is still active. NR. [U.S. Coast Guard]

Eldred Rock light, one of the oldest lighthouses in Alaska.

JUNEAU

Erected on the north side of the entrance to Cross Sound, the Cape Spencer light guided vessels into the north entrance of the Inside Passage. Although an untended acetylene beacon had been here as early as 1913, this lighthouse was the first major aid to navigation at the site. It is a square reinforced-concrete tower 25 feet tall rising from a flat-roof, rectangular one-story reinforced-concrete structure, which housed the fog signal and also served as the residence for the three keepers. The station received a radio beacon, the first in Alaska, in 1926. The flashing white light, 105 feet above sea level, is now automated and still active. The station is within the boundaries of Glacier Bay National Monument. NR. [U.S. Coast Guard]

■ **Cape Spencer Lighthouse**
Entrance to Cross Sound
Glacier Bay National
Monument
1925

Above: Cape Spencer light on an island typical of Alaska's rugged sites. Gear is landed and hauled up on the left. Left: Second lighthouse erected for the Five Finger Islands, another Moderne-style structure with a basement and one story.

The two earliest lighthouses built in Alaska—Five Finger Islands and Sentinel Island — were lighted on the same day in 1902. The first one here, a square tower rising from the center of the roof of the square two-story dwelling, served to guide vessels into the passage to Juneau. The Five Finger Islands light tower and dwelling burned in 1933, and the Bureau of Lighthouses relocated the station to a nearby island and built a 1½-story structure that housed the three keepers and all the equipment. The last staffed lighthouse in Alaska, the station was equipped with a fog signal and radio beacon and had the usual complement of buildings. The light, originally a fourth-order lens, is still active. [U.S. Coast Guard]

■ **Five Finger Islands Lighthouse**
Frederick Sound
1902, 1935

Cape St. Elias light showing the aerobeacon within the helical-bar lantern.

KAYAK ISLAND

■ **Cape St. Elias Lighthouse**
Southwest point of
Kayak Island
1916

In the days before Alaska received navigational aids, Mount St. Elias, northeast of Kayak Island, was an important landmark. The light at Cape St. Elias in the Gulf of Alaska not only guided ships along this section of the Pacific coastline but also warned them of the hazards here. The 55-foot square tower rose out of a corner of the reinforced-concrete fog signal building. Its light was 85 feet above sea level. Never rebuilt, the lighthouse served well through the years. Still active, it was automated in 1974, and its light can be seen 11 to 15 miles. NR. [U.S. Coast Guard]

SKAGWAY

■ **Sentinel Island Lighthouse**
Frederick Sound
1902, mid-1930s

A square tower attached to one end of a wood double dwelling, this lighthouse helped ships into and through the Lynn Canal to Skagway. It was replaced in the mid-1930s by a fog signal building with a light tower that rose from the roof of the two-story structure. The Coast Guard automated the light in 1966 and burned down the double keepers' dwelling in 1971. At the station were a fog signal, radio beacon and other typical buildings. The light, originally a fourth-order lens, is still active. [U.S. Coast Guard]

Above: Sentinel Island light station near Skagway, 1951, with a tramway on the left to transport supplies. Left: Sentinel Island's keeper's residence when the light tower was attached to the structure. The dwelling no longer exists.

■ ■ ■ ■ ■ ■ CALIFORNIA ■ ■ ■ ■ ■ ■

BIG SUR

The site selected for the Point Sur lighthouse south of Monterey was a steep-sided, rugged sandstone hill separated from the coastal mountain range by a half-mile stretch of low sandy soil that is covered by water during storms. From the sea the hill has the appearance of a high, somewhat rounded island. At this point southbound ships left the coast and northbound ships returned to it. The Lighthouse Board began requesting funds for the lighthouse from Congress in 1876, but not until the board had reduced the cost for the station nine years later did Congress appropriate $50,000 to start the work. Railroad track was laid and trestles were built to haul the building materials up the rugged hill. The keeper's stone dwelling was constructed at the pinnacle and the light at a lower site. The short, gray stone tower, 50 feet tall, received a first-order lens that for many years gave off a red-and-white flashing light. The light went into

■ **Point Sur Lighthouse**
Pfeiffer Big Sur State Park
Route 1 south
1889

Point Sur light station near Big Sur, where the light tower and its work room are some distance from the residence.

service in 1889 with a focal plane 250 feet above sea level. Over the years the station grew with the addition of more quarters, a foghorn, radio beacon and 20,000-gallon tank to hold rainwater that ran off the roofs of the structures. Ultimately, it became a four-family light station. In 1950 the light was changed to a flashing white one, and today the light is automated. The station now is within the boundaries of Pfeiffer Big Sur State Park. [U.S. Coast Guard]

CAMBRIA

■ **Piedras Blancas Lighthouse**
Route 1 north of Cambria and San Simeon
1875

Because there was no light between Point Conception, near Lompoc, and Pigeon Point, near Pescadero, except Point Pinos, which was primarily a harbor light on Monterey Bay with limited visibility, the Lighthouse Board decided to erect a seacoast light at Piedras

Piedras Blancas light station's fog signal building and truncated light tower, now equipped with an aerobeacon. The residence is behind the tower.

Blancas, the point at which coasting vessels left the coast. Landing materials through the surf, workers built a brick conical tower about 90 feet tall. On February 15, 1875, the keeper lighted the lamp of the first-order lens, whose light was 142 feet above sea level. The board added a foghorn to the station in 1906. In 1949 the Coast Guard removed the lantern and its lens from the tower, thus ruining its symmetry, and placed an aerobeacon on the flat area that became the top of the 74-foot tower. The lens is now on display a few feet off Route 1 at Cambria. Exposure to the sun has discolored the glass prisms. [U.S. Coast Guard]

CRESCENT CITY

Located close to the Oregon line on the seaward side of a small islet off Battery Point, this lighthouse—a Cape Cod dwelling with a brick tower, plastered and painted white —is typical of the early West Coast lighthouses. Cape Cod structures seem an architectural anachronism in California, with its strong Spanish heritage. The explanation is simple. The early western lighthouses were designed in Washington, D.C., by eastern architects with little understanding of California who sought to develop a standard lighthouse design. Except for the one at Cape Disappointment near Ilwaco, Wash., all of the first eight lighthouses were to be of this same design. The Cape Cod style set the pattern for lighthouses built on the West Coast for many decades. The Spanish influence on California lighthouses did not come until the 1920s, when the Spanish Revival style became popular.

Originally, this tower supported a red lantern containing a fourth-order lens that exhibited a fixed light interrupted every 90 seconds by a white flash. The dwelling was left unpainted in the beginning, but in time it received a coat of whitewash. In 1907 the Lighthouse Board removed the original lens and installed a new fourth-order panel lens, which had four panels of glass separated by a metal panel, producing an even more distinct flash. The Coast Guard automated the light in

■ **Battery Point (Old Crescent·City) Lighthouse**
Off Battery Point
West side of harbor
1856

Battery Point light station, where a light tower rises from a Cape Cod–type dwelling, typical of early West Coast lights.

1953 and a few months later leased it to the Del Norte County Historical Society, which maintains the lighthouse and opens it to the public. The society has relighted the old tower, so that it is once again in the *Light List,* this time as a private aid to navigation under the name Battery Point light. NR. [U.S. Coast Guard. Leased to Del Norte County Historical Society]

■ **St. George Lighthouse**
Off Point St. George
North of Crescent City
George Ballantyne
1892

Considered an engineering feat and completed under the direction of George Ballantyne, on-site engineer also for the Tillamook Rock, Ore., light, this important lighthouse was built off shore to guard ships against the rocks and reefs off Point St. George in far northern California. On this reef in 1865 the sidewheeler U.S.S. *Brother Jonathan* went down with a loss of about 200 lives. Not until 1882 did the Lighthouse Board settle on a site for a lighthouse and have an engineer survey the rock. Work started in 1883 but soon stopped because Congress failed to appropriate money. It finally provided funds in 1887, and work resumed. Carving out a foundation on the rock, workers built an elliptical base of granite that was filled with reinforced concrete. On the top was constructed a square granite light tower on which was placed a first-order lantern and lens. Work was difficult because of treacherous storms that swept the area. The winds could toss $3\frac{1}{2}$-ton granite blocks into the air as if they were children's building blocks. Capricious waves rolled over the island, damaging the work in progress and injuring the workers; one was even swept off the rock. Winter storms were so severe that work ceased for part of the year. In time the lighthouse was completed, and the keepers displayed the light on October 20, 1892.

St. George lighthouse, an especially dramatic light evoking the movement of a ship's prow. The boom on the right was used to lift supplies to the landing below.

For the keepers, the St. George Reef light was a dangerous place to work, and many injuries were

reported, ranging from a broken leg to mental breakdown to drowning. The most severe disaster occurred in 1951; three members of the Coast Guard died when the station boat swamped while being lowered into the water. In 1975 the Coast Guard closed the St. George lighthouse and placed a large navigational buoy near the rocks and reefs. Technology had caught up with another lighthouse, and in this case we can say, "Thank goodness." The lighthouse is not accessible to the public. [U.S. Coast Guard]

FERNDALE

Cape Mendocino in northern California, south of Eureka, is a prominent land mass known for its dangerous waters. As early as 1565 the Spanish used the cape as a landmark to guide them past this dangerous area. The government's *Coast Pilot* noted that "Cape Mendocino is the turning point for nearly all vessels bound north and south, and in view of the dangers in its vicinity, should be approached with considerable caution in thick weather. . . . Fog is more prevalent southward and the rainfall heavier northward."

The site of the lighthouse is as hard as rock in the dry season, but with rain it becomes soft, susceptible to landslides. For this reason a hole was dug two feet deeper and larger in circumference than originally planned. The hole was filled with concrete, and on this foundation was constructed a 16-sided iron pyramidal tower. The tower held the light 43 feet above the ground, but the high promontory raised it to 422 feet above sea level. After 1891, when the old Point Loma lighthouse in San Diego was closed, the Cape Mendocino lighthouse boasted the highest light in the Lighthouse Service. Lighted on

■ **Cape Mendocino Lighthouse**
Coastal road south of Ferndale and through Capetown
1868

Cape Mendocino light, whose short height was made up by its elevated location. Handles on the lantern's glass panes permitted keepers to clean the glass safely.

December 1, 1868, the light tower experienced uneven settling, and several times over the years it was severely rattled by earthquakes. Strong winds, a common problem, were particularly rough on the wood dwelling. Despite these vicissitudes, the tower survived and continued to send its welcome beam to mariners.

Automated in 1950, the old first-order lens was moved to the Humboldt County Fairgrounds in Ferndale, where it is on display. Two aerobeacons replaced the lens, but eventually they were removed, and the light was moved to a steel skeleton tower nearby. The Coast Guard destroyed the dwellings and outbuildings because of a problem with squatters; now all that remains of the station is the abandoned tower, the skeleton tower, a radio antenna and a small building holding the electrical generators and radio equipment. The light station is not open to the public. [U.S. Coast Guard]

LOS ANGELES

■ **Los Angeles Harbor (San Pedro Harbor) Lighthouse**
San Pedro
End of harbor breakwater
East of Pacific Avenue at
Paseo del Mar
1913

Originally known as the San Pedro Harbor light, this lighthouse was built on the outer end of the San Pedro Harbor breakwater. The tower, a cylindrical structure with black pilasters built on a pentagonal concrete block, holds the light 69 feet above the breakwater and 73 feet above mean high water. The lighthouse is exposed to the weather and over the years has been buffeted by some memorable storms. The light is now automated. NR. [U.S. Coast Guard]

Los Angeles Harbor light, one of the more ornately decorated light towers on the West Coast.

■ **Point Fermin Lighthouse**
San Pedro
Paseo del Mar west of
Pacific Avenue
1874

By the 1870s shipping traffic had increased along the southern California coast, and many of the vessels stopped in San Pedro Harbor; consequently, a lighthouse was needed to guide these vessels into the harbor. The Lighthouse Board ordered construction of a lighthouse on a cliff at Point Fermin at the entrance to the harbor, and on December 15, 1874, the keeper displayed the light of the fourth-order lens. This Italinate-style light station consisted of a square tower that rose up through a keeper's dwelling. Later, during World War II, the iron lantern atop the tower was removed and in its place a lookout room was constructed, seriously altering the old structure's historic appearance. At the end of the war, however, the light was relighted on a steel skeleton tower at the edge of the cliff. Later, the city of Los Angeles acquired the land around the lighthouse and created a city park. The Sons and Daughters of the Golden West, a preservation group, assumed responsibility for the lighthouse, subsequently removing the lookout room from the tower and replacing it with a metal lantern. Today, the refurbished lighthouse is the popular centerpiece of the city park. NR. [City of Los Angeles. Sons and Daughters of the Golden West.]

Point Fermin lighthouse, 1893. This light has seen many changes over the years but has been restored.

About 10 miles northwest of the Point Fermin light, the Bureau of Lighthouses built a lighthouse to serve as both a light for coasting vessels and as a guide to San Pedro Harbor. The masonry light tower is cylindrical and painted white. Dwellings and outbuildings are in the Spanish Revival style. The light is 67 feet above the ground and 185 feet above sea level and is visible 20 miles seaward. The light is now automated. NR. [U.S. Coast Guard]

■ **Point Vicente Lighthouse**
Rancho Palos Verdes
North of Marineland
Off Palos Verdes Drive
1926

Point Vicente light.

MENDOCINO

The only lighthouse between Point Arena and Cape Mendocino, the Point Cabrillo light was intended to serve coasting traffic. The lighthouse, strongly reminiscent of the first lighthouses built along the California coast, appears to be a Cape Cod dwelling with a tower at one

■ **Point Cabrillo Lighthouse**
Off Route 1
1909

Point Cabrillo light near Mendocino in 1909, a tower rising from a fog signal building. Other facilities are located some distance from this structure.

end. Actually, the light tower, a 47-foot frame structure, is part of the fog signal building. The lantern with its diamond-patterned glass held a third-order lens. The light station complex is more spread out than usual, with the three two-story dwellings, more spacious than most, located some distance from the lighthouse. Behind the dwellings were garden plots and sheds for the keepers to store their goods; the station even had enough land that each keeper could keep cows and hogs. Both its accommodations and its location near a town with schools made this lighthouse a popular station with keepers and their families. The light is now automated, and the fog signal has been replaced by a buoy with a sound signal. Coast Guard personnel now occupy the dwellings. The complex is closed to the public but can be viewed at a distance from the highway. [U.S. Coast Guard]

MONTEREY

■ **Point Pinos Lighthouse**
Pacific Grove
Lighthouse Avenue between
Sunset Drive and Asilomar
Avenue
1854

Now the oldest active lighthouse on the West Coast, the Point Pinos light was the third one built on the coast and the second one lighted. The federal government's Coast Survey suggested three sites for the lighthouse, and the contractors chose the one at the south side of the entrance to Monterey Bay, because, according to local tradition, the site was nearer the stone needed for the dwelling. Although the lighthouse inspector criticized the site after the structure had been built, over the years no serious attempts have been made to move it. A stone Cape Cod structure with a 43-foot tower rising through the center, this lighthouse has changed only a little from the time it was constructed. In 1907, as a result of damage incurred in the earthquake of the previous year, the shed attached to the rear of the dwelling was extended, the entranceway was enclosed, a large dormer was added to the front roof of the dwelling, and two smaller dormers were added to

the rear roof. During its active years, the lighthouse had several women keepers and assistant keepers, not an unusual phenomenon in the Lighthouse Service in the 19th century, particularly on the West Coast. The board expected them to do the work of a man lighthouse keeper, but it did permit the crew of supply vessels, if they had the time, to do some of the more physically strenuous work for the women keepers. Although it is an active light with its original Fresnel lens, the Coast Guard has leased the lighthouse, now automated, to a local historical society, which has opened it to the public. NR. [U.S. Coast Guard. Leased to Town of Pacific Grove]

Point Pinos light, the oldest active lighthouse on the West Coast.

OAKLAND

Like its sister ship *WAL-604* in Astoria, Ore., this light vessel was built at East Boothbay, Maine, and was launched and commissioned in 1950. The Coast Guard first assigned it to the Overfalls station off Cape May, N.J., where it remained until 1960, when the station was discontinued. From there the Coast Guard sent the vessel to the Pacific Coast and assigned it to Blunts Reef off Eureka, Calif. It served on that station until 1969, when the Coast Guard made it the relief lightship for the Pacific Coast, its assignment until it was retired in 1975. The Coast Guard decommissioned the vessel on January 1, 1976.

This steel-hulled ship is 128 feet long, with a 30-foot beam and a draft of 11 feet. It was equipped with a 500-millimeter lens when commissioned, but in 1964 it received the more powerful "black box" light, a four-sided lantern that contained six locomotive lights on each side. It also had twin diaphone fog signals and a fog bell. Its mushroom anchor, which fitted into the hawse in the stem when under way, weighed 7,000 pounds.

After the lightship was decommissioned, the government sold it to the State Capital Museum Association of

■ **Lightship Relief (WAL-605)**
Waterfront
1950

Olympia, Wash. The association operated it unsuccessfully as a floating historic ship. The lightship was sold at auction to a private owner, who used the vessel occasionally for fishing before giving it to the U.S. Lighthouse Society, a nonprofit organization, several years ago. The society has been restoring the lightship and plans to open it to the public in the near future somewhere in the Bay Area. The lightship, essentially the same as it was when it was launched, is now located on the waterfront in Oakland. It has not yet found a permanent berth, thus it is advisable to contact the U.S. Lighthouse Society at (415) 362-7255 before visiting. [U.S. Lighthouse Society]

WAL-605, c. 1968, when assigned to Blunts Reef station.

Point Montara lighthouse and one of the dwellings. Most structures at the light station have been converted into a youth hostel.

PACIFICA

■ **Point Montara Lighthouse**
Route 1 south
1872, 1900, 1926

This station was established as a fog signal to warn ships off shore just south of San Francisco and north of Half Moon Bay. A light tower was added in 1900 and was rebuilt in 1926. The present 30-foot conical tower puts the light 70 feet above sea level; it can be seen 14 miles at sea. Today, the light is automated, but the fog signal is gone. The dwellings and other buildings have been leased to an organization that operates a youth hostel here. [U.S. Coast Guard. Leased to American Youth Hostels]

PESCADERO

Although early on considered important as sites for lighthouses, Pigeon Point and nearby Ano Nuevo Island between San Francisco and Santa Cruz were to witness a number of shipwrecks, often with heavy loss of life, before aids to navigation were established here. Indeed, Pigeon Point received its name from the clipper ship *Carrier Pigeon* that broke up on its shoals in 1853. Finally, in 1871 the Lighthouse Board decided to erect a fog signal at both sites and also to build a lighthouse at Pigeon Point. In September 1871 the fog signal at Pigeon Point went into service, and a little more than eight months later the one at Ano Nuevo was activated. Ano Nuevo received a small lens lantern in 1900, but the Coast Guard replaced it in recent years with a buoy just off shore.

The Pigeon Point light tower, a 115-foot brick circular structure, held a first-order Fresnel lens whose light was first exhibited on November 15. A low brick structure containing an oil room and work room was attached to the front of the tower — a not uncommon design in the 1870s. A double keepers' dwelling of plain Victorian style completed the new station. In 1960 the Coast Guard took down the double keepers' dwelling and in its place constructed four bungalows. In its 100th year an aero-beacon replaced the first-order Fresnel lens as the tower's light, which is now automated. The station has been leased to the California Department of Parks and Recreation, which has subleased it to the American Youth Hostels for use as a hostel. A local interpretive group, under an agreement with the hostel organization, conducts tours of the light station. NR. [U.S. Coast Guard. Leased to California Department of Parks and Recreation. Subleased to American Youth Hostels]

■ **Pigeon Point Lighthouse**
Route 1 south
1872

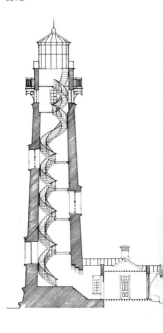

Pigeon Point light showing the attached work room. The spiral stairway, with landings attached to the opposite side of the tower, is an unusual design.

POINT ARENA

■ **Point Arena Lighthouse**
Lighthouse Road north
1870, 1908

Point Arena light, a
cylindrical lighthouse
constructed after an
earthquake had damaged the
first tower.

South of Point Arena the coast trends northeast-south-west, and to the north it trends more northerly. The point thus is an advantageous site for a lighthouse, because a light lets coasting traffic know when to alter course. Consequently, the Lighthouse Board erected a tall masonry tower here, south of the town of Mendocino, and lighted its first-order Fresnel lens on May 1, 1870. A year later it placed a fog signal at the station. The earthquake of 1906 damaged the tower beyond repair and destroyed the lens, as well as the dwelling. The board immediately ordered that a temporary tower be erected, and for more than two years this tower with its second-order lens guided ships along this section of the coast.

The new permanent tower, a cylindrical structure made of reinforced concrete and crowned with a first-order lens, was completed and lighted in September 1908. The light, 115 feet above the ground and 155 feet above sea level, has served since that time; it is now automated. The Point Arena Lighthouse Keepers Association, which has leased the property from the Coast Guard, maintains the site and buildings and makes them available to the public. It provides guided tours of the tower and fog signal building, which has a small museum. To help defray maintenance expenses, the association rents the houses on a daily basis. [U.S. Coast Guard. Leased to Point Arena Lighthouse Keepers Association]

POINT REYES

■ **Point Reyes Lighthouse**
Point Reyes National
Seashore
Off U.S. 1
1870

As early as 1854 Congress appropriated money to build a lighthouse at Point Reyes, north of San Francisco, but the cost of land and unclear ownership combined to delay government acquisition of the site until 1869. Construction began the following year. Point Reyes is a high,

Point Reyes light, a 16-side
tower that takes advantage c
its elevated site north of San
Francisco Bay.

rugged and precipitous piece of land overlooking the Pacific Ocean, Drakes Bay and the entrance to San Francisco Bay, and the wind here blows strong. The site for the lighthouse was 200 feet below the top of Point Reyes but still 300 feet above sea level. Construction was slow and dangerous. With little space to build on, workers had to carve out a flat area for the light tower. A short iron tower was bolted to a base of concrete, and on the tower a lantern with a first-order lens was placed. The dwelling, similar to the one at Point Bonita, was built nearly 500 feet from the edge of the cliff. The new 16-sided lighthouse went into operation on December 1, 1870, and its rotating lens gave off a flashing white light that could be seen for more than 20 miles at sea.

The site, more than all others on the West Coast, needed a first-class fog signal. The spot selected for one was more than 150 feet below the light tower, and here the Lighthouse Board erected a steam fog signal. A shortage of water hindered operation of the fog signal in the early 1870s, and when it did begin operation, the signal was not effective. In the 1880s the board substituted twin siren fog signals, which in 1890 were replaced by two whistle signals. In 1910 the station went back to a siren signal, but that one received numerous complaints. In 1915 the Bureau of Lighthouses installed a diaphone fog horn, and this one seemed to be effective. In 1934 the bureau had the diaphone fog signal moved southwest.

Through the years the lighthouse has served well, guiding ships both along the coast and to the entrance to San Francisco Bay. In 1975 the Coast Guard transferred the station to the National Park Service to become part of the Point Reyes National Seashore. At that time the Coast Guard automated the light with a modern apparatus placed on the fog signal building. With the exception of the light tower, the buildings transferred were of comparatively recent vintage. The 19th-century structures — dwellings, catch basin, barns, walkways, wind fences, blacksmith shop, coal sheds and wood bulkheads — are gone, and the structures that replaced them reflect the 1960s in both style and materials. The original light tower survives, and the complex is open to the public. [National Park Service]

SAN DIEGO

■ Old Point Loma Lighthouse
Cabrillo National Monument
End of Point Loma
Route 209
1855

Located at the end of Point Loma (Spanish for "hillock"), the most southwestern point in the United States, this lighthouse guided ships along the coast and into San Diego Harbor for 36 years. The stone Cape Cod structure was one of the first eight lighthouses on the West Coast and has a cylindrical brick tower rising from the center. Although its light from a third-order lens was 462 feet above sea level, in time the Lighthouse Board realized that clouds often obscured the light, whereas at a lower level visibility was good. The board thus decided to erect a new tower at the tip of Point Loma on a site only a few feet above sea level (see next entry).

In 1891 the old Point Loma lighthouse went out of service. The stone dwelling and its brick tower lay idle, slowly deteriorating, for a number of years. At one time it was nearly torn down to make way for a 150-foot statue of the explorer Juan Rodriguez Cabrillo. The statue never materialized, however, and in 1933 President Roosevelt turned over the lighthouse, now a national monument, to the National Park Service. Restored in 1935, the old lighthouse became a tea room and later a bookstore and office space for park staff. Subsequently, the National Park Service refurnished the old building to depict the life of a light keeper and his family. Of the ancillary structures that once made up the light station — a barn, assistant keeper's quarters, catch basin and cistern — only the cistern survives. The two-story, 20-by-40-foot dwelling has two rooms on each floor, a basement and a small shed attached to the rear.

Old Point Loma lighthouse, another Cape Cod–inspired structure now part of Cabrillo National Monument.

The view from the lighthouse today is a spectacular seascape, one of the three great harbor views of the world (together with the bays of Naples and Rio de Janeiro). In the winter months the park provides a platform to view the migrating gray whales. During its active years, numerous San Diegans came out to the lighthouse to watch the whalers in action; the keeper's children, when they had spotted the animals, would signal the whalers at nearby Ballast Point, for which information the spotters were rewarded. Now the centerpiece of Cabrillo National Monument, the lighthouse is open daily to visitors. NR. [National Park Service]

When the Lighthouse Board realized that the lighthouse atop Point Loma would have to be replaced, it erected two new lighthouses—a coastal light to guide ships along the coast and toward San Diego Harbor and a harbor light to guide ships into the harbor. The board placed the harbor light near the end of Ballast Point, a protrusion of land perpendicular to Point Loma that marks the entrance to the harbor. The site the board selected for the new Point Loma light was the tip of this point, 18 feet above sea level.

The board erected a pyramidal iron skeleton tower, with a white shaft containing the stairway and a black lantern. A third-order Fresnel lens had been ordered from France for the new lighthouse, but it was such a fine example of its type that the Lighthouse Board decided to display it at the World's Columbian Exposition in Chicago in 1893. In searching for a replacement lens for the new Point Loma lighthouse, it found that the third-order lens for the Alligator Reef light in Florida was available and shipped that one to Point Loma. When the exposition was over, the board sent the lens originally intended for Point Loma to the newly completed Chicago Harbor light. The focal plane of the Point Loma light is 88 feet above sea level. The Lighthouse Board provided twin

■ Point Loma Lighthouse
On shore below old Point Loma lighthouse
1891

Newer Point Loma light station, with a foghorn perched at the base of the skeleton tower.

dwellings that were simple but more commodious than the old Cape Cod structure at the former station, as well as a barn, catch basin and above-ground water tank at each dwelling, along with the standard outbuildings. The Bureau of Lighthouses later added another dwelling in the Spanish Revival style and installed a foghorn.

Today, the three dwellings, barn and foghorn, along with the light tower, survive. It is best to view this light station first from the top of Point Loma; with its mature palm trees, the light station is one of the most pictur-esque, suggesting a southern California of more than 50 years ago. The original Ballast Point light station went out of service in the 1960s. The sixth-order Fresnel lens from this station is now at Cabrillo National Monument. [U.S. Coast Guard]

SAN FRANCISCO

■ **Alcatraz Island Lighthouse**
Golden Gate National
Recreation Area
By boat from Fisherman's
Wharf
1854, 1909

First Alcatraz Island lighthouse in the distance, as depicted in a watercolor by T. E. Sandgren based on a sketch by Maj. Hartman Bache, who documented U.S. lighthouses in the mid-1800s.

The first lighthouse on the West Coast was placed on Alcatraz Island. Construction began in December 1852 on its Cape Cod dwelling with a cylindrical brick tower rising through the center, and by early spring it was near completion. More than a year passed before the new lighthouse received its third-order Fresnel lens, which first exhibited its fixed light on June 1, 1854. Two years later the addition of a fog bell increased the station's effectiveness. In 1858 U.S. military troops began fortify-ing Alcatraz Island, and the military's presence soon dominated the island. Old photographs show pyramidal stacks of cannonballs near the lighthouse. In time the island became a military prison for Indians and soldiers. In 1902 the third-order fixed lens of the lighthouse was removed and later displayed at the 1915 Panama-Pacific Exposition; it was replaced by a fourth-order flashing lens.

In 1909 the lighthouse was torn down to make way for a maximum-security prison. A new lighthouse, an

octagonal tower of reinforced concrete, was constructed just outside the prison. The focal plane of its light was 214 feet above sea level. For 61 years, except for the interruption of World War II, the white tower flashed its light to guide traffic in San Francisco Bay. In 1970 the site, then abandoned as a prison, served as a backdrop for a Native American protest. The light, automated since 1963, was turned off and the tower partially painted red. A fire, begun during the Native American occupation, gutted the old keeper's quarters. In time the protesters dwindled, and in 1971 the government evicted the last few. The light resumed service and continues to function. Alcatraz Island has become part of the Golden Gate National Recreation Area and is open to the public daily. [U.S. Coast Guard]

Alcatraz Island light station before the keeper's quarters were gutted by fire. The light station site is the oldest on the West Coast.

Had there not been a disagreement over the price of the land, this light station would have been located on the mainland, on Point San Pablo, rather than on East Brother Island, which was about one-third acre in size. The need for a light station and fog signal for the increasing traffic through the San Pablo Straits was apparent in the 1860s, and after delays brought about by negotiations for a mainland site, the Lighthouse Board started work on a lighthouse and fog signal on the island in 1873, blasting off the top of the island to get a level surface. Construction was completed the following year, and the flashing light was exhibited on March 1. The fog signal went into service two months after the light. The square light tower was attached to the dwelling, and both were of Stick Style design. Over the years the structures lost their Victorian appearance as "modernization" occurred. In addition, several ships ran into the island, damaging the station's wharf, and in 1940 a keeper accidentally kicked over a lantern, starting a roaring fire

■ **East Brother Island Lighthouse**
Richmond
East Brother Island
Off Point San Pablo
1874

East Brother Island light in Richmond, when it was tended by four keepers. The station now is a bed-and-breakfast inn, and the light has been automated.

that destroyed the wharf, boat house, tramway, fencing and four boats.

In 1969 the Coast Guard automated the station. Because it had no more use for the buildings, it planned to demolish them to discourage vandalism and erect a simpler concrete or steel structure that would better protect the light and fog signals from damage. Several local groups, alarmed at the Coast Guard's intentions, petitioned to save the structures. In time a group of private citizens formed the nonprofit East Brother Light Station, Inc., with the intent of establishing a bed-and-breakfast operation. With fund-raising efforts, extensive historical and architectural research and volunteer labor, the group restored the dwelling and tower to their original appearance, refurbished the fog signal house, wharf, fences, water tanks and other outbuildings and constructed a new catch basin. The organization opened the lighthouse for business in 1980, and since that time it has been a successful bed-and-breakfast inn. The light is still in operation, as is the foghorn. NR. [U.S. Coast Guard. Leased to East Brother Light Station, Inc.]

■ **Fort Point Lighthouse**
Fort Point National
Historic Site
Marine Drive north of
Crissy Field
Under the Golden Gate
Bridge
1853, 1855, 1864

Fort Point is located at the edge of San Francisco Bay, almost under the Golden Gate Bridge. When the Americans arrived on the Pacific coast, the Mexicans had been using a bluff here as the site for a battery for the defense of the bay. On this bluff, then known as Battery Point, the second lighthouse on the West Coast was constructed, built at the same time as the first Alcatraz lighthouse. Shortly after it was completed in 1853, however, the Army determined to fortify Battery Point. Troops tore down the newly completed lighthouse and cut away the bluff to erect a large brick fort named Fort Winfield Scott. The area then became known as Fort Point.

Fort Point lighthouse atop Fort Winfield Scott. The light is the third for this site.

In 1855 the Lighthouse Board constructed outside the fort a wood tower that held a fifth-order lens and a year later installed a fog bell on the outside wall of the fort near the lighthouse. During the Civil War the Army decided to extend the seawall in front of the fort, necessitating the removal of the lighthouse. In 1864 the Lighthouse Board erected a metal light tower over the stairway of the fort's northwest corner but left the fog signal on the outside wall. In 1904 the fog bell was placed on the lighthouse. Thirty years later the Bureau of Lighthouses decommissioned the Fort Point light. For the next 40 years the light tower stood rusting, exposed to the sea climate. In 1970 Congress established the Fort Point National Historic Site, administered by the National Park Service. One of the first restoration efforts at the park concentrated on the old light tower; work was completed in early 1973. The site is now open to the public on a daily basis. NR. [National Park Service]

■ Point Bonita Lighthouse
Point Bonita
Golden Gate National
Recreation Area
Off U.S. 101 (north) to
Alexander Avenue or (south)
to Sausalito exit, then follow
signs to Forts Barry, Baker
and Cronkhite
1855, 1877

Lighted on April 30, 1855, this lighthouse on the ocean side of the Marin Peninsula was the third one in the San Francisco Bay area and the third to be lighted on the West Coast as well as the first one on the West Coast to be built by local contractors and to have a fog signal. Three shipwrecks on nearby shoals prompted the light's installation — the most serious being that of the *Tennessee* in 1853. The next year the appropriation for the light was approved. The site selected for the cylindrical brick tower surmounted by a lantern housing a second-order Fresnel lens was 306 feet above sea level. The dwelling, a simple Cape Cod structure, was located one-fourth mile away and at a lower point.

Needed almost as much as the light was a fog signal. A few months after the light began operation, the light-

Point Bonita lighthouse is not far from Sausalito, a station that boasts a variety of structures and amenities to accommodate the difficult site, a 1½-mile hike from a parking area.

house district inspector shipped a 24-pound cannon to the light station and dispatched an Army sergeant to the station to fire the cannon during fog. This fog signal was not a great success, because fog in the area sometimes lasted for days and the sergeant had difficulty getting relief. Moreover, many ship captains reported not hearing the cannon. But more important to the Lighthouse Board was the fact that powder had risen substantially in price. Consequently, a year after it went into service, the cannon was replaced with a fog bell. The old cannon is now at the Coast Guard barracks at Alameda. In the 1870s a fog siren replaced the fog bell.

A problem similar to that at the old Point Loma lighthouse continued to plague Point Bonita: fog or low clouds, which obscured the light for ships entering the Golden Gate. The Lighthouse Board in 1877 thus had a new tower erected on the western extremity of the point, which was below the fog line. The lantern room and lens of the 1855 lighthouse were moved to this new light. Resting on a one-story rectangular structure with two wings — one for oil and the other for a watch room — this short tower had a lantern whose light was 140 feet above sea level. The original tower served as a daymark until 1907, when Army troops took it down to make way for military structures.

The site is a precipitous and rugged piece of land that has been subject to crumbling and erosion over the years. To accommodate the changing site conditions, an interesting collection of structures has evolved here, including a suspension bridge, tunnel, tramway and hoist to get supplies to the light tower, fog signals, dwellings, radio antenna towers, rail incline, oil tank, military buildings and other structures. Many of the structures still stand, and remains of the others are discernible. The light station, now within the bounds of the Golden Gate National Recreation Area, is open to the public, a 1½-mile hike from the parking area. [U.S. Coast Guard. National Park Service]

TRINIDAD

Established to illuminate a dark area of the coast north of Cape Mendocino and to aid traffic sailing close to the coast, this small lighthouse, 25 feet tall, had a fourth-order lens. The short square brick tower and its light were perched on the hillside, 196 feet above ocean level. The lighthouse, little changed since it was first erected, continues to serve ocean traffic. The light, a 375-millimeter modern optic, is automated, and a foghorn has replaced the fog bell. Although the original bell house remains, the Coast Guard tore down the dwelling and in its stead put up a triplex. Although the lighthouse is still in operation, local citizens some years ago erected an almost identical structure closer to the usual tourist route. The lantern of the replica contains the original lens and the original fog bell is positioned beside the tower. [U.S. Coast Guard]

■ **Trinidad Head Lighthouse**
Off U.S. 101
1871

Trinidad Head light, with its newer triplex dwelling. A walkway to the right permitted easy access to the foghorn building.

VENTURA

In the 1860s the Lighthouse Board had wanted to erect a light on Anacapa Island to mark the entrance to the Santa Barbara Channel, a natural channel formed by the mainland and the four northern Channel Islands. Instead, it placed the light station on the mainland at Port Hueneme, most likely because it was vastly less expensive to build a lighthouse there than on an island, particularly one of Anacapa's configuration. In 1910, at the Lighthouse Board's request, Congress voted an appropriation to place a lighthouse on Anacapa, which is composed of three islets (actually peaks of mountains that sank below the water a million or so years ago). The site selected for the tower was East Anacapa, which is steep; access from a boat is a ladder that runs vertically up the side. On top, where the lighthouse is located, the area is gently undulating. In 1912 the light on the steel tower went into service. This light served until 1932, when the Bureau of Lighthouses replaced the tower with

■ **Anacapa Island Lighthouse**
Channel Islands National Park
By boat from Ventura
1912, 1932

Anacapa Island light off Ventura, where the government once imported rabbits to ensure a food supply during World War II. Eventually the rabbit population was destroyed in the interest of preserving native species of vegetation.

a short cylindrical masonry tower painted white. The bureau also added a foghorn. The light is automated, and the station is now part of Channel Islands National Park. Many of the structures survive, including the tower, bungalows that served as keepers' quarters and a small churchlike structure that contains two redwood water tanks. Reportedly, fishers used to shoot at the water tanks, but when the structure resembling a mission was built around them, the target practice ceased. The light station is open to the public. [U.S. Coast Guard. National Park Service]

■ ■ ■ ■ ■ ■ ■ ■ HAWAII ■ ■ ■ ■ ■ ■ ■ ■

KAUAI

■ **Kilauea Point Lighthouse**
Kilauea Point National
Wildlife Refuge
North side of Kauai
Off Route 56
1913

This northernmost lighthouse in the Hawaiian Islands went into service with the prime purpose of aiding westbound traffic, just as the Makapuu Point light on Oahu served eastbound traffic; in other words, it was a landfall light for ships coming from the Orient. The light tower, "slightly conical in shape," was 53 feet tall. The site had an elevation of 180 feet, which placed the focal plane of the second-order lens at 216 feet above sea level. This was the last staffed lighthouse in the Hawaiian Islands. The light was fully automated in 1976, when the Coast Guard moved its aerobeacon to a new stand, a monopole. That light is still active.

The Coast Guard allowed the Fish and Wildlife Service to use the station as a wildlife refuge for colonies of birds at the point. In 1985 the area officially became the

Kilauea Point National Wildlife Refuge, at which time the Coast Guard transferred the old light station to the Fish and Wildlife Service. The lighthouse is now part of the refuge and is accessible to the public. In addition to the tower, the keepers' dwellings survive. Exhibits on the lighthouse have been placed at the entrance to the tower, and an interpretive center provides tours. NR. [U.S. Fish and Wildlife Service]

Above: Kilauea Point light, a conical tower replaced by an aerobeacon on a pole. Left: Molokai light the day after a tidal wave struck the station.

MOLOKAI

The construction expense of this station's structures, including the 138-foot octagonal concrete tower, dwellings, work sheds and oil house, was a costly $60,000. The light from the tower's revolving two-panel lens was 213 feet above sea level, giving it a range of 25 miles. The station's proximity to the noted leprosy sanitarium on Molokai, now a national historical park, caused some concern to the early keepers. The light, which once measured 2-million candlepower, was automated in 1970. It is still active, providing its assistance to traffic on the northern side of the islands. The light station is not open to the public, but the park may be reached by plane or mule. The Lahaina Restoration Society has placed the tower's two-panel lens on display in Lahaina on nearby Maui. NR. [U.S. Coast Guard]

■ **Molokai Lighthouse**
North Shore
Adjacent to Kalaupapa
National Historical Park
1909

OAHU

When the Lighthouse Board took charge of Hawaiian navigational aids in 1904, it found that "the lighthouses are generally of a very rude character. . . . The lights used in the lighthouses throughout the islands, except Diamond Head light, are ordinary oil lights, either double wicks or circular burners." The exception to this gloomy picture was a full-fledged lighthouse — a square masonry tower with a third-order Fresnel lens — that had been built in 1899 on Diamond Head, southeast of Honolulu. By 1917 cracks were evident in the cement work of the tower, and the Bureau of Lighthouses decided to build a

■ **Diamond Head Lighthouse**
Off Route H1
1899, 1917

Oahu's Diamond Head light, a square pyramidal structure that is the second tower for this site.

replacement tower. The lantern and watch room were removed from the old tower and placed on a temporary wood tower. Then the old tower was dismantled down to the foundation. On the old foundation a new reinforced-concrete tower with a new iron spiral staircase was erected, and the third-order Fresnel lens was moved and relighted. The height of the tower and focal plane of the light remained virtually, if not exactly, the same — 147 feet above sea level. Automated in 1924, the light is still active. A 1921 bungalow that served as the keeper's quarters also remains. It has been expanded considerably and, since automation, has served as the lighthouse district superintendent's residence and, since 1939, as the home of the commandant of the 14th Coast Guard district. The grounds at this time are not open to the public. NR. [U.S. Coast Guard]

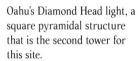

■ **Makapuu Point Lighthouse**
Makapuu Point
Off Route 72
1909

Makapuu Point light's hyper-radiant lens, the largest in the United States.

The Lighthouse Board early recognized the need for a lighthouse at this point, on the eastern side of Oahu. In its 1905 report it noted that "all deep-sea commerce between Honolulu and Puget Sound, the Pacific Coast of the United States, Mexico and Central America, including Panama, passes Makapuu Head, and . . . there is not a single light on the whole northern coast of the Hawaiian Islands to guide ships or warn them of the approach to land, after a voyage of several thousand miles." Congress's response was to appropriate $60,000 for a lighthouse. The board selected a site nearly 400 feet above sea level; consequently, there was no need for a tall tower. The white cylindrical concrete tower was 46 feet tall, and the board assigned to it one of the new hyper-radiant lenses. It was the largest lens in use in a lighthouse in the United States, having an inside diameter of 8½ feet. The focal plane of its light was 420 feet above sea level, making it visible for 28 miles. The station received a radio beacon in 1927. Still active, the light of its old hyper-radiant lens is now automated. After automation, the light station became the victim of vandals. The dwellings and other structures sustained heavy damage, as did the hyper-radiant lens, which was fired on. After a group took possession of the station in a dispute over

ownership of the land, the Coast Guard leveled all structures here except the old light tower. The site is accessible but the light at present is not open to the public. NR. [U.S. Coast Guard]

Makapuu Point light at the end of a walkway to the former dwelling.

■ ■ ■ ■ ■ ■ ■ OREGON ■ ■ ■ ■ ■ ■ ■

ASTORIA

Built at the Rice Brothers Shipyard in East Boothbay, Maine, this lightship, the last on the Pacific coast, spent its entire career at one site, the important Columbia station just outside the Columbia River Bar and southwest of Cape Disappointment, Wash. The shipyard launched *WAL-604* in April 1950, the Coast Guard commissioned it in December, and it took its position at the station in 1951. Three lightships had preceded it at the station, which was established in 1898. *WAL-604* remained here, except for the usual reliefs, until 1979, when

■ Lightship Columbia
(WAL-604)
1792 Marine Drive
1950

Lightship Columbia on station. An auxiliary anchor is on the stern.

it was replaced by a lighted horn buoy. This steel-hulled light vessel is 128 feet long with a beam of 30 feet. It drew 11 feet of water, displaced 617 tons and carried a 7,000-pound mushroom anchor. Both the masts are steel, as is the deckhouse. The foremast carried a 500-millimeter lens lantern, but in 1964 the Coast Guard changed the light to a modern high-intensity light. It also carried twin diaphone fog signals. This lightship, with typical 20th-century lines, is one of the six built under the administration of the Coast Guard; of the five that remain, *WAL-604* has the best structural integrity. When the Coast Guard decommissioned the lightship in 1979, the Columbia River Maritime Museum acquired it and moored it on the waterfront in Astoria. This vessel is still in operational condition, and the museum displays it as a historic ship open to the public. [Columbia River Maritime Museum]

BANDON

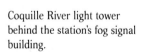

■ **Coquille River Lighthouse**
Bullards Beach State Park
Off U.S. 101 north
1896

Established north of Cape Blanco at the mouth of the Coquille River to mark the entrance to that waterway, this lighthouse, a 40-foot conical brick tower covered with stucco, had a fourth-order lens whose light was 47 feet above sea level. The station, south of Coos Bay, included a fog signal building attached to the tower, a 1½-story double keepers' dwelling and a barn. The light served until 1939, when it was discontinued. It was vandalized and by the mid-1970s was in dreadful condition. In 1960 the Corps of Engineers acquired the old light station property. The barn and keepers' dwelling were no longer

Coquille River light tower behind the station's fog signal building.

standing. The state of Oregon leased the property from the Corps of Engineers and made it part of Bullards Beach State Park. Both restored the station, which is open daily during the summer months. NR. [U.S. Army Corps of Engineers. Leased to Oregon State Parks]

CHARLESTON

Oregon's second lighthouse, the Cape Arago light went into service on November 1, 1866. Located at the entrance to Coos Bay, it served both as a coastal guide and as an aid for ships approaching the bay. This area, with its rocks and reefs, is a dangerous one, and a number of shipwrecks have occurred here both before and after the lighthouse was established. The original iron tower, in time, was threatened by erosion, and in 1908 the Lighthouse Board erected another light tower at a safer location and placed the original fourth-order lens in it. It was not a permanent move, for less than 30 years later, because of continued erosion, the Bureau of Lighthouses erected a concrete tower attached to the fog signal house and moved the fourth-order lens once again. The focal plane of the light on the 44-foot tower is 100 feet above sea level, permitting the light to serve its dual function. The light has been automated for more than 20 years. The dwellings have been removed, and visitors to the site require the special permission of the local Coast Guard unit. [U.S. Coast Guard]

■ **Cape Arago Lighthouse**
1½ miles southwest of entrance to Coos Bay
1866, 1908, 1934

Cape Arago light, the third for the site, as it currently appears without the dwellings.

FLORENCE

Lighted on March 30, 1894, this 56-foot conical masonry tower was erected to guide ships along this section of the coast north of the Siuslaw River. Its first-order Fresnel lens, whose focal plane is 205 feet above sea level, lighted a dark area between Yaquina Head and Cape Arago, a distance of some 90 miles. The light is automated, and a number of buildings survive, including the oil house near the tower and one of the old dwellings on Forest Service land. The picturesque setting of the lighthouse on this rugged, rocky coast has made the old structure a popular

■ **Heceta Head Lighthouse**
Adjacent to Devil's Elbow State Park
Siuslaw National Forest
Off U.S. 101 north
1894

Heceta Head light station in its picturesque location near Florence, with a first-order lens whose focal plane is 205 feet above the water. Its light can be seen 21 miles out to sea.

subject for photographers. The grounds of the old light station are open to the public, but entrance to the lighthouse is only by permission of the Coast Guard. The dwelling, restored by the Siuslaw National Forest, is leased to Lane Community College. NR. [U.S. Coast Guard. U.S. Forest Service]

NEWPORT

■ **Yaquina Bay Lighthouse**
Yaquina Bay State Park
Off U.S. 101
1871

This lighthouse was in service for only three years. The square wood tower rose from the back elevation of a two-story wood dwelling. The light from the fifth-order lens guided vessels into the bay until 1874, when the Lighthouse Board thought that it had become superfluous because of the new Yaquina Head lighthouse just a few miles away (see next entry). The lighthouse and dwelling lay idle for a number of years, although they were used for a considerable period of time by the Corps of Engineers and the Life Saving Service. In 1934 the site was transferred to the state of Oregon. The state planned to demolish the lighthouse in 1946, but local citizens opposed this decision and saved it. The Lincoln County

Historical Society has maintained a museum in the lighthouse since 1965. In 1975 the state restored the old building. It is open to the public. NR. [State of Oregon. Leased to Lincoln County Historical Society]

In its early days this light station was known as the Cape Foulweather light, because Cape Foulweather, which is four miles to the north, is where the lighthouse was to have been built. The materials, however, were inadvertently landed at this point. Construction did not go smoothly. Landing materials was a difficult and dangerous task, and several lighters overturned and lost their cargoes. Even part of the first-order lens was lost in transit from the East. Despite these vicissitudes, the work was completed, and the keeper lighted the lamp in the lens on August 20, 1873. The brick tower, decorated with Italianate support braces, is 93 feet tall, placing the light 163 feet above sea level. The light, with its original lens in place, is still active. The dwellings have been torn down. [U.S. Coast Guard]

■ **Yaquina Head Lighthouse**
Lighthouse Road
Off U.S. 101, 4 miles north of Newport
1873

Below left: Yaquina Head light station before the dwellings were torn down. Below: Cape Blanco light and work room.

PORT ORFORD

This cape, which takes it name from its white face, was well known to Spanish navigators as early as the 17th century, especially those piloting the Manila galleons. The cliff appears beautiful, with wild flowers and spectacular views of sea, coast and land, but to mariners of the area it is filled with treacherous waters, and many vessels have crashed on its rocks and reefs. On this cape the Lighthouse Board erected a conical masonry tower, 59 feet tall. The light of its original first-order Fresnel lens, 245 feet above the sea, is rated at 1-million candlepower. Today, the light is automated and still guides ships along this section of the coast. The original brick dwelling, along with other original outbuildings, has disappeared, replaced by other structures over the years. The light station at present is closed to the public and can be visited only with special permission of the local Coast Guard unit. [U.S. Coast Guard]

■ **Cape Blanco Lighthouse**
Adjacent to Cape Blanco State Park
Off U.S. 101 north
1870

TILLAMOOK

■ **Cape Meares Lighthouse**
Cape Meares State Park
Three Capes Loop Road
Off U.S. 101, 7 miles west of
Tillamook
1890

A 38-foot octagonal brick tower sheathed in sheet iron with a first-order Fresnel lens, Cape Meares light guided shipping along the coast until 1963. Then, the Coast Guard erected a replacement nearby, a 17-foot masonry tower that was really little more than a square concrete box with an automated light 232 feet above the sea and rated at 800,000 candlepower. In 1985, over the protest of area fishers, the Coast Guard also eliminated the second light. The Coast Guard, however, had a change of mind and reactivated it. The current *Light List* shows it as being visible for 25 miles. Meanwhile, the original tower with its Fresnel lens had become a tourist attraction. Unfortunately, some visitors broke into the old tower and vandalized the lens. The Coast Guard fenced off the area to prevent further damage. Cape Meares State Park repaired and refurbished the damaged lens and light tower and reopened it to the public. The old tower is still a popular attraction in the park. [U.S. Coast Guard. Leased to Oregon State Parks]

■ **Tillamook Rock
Lighthouse**
1⅓ miles west of Tillamook
Head
George Ballantyne
1881

Tillamook Rock is rough and craglike, surrounded by a turbulent sea. Landings can be made on only one side of the rock. With great difficulty workers carved out a foundation on the rock and erected a lighthouse from plans based on measurements taken by an engineer with a pocket tape measure. To prepare the foundation and build the one-story dwelling and the square tower took 18 months. Lighted on February 1, 1881, the light served until 1957, when it was decommissioned and replaced by a whistle buoy. Through the years keepers had their nerves tested by the turbulent sea; one keeper in 1882 reported green water sweeping over the top of the 150-foot light tower. The lighthouse passed through private hands in the years after its closing, and today it is a columbarium. NR. [Eternity at Sea, Inc.]

WINCHESTER BAY

■ **Umpqua River Lighthouse**
Adjacent to Umpqua
Lighthouse State Park
Off U.S. 101
1857, 1894

Although Congress had authorized and appropriated money for this light in 1851, the first lighthouse at this site was not built until six years later and then with some difficulty. Indians in the vicinity were generally friendly, but a theft of a lighthouse construction worker's tool led to a general melee, which the Indians might have won had not one of the foremen set off a stick of dynamite. The explosion frightened the Indians, who hastily departed the field of battle. Construction resumed, and tensions between the adversaries remained under control. Six years after the light station was completed, a severe storm washed away a portion of the lighthouse. Fearing that another storm would destroy the building, the Lighthouse Board ordered that the lens be taken down. Workers completed that task and began taking the lantern apart when they felt the structure shake. The movement became more violent, and they swiftly descended the stairs and ran out of the building. As they

Above: Cape Meares light, near Tillamook, which is no longer active. Left: Tillamook Rock light, Tillamook, now serving as a repository for ashes of the dead. Below: Umpqua River light station, Winchester Bay, a large complex that guided traffic along the coast and to the mouth of the river.

stood on the ground looking up at the building, it collapsed. The Lighthouse Board then erected a replacement light at Cape Arago off Charleston in Coos Bay.

Some years passed before the board realized that a light was needed at the Umpqua River, and a second was constructed here in 1892–94. In addition to the 65-foot conical tower, which supported a first-order lens, the light station had two dwellings, two galvanized-iron oil houses and other outbuildings. The tower's light, whose focal plane is 165 feet above the sea, has remained in operation and is now automated. NR. [U.S. Coast Guard]

■ ■ ■ ■ ■ ■ ■ WASHINGTON ■ ■ ■ ■ ■ ■ ■

COUPEVILLE

■ Admiralty Head Lighthouse
Fort Casey State Park
Off Route 20, 3 miles south
of Coupeville
1903

Admiralty Head lighthouse, a handsome masonry complex anchored by its tower.

The first lighthouse built to guide ships from the Strait of Juan de Fuca into Puget Sound through Admiralty Inlet was located at Admiralty Head on Whidbey Island. It was lighted in 1861 and served until 1903, when it got in the way of the Army's construction of fortifications at the site. The light was then moved a short distance to the north. Here, the Lighthouse Board erected a sturdy masonry structure that consisted of a two-story dwelling with an attached light tower of equal height. The fourth-order Fresnel lens in the tower went into service in 1903, and its light could be seen for 17 miles. In the 1920s the light was deemed no longer useful to shipping traffic, which had come to rely on the Point Wilson light on the opposite shore. In 1927 the lantern was removed for use at another lighthouse, and thereafter the dwelling and tower lay idle. During World War II the Army renovated the old structure for quarters, but after the war the dwelling and light tower again fell into disuse. In time, the Army no longer needed the fortifications, now known as Fort Casey, and declared the land surplus. The Washington State Park System acquired the fortifications and old lighthouse, and with the aid of the Island County Historical Society restored the lighthouse and reconstructed the lantern. The lighthouse is now part of Fort Casey State Park and is open to the public. NR district. [State of Washington]

ILWACO

■ Cape Disappointment Lighthouse
Cape Disappointment
Route 2
1856

The mouth of the Columbia River was a dangerous place to navigate, especially in the days of sailing ships—a fact that the builders of the first lighthouses on the Pacific coast confirmed for themselves. The work crew had just completed building the Southeast Farallon Island lighthouse near San Francisco in 1853, and the lighthouse at Cape Disappointment was next on their list. The vessel that carried them and the materials for the lighthouse became a victim of the vagaries of the wind and drifted onto the rocks. The ship sank almost immediately, with the loss of all the materials but, fortunately, no lives. The crew returned to San Francisco, purchased more mate-

rials, chartered another vessel and hurried back to Cape Disappointment, arriving in November 1853, just two months after their ship had gone down. By the following July, the 53-foot conical tower and the separate stone-and-brick Cape Cod dwelling were completed. The government inspector found that the tower and dwelling exceeded specifications, but the top of the tower was too small to support a first-order lantern and lens, so he had it enlarged to accommodate the first-order light. Two years after the tower had been completed, the lantern and Fresnel lens were installed, and the light went into service on October 15, 1856.

The Army built fortifications adjacent to the light station, and in 1871 an artillery shell came so close to the fog signal that the concussion destroyed the apparatus and broke 11 panes of glass in the lantern. In 1898 the Lighthouse Board, realizing that the light could not be seen well from the north, established a new light station at nearby North Head (see next entry) and moved the first-order lens from Cape Disappointment there. The Cape Disappointment tower received a new fourth-order lens for its old lantern and became a harbor light. The light, 220 feet above sea level, is still active. The grounds of the old station are open to the public, but the tower is closed. The station can be reached by a well-marked road to the cape. NR district. [U.S. Coast Guard]

On the ocean side, north of the Cape Disappointment light, is North Head. The Lighthouse Board built a new lighthouse here in 1898 and transferred the first-order lens from Cape Disappointment to the new 65-foot conical masonry tower. The focal plane of the light is 194 feet above sea level. This lens served until 1939, when the Coast Guard assumed responsibility for the nation's

Cape Disappointment light, illustrated by T. E. Sandgren after an 1859 sketch by Maj. Hartman Bache. The tower is much the same today.

■ **North Head Lighthouse**
Cape Disappointment
Route 2
Through Fort Canby
State Park
1898

North Head lighthouse, a coastal light on the ocean side of Cape Disappointment.

lighthouses. The Coast Guard replaced the lens with one of the fourth order and moved the old first-order lens to the museum at Fort Columbia. The light was automated in 1961. Visitors can hike out to the site for a spectacular view of the Columbia River Bar and Washington's Long Beach Peninsula. NR district. [U.S. Coast Guard]

KIRKLAND — SEATTLE

■ **Lightship Relief (LV-83)**
Lake Union
Northwest Seaport Museum
1002 Valley Street
1904

LV-83 is one of the two oldest lightships in the country, and during its career it served to guide ships into three major ports. This steel-hulled light vessel was built in 1904 in Camden, N.J. Originally 112 feet long with a beam of 28.6 feet and a draft of 12.6 feet, the hull in 1929 was lengthened to 129.8 feet. It displaces 668 tons. The ship was first sent to the West Coast to serve at the Blunts Reef station, a large and dangerous stretch of submerged

LV-83 under way in San Francisco Bay in 1947. The mushroom anchor is visible in the hawse hole on the bow.

rocks off Cape Mendocino, and near Eureka, Calif., a busy port deeply involved in the redwood trade. The ship served on this station until 1930; during its years there it survived several terrible storms that blew it off station and withstood ramming by a steam schooner. It once provided refuge for 155 survivors from a stranded coastal schooner. The Bureau of Lighthouses reassigned the lightship to San Francisco Bay, and for the next 21 years the vessel guided ships into the bay. In 1951 *No. 83* became a relief lightship and served the Northwest coast at the Columbia River Bar, Umatilla Reef and Swiftsure Banks at the mouth of the Strait of Juan de Fuca. Decommissioned in 1960, the ship was acquired by an organization now known as Northwest Seaport. It awaits restoration and is occasionally open to the public. The lightship retains its original marine steam engine and machinery. It also has its bell, made in 1904, which served as its auxiliary fog signal. In the 1930s a 375-millimeter lens with a 1,000-watt lamp replaced the reflector lights, which originally had been fueled by oil and later by electricity. The lens increased the range of the light to 15 miles. Also in the 1930s the Bureau of Lighthouses installed a diaphone fog signal to replace the original steam whistle. The red lightship, with buff-colored masts and fittings, was recently moved across Lake Union to Seattle adjacent to the *Wawona*. The name *Relief* is printed on the side of the hull. [Northwest Seaport Museum]

Mukilteo light station, where all but the tower and fog signal structure have been demolished.

MUKILTEO

This lighthouse, located in Possession Sound, near the landing of the ferry that runs from Mukilteo to Whidbey Island, was intended to guide traffic through the sound and on to Everett. The octagonal wood tower is attached to the fog signal building, also made of wood. Both structures are painted white. The tower is 30 feet tall, and the focal plane of the light is 33 feet. The dwelling and other subsidiary structures have been removed. The Coast Guard has installed in the lighthouse a photo-graphic exhibit on Puget Sound lighthouses. The light-house is open on weekends from noon to 4 p.m. NR. [U.S. Coast Guard]

■ **Mukilteo Lighthouse**
Near Mukilteo ferry landing
1906

Right: Cape Flattery lighthouse c. 1965, showing the tall tower rising from the masonry dwelling. Below: Cape Flattery light station after its expansion, with its whitewashed dwelling. The complex behind the station is a weather station, many of whose structures are now gone.

NEAH BAY

■ Cape Flattery (Tatoosh Island) Lighthouse
Route 112 to end, then 2 miles over dirt road
1858

Erected on Tatoosh Island, just off the tip of Cape Flattery, the most northwestern point of the continental United States, this lighthouse was one of the first 16 built on the West Coast. During its construction workers had to contend with the proximity of an Indian tribe, the Makah, who resented the presence of outsiders in their territory. No hostilities broke out, perhaps because the workers had built and armed a fortification. Work proceeded slowly, but the lighthouse was finally completed and was lighted on December 28, 1858. The 65-foot stone tower rose out of the Cape Cod dwelling, as did most of the other early lighthouses on the West Coast; this tower, however, was much taller than the other early lights, such as the one at Point Pinos in Monterey. The tower contained a first-order lens that had been purchased for the old lighthouse at Point Loma in San Diego. This lens was replaced many decades later by a smaller one. The island rises abruptly out of the sea, making the focal plane of the light 165 feet above sea level. The light is still active and can be seen from a hazardous viewpoint at the end of a two-mile dirt road. NR. [U.S. Coast Guard]

PORT TOWNSEND

Placed at the turning point for entering Admiralty Inlet from the Strait of Juan de Fuca, this lighthouse marked a dangerous area. The 46-foot wood tower, which rose out of the dwelling, had a fixed white light with a red flash every 20 seconds. In 1913–14 the Lighthouse Board built a new and taller tower, as well as a more modern fog signal. The new lighthouse was an octagonal concrete structure with a hipped-roof wing on each side, and its light was 51 feet above the water. This important light, now automated, is still active. The station includes a two-story dwelling and a smaller ranch-style one. NR. [U.S. Coast Guard]

■ **Point Wilson Lighthouse**
Fort Worden
1½ miles north of Port Townsend
1879, 1914

Point Wilson lighthouse, rising from the fog signal building, the second tower on the site.

SEATTLE

This lighthouse was established on the east side of Puget Sound, because at this point ships made their turn to head into the port of Seattle. With the completion of the Lake Washington Ship Canal, the lighthouse took on the additional duty of marking the turn into Shilshole Bay. The 23-foot white square brick tower covered with stucco is located close to the water's edge. Debris thrown up on the grounds from the sound has damaged the tower, so the Coast Guard has piled heavy stone at the tower's base

■ **West Point Lighthouse**
West Point
Fort Lawton
West off Route 99, south of the George Washington Memorial Bridge
1881

West Point light station, which guides ships into the port of Seattle. Note the lumber washed up along the shore.

to keep off the debris. The focal plane of the fourth-order lens is 27 feet above the level of the sound. Two frame keepers' dwellings, an oil house and a fog signal building complete the station. NR. [U.S. Coast Guard]

TACOMA

■ Point Robinson Lighthouse
Robinson Point
East end of Maury Island
By ferry from Tacoma and
Seattle to Vachon Island
1885, 1915

To guide naval traffic through the Strait of Juan de Fuca and into the various sounds and passages that lead to the bays and harbors of Seattle, Tacoma and Everett, the Lighthouse Board and its successor, the Bureau of Lighthouses, added aids to navigation as they were needed. Some of these sites evolved over the years. A typical example is the Point Robinson lighthouse, whose roots go back to a fog signal established in 1885 on Maury

Island, just off the larger Vachon Island. Two years later a lantern was added, and in 1915 the Bureau of Lighthouses built a full-fledged lighthouse. The 38-foot octagonal masonry tower, attached to the fog signal building, was crowned with a lantern holding a fifth-order lens; the focal plane of its light is 40 feet above sea level. At the same time two keepers' dwellings were constructed. [U.S. Coast Guard]

Below left: Point Robinson light and fog signal building. Below: Grays Harbor light, an octagonal pyramidal tower.

WESTPORT

Grays Harbor is a treacherous area with surprise squalls; an estimated 50 ships and numerous smaller fishing and pleasure vessels have been victims of these perilous waters west of Aberdeen in the middle of Washington's Pacific coastline. In the 1920s the *Coast Pilot* reported that the harbor was "probably the leading lumber port in the United States." This lighthouse was established not only to guide ships into the harbor but also to light the dark coast between the Cape Disappointment light to the south and the Destruction Island light to the north, which had been put into service in 1892 on the picturesque, rugged and stormy island off the Washington coast. The octagonal light tower at Grays Harbor, 107 feet from the ground to the top of the lantern's ventilator ball, is brick painted white, except for the top 12 feet and the lantern, which are painted black. The focal plane of the light is 123 feet above sea level. The white part of the red-and-white light from the tower's third-order Fresnel lens is visible 23 miles. The station, now automated, has a radio beacon and a diaphone fog signal, which replaced an earlier siren fog signal. NR. [U.S. Coast Guard]

■ **Grays Harbor (Westport)**
Lighthouse
Point Chehalis
South side of harbor
entrance
Route 105
1898

■ ■ ■ ■ ■ ■ ■ ■ ■ ■ ■ ■ ■ ■ ■ ■ ■

EPILOGUE:
LOST LIGHTS AND LOSING BATTLES

Many lighthouses and lightships over the years have been lost, for the most part because of natural causes — erosion, storms, fire and ice — but also because people have sometimes been careless keepers.

EROSION AND STORMS

The first Ponce de Leon Inlet lighthouse (1835) in Florida fell victim to erosion before it was even lighted. Cape San Blas, west of Apalachicola, Fla., saw erosion claim three towers in 1851, 1856 and 1882. North Carolina's migrating Oregon Inlet took the first lighthouse (1848) on Bodie Island in 1859 and probably would have swallowed the second one (1859) if the Confederates had not destroyed it in 1861. Erosion in 1941 also took the first Willapa Bay lighthouse (1858) at Cape Shoalwater, Ore., one of the West Coast's original 16 lights. The colonial light tower (1767) at Cape Henlopen, Del., toppled in 1926, after the wind had eaten away the sand bank on which it was built. A migrating inlet threatened the Barnegat light tower (1859) until the state of New Jersey dumped heavy riprap on the inlet side of the lighthouse to halt the erosion.

Storms, of course, speed erosion, but they can and have done serious damage to lighthouses directly. A severe hurricane in the Florida Keys took down the first Key West lighthouse (1825) on Whiteheads Point and killed the keeper and his family in 1846. Nearby, the stone tower (1827) at Sand Key was lost with the keeper's house the same year; the screwpile tower built to replace it in 1853 stood out another hurricane in 1865 even though the entire island was washed away (but later reappeared). The terrible hurricane of 1938 smashed into New England and did substantial damage to lighthouses along its coast. At Palmer Island (1849), New Bedford, Mass., it not only left destruction but also took the life of the keeper's wife. At Prudence Island (1823), Portsmouth, R.I., it swept the site clean except for the tower and caused the death of the keeper's family and visiting friends. In more recent years, a tidal wave in 1946 covered the Scotch Cap light station (1940) in Alaska's Aleutian Islands, taking all the structures and three keepers.

Fire and ice likewise have wreaked havoc with America's lighthouses. In the Chesapeake Bay, floating ice has injured screwpile lights and in some cases destroyed them. In 1893 floating ice ripped the Wolf Trap light (1870) from its foundation; it was found floating toward the capes. The Thimble Shoals light (1870) near Hampton Roads, Va., burned in 1880. Replaced in 55 days, the new structure was later hit by a barge and a ship, and in 1909 a schooner banged into the hapless lighthouse and set it on fire. This time the Lighthouse Board erected a caisson light at the site.

Opposite: Cape Hatteras lighthouse (1870), near Buxton, N.C. — probably the most conspicuous current victim of the sea's eroding power.

Above: First Minots Ledge lighthouse (1850), off Cohasset, Mass., falling in 1851 to a battering sea. The loss was a combination of the exposed Atlantic site and improper iron skeleton construction. Right: Chandeleur Island light station (1856), near New Orleans, tilting after an 1893 storm. The second light at the site, it was replaced by a third tower, whose foundation used broken brick from the old lighthouse as fill. Below: Ice surrounding the Love Point, Md., screwpile lighthouse in the Chesapeake Bay.

Left: Sand Key light (1853) in the Florida Keys. This tall screwpile structure replaced an 1827 lighthouse destroyed by a hurricane and has itself withstood many storms, including one in 1865 that washed away the island.

Above: Cat Island light station (1871), off the coast of Mississippi near Gulfport. Stabilized by rocks under and around it, the screwpile light rode out hurricanes that severely damaged its 1831 predecessor. Left: Humboldt Harbor, Calif., lighthouse (1856). The eighth built on the West Coast, it fought a losing battle with the sea.

ACCIDENTS AND WAR

Top: Mobile Point, Ala., light tower (1822), bombarded beyond repair during the Civil War because it was close to Fort Morgan. Above: Breakwater light in Buffalo Harbor, N.Y., showing the effects of a run-in with a ship.

Lightships were regularly knocked about — Willard Flint in his *Lightships of the United States Government* documented 150 collisions involving these vulnerable vessels. One lightship serving the Nantucket South Shoals station was hit by a liner in 1934, resulting in its sinking with a heavy loss of life. Like lightships, lighthouses are not immune to accidents. Rhode Island's Newport Harbor light (1865) on Goat Island was rammed by a submarine in the 1920s. Screwpile lighthouses in the Chesapeake Bay also suffered collisions on a number of occasions.

Beginning with the tribulations of the Boston Harbor light (1716) during the Revolution — saved by the Americans in 1775 only to be blown up by the British a year later — lighthouses also have seen unwanted action during war. During the Civil War, the Confederates damaged many lighthouses so that they could not give aid to the enemy. In the cases of Bodie Island, N.C. (1859), St. Simons Island, Ga. (1810), and probably Hunting Island (1859) near Beaufort, S.C., they destroyed the towers beyond repair.

VANDALISM AND NEGLECT

Vandals, too, have struck at lighthouses. A notable loss occurred in the late 1970s when two Canadian runaways burned down the St. Croix River light (1855) on Dochet Island, Maine, when a fire quickly got out of control in high winds. The old lighthouse was then out of service after having been replaced by a steel skeleton tower; it had just been brought into the National Park Service. During its active years this station occupied the number one place in the *Light List* because of its closeness to the United States–Canada border.

The government has been automating lighthouses since the widespread adoption of electricity in the early 20th century. Preservation of the nation's lighthouses has never been the lighthouse system's key mission; providing aid to mariners is its priority. Thus, when technological developments made historic lighthouses nonessential, the Coast Guard sometimes undertook what seemed to be appropriate action — to demolish unnecessary structures. A number of light station buildings were lost in this way over the early years of automation. A few obsolete light towers were dealt with by removing their lanterns and lenses. Fortunately, in recent years, greater preservation awareness, protective laws and public interest have encouraged the Coast Guard, even with an inadequate budget, to maintain its lighthouse inventory.

In some cases, the new owners of lighthouses have been careless keepers with their historic charges. The New Dorp lighthouse (1854), a small range light on Staten Island in New York, was used as a residence for a number of years after it was sold and retained its original features. Recently, the owners enlarged the structure, seriously altering its historic character. The Sabine Pass, La., light station (1908), the one with the rocket-shaped light tower, has suffered the reverse: it has lost structures. The Coast Guard transferred the site to the state of Louisiana for a park, but funding was not authorized. The old station languished, used off and on by people

Top and above: St. Croix River light (1855) on Dochet Island, Maine, before it was burned by runaways. The fog bell was housed in the metronome-shaped structure built over the water. The drawing details the dwelling with the tower rising through the roof.

studying the area's environment. The state eventually sold the site at public auction, and in private hands it fared no better — indeed, a little worse, for a fire swept the site, burning all the structures but leaving just the light tower. Its future today is no brighter than it has ever been since leaving Coast Guard hands.

CAPE HATTERAS AND THE SEA

Today, for some lighthouses, the new threats from nature are as strong as anything humans could devise. The Sand Island light (1873) near Mobile, Ala., is resting on the remains of a 400-acre island that is now little larger than the base of the lighthouse. Rubble piled around the tower's base is impeding the progress of erosion, but it will not stop it. The old Charleston, S.C., lighthouse (1876) on Morris Island is standing in water because channel dredging has changed erosion patterns, causing the island to fall away. In the Chesapeake Bay the Cedar Point lighthouse (1896), consisting of a house with a tower resting on its roof, is less than a shell of itself; its walls are slowly crumbling as the water swirls around it.

The most conspicuous victim of erosion — also one of the most conspicuous and beloved lighthouses in the country — is the Cape Hatteras lighthouse (1870) in North Carolina. Regarded as the most important lighthouse during much of the 19th century, this landmark faces erosion, the water now less than 100 feet from the well-known striped tower. The lighthouse has been threatened by erosion several times already, with the water coming almost to the structure's foundation. It happened in the 1930s and again in the 1960s. Each time the government placed groins and sandbags to impede the advance of the Atlantic Ocean, and each time these efforts were ineffective. But on both these occasions, as before, the water relented as though it had been teasing the old lighthouse, and in subsequent years, the ocean

Cape Hatteras light on its eroding site. The famous candy-striped tower has fought a valiant fight with the Atlantic Ocean.

would wash sand between it and the light tower. Today's erosion is more extensive and thus more than a threat. One now has the feeling of impending doom. Erosion has already claimed the land on which the first Cape Hatteras light tower (1803) stood. Usual protection methods have been tried, along with some of the newer ones such as plastic "grass" supposed to trap sand. They perhaps slowed the erosion somewhat, but the ocean kept nibbling away at the beach. All agree that in time the ocean will topple the tower. Some people speculate that if a strong hurricane were to take aim at Cape Hatteras and hit dead on, or if two storms occurred close together, the tower would be gone.

Why now has the ocean stopped teasing the light tower, and why is it bent on consuming it? A new factor has been thrown into the erosion equation. The ocean has risen because of the melting ice cap, and this change has altered patterns of erosion.

National Park Service officials know that unless something is done, the tower (located in the Cape Hatteras National Seashore) will eventually topple into the ocean. A proposal by the Corps of Engineers called for saving the structure by building a large and rather tall revetment around the tower. Ultimately, the sand would be washed away and leave the light tower and revetment on an island just off shore. Others broached a program of sand replenishment, which would have to be done on a regular basis for an incalculable length of time, and each replenishment effort would be expensive. Some suggested a groin field to halt erosion. Another group counseled moving the light tower back from the water's edge. Many of the local people who have lived their entire lives on the Outer Banks and have a strong emotional tie to the lighthouse thought that this venerable tower, like an old and beloved relative, should have a dignified death and be permitted to fall into the ocean. They did not believe that the tower should be put on artificial life support.

The National Park Service, with all this conflicting advice, and knowing that the old light tower is a well-known national landmark and an important symbol of the state of North Carolina, turned to the National Academy of Sciences for advice. The academy directed its National Research Council to gather a team of experts from various disciplines, study the problem and recommend a course to follow. The National Research Council's team had experts from many disciplines — lawyers, engineers, erosion specialists, historic preservationists, geographers, a marine scientist and an economist. After examining the site, talking to concerned groups, reading past reports and deliberating over the various issues, the committee recommended several options to the National Park Service. Its preferred option was to move the lighthouse. The Park Service held public hearings on the options and planned to make its decision in 1989.

How many other historic light towers that once were thought to be secure are now threatened by similar new turns of nature?

BIBLIOGRAPHY

See also Further Reading in Lighting America's Shores.

"Aging Cape May Lighthouse Is Symbol of the Past." *New York Times*, March 18, 1984, p. 46.

Aikin, Ross R. *Kilauea Point Lighthouse: The Landfall Beacon on the Orient Run*. Kauai: Kilauea Point Natural History Association, 1988.

Apostle Islands National Lakeshore. *Lights of the Apostles*. Philadelphia: Eastern National Park and Monument Association, 1988.

Bang, Henry R. *The Story of the Fire Island Light*. Long Island, N.Y.: Author, 1988.

Barry, Elise, and Wayne Wheeler. "Hudson River Lighthouses Get a New Lease on Life, Part III." *The Keeper's Log*, vol. III, no. 4 (Summer 1987).

Bearss, Edwin C. *Basic Data Study, History: Assateague Island National Seashore*. Washington, D.C.: Division of History, National Park Service, 1968.

Bleyer, Bill. "A Lighthouse Tradition Fades Out," New York *Newsday*, February, 18, 1986, p. 6.

_____ . "The Lighthouse Finds a Keeper." New York *Newsday*, April 5, 1986.

Boucher, Jack E. *Atlantic City's . . . Historic Absecon Lighthouse*. Somers Point, N.J.: Atlantic County Historical Society, 1964.

Caldwell, Bill. *Lighthouses of Maine*. Portland, Maine: Guy Gannett Books, 1986.

Clemensen, A. Berle, and William W. Howell et al. *Historic Structure Report: Three Sisters Lighthouses — Cape Cod National Seashore, Massachusetts*. Denver: Denver Service Center, National Park Service, 1986.

Cox, Rachel, and Michael Bowker. "The Lighthouse: Endangered Species." *Historic Preservation*, vol. 37, no. 6 (December 1985).

Delgado, James P. *Alcatraz Island: The Story Behind the Scenery*. Las Vegas: KC Publications, 1985.

_____ , and Kevin J. Foster. *Nominating Historic Lighthouses and Aids to Navigation to the National Register of Historic Places*. Bulletin no. 34. Washington, D.C.: National Register of Historic Places, National Park Service, 1989.

De Wire, Elinor. *Guide to Florida Lighthouses*. Englewood, Fla.: Pineapple Press, 1987.

de Zafra, Dorothea. *Charlotte's Lighthouses and Its River: How They Came to Be*. Rochester, N.Y.: Charlotte-Genesee Lighthouse Historical Society, 1984.

Faber, Harold. "Lighthouse on Hudson Is Becoming a Museum." *New York Times*, September 17, 1984, p. B-4.

Feller-Roth, Barbara. *Lighthouses: A Guide to Many of Maine's Coastal and Offshore Guardians*. Freeport, Maine: De Lorne Publishing, 1985.

Fisher, Charles C., Jr. "Cedar Keys Lighthouse." *The Keeper's Log*, vol. III, no. 4 (Summer 1987).

Fraser, Robert. "Scituate Lighthouses." *The Keeper's Log*, vol. III, no. 2 (Winter 1987).

Gallant, Cliff. "Mind the Light Katie." *The Keeper's Log*, vol. III. no. 3 (Spring 1987).

Gibbs, James A. *West Coast Lighthouses: A Pictorial History of the Guiding Lights of the Sea*. Seattle: Superior Publishing, 1974.

Glunt, Ruth R. *Lighthouses and Legends of the Hudson*. Monroe, N.Y.: Library Research Associates, 1975.

Hall, Stephen P. *Split Rock: Epoch of a Lighthouse*. Minnesota Historic Sites Pamphlet Series, no. 15. Minneapolis: Minnesota Historical Society, 1978.

Historic Place Restoration Feasibility Study: Point Iroquois Light Station. Hiawatha National Forest, Near Sault Ste. Marie, Michigan. Detroit: William Kessler and Associates, 1978.

Holden, Thom. *Above and Below: A History of Lighthouses and Shipwrecks of Isle Royale*. Houghton, Mich.: Isle Royale Natural History Association, 1985.

Holland, F. Ross, Jr. *The Aransas Pass Light Station: A History*. Corpus Christi: Charles Butt, 1976.

————— . *A History of Bodie Island Light Station*. Washington, D.C.: Division of History, National Park Service, 1967.

————— . *A History of Cape Hatteras Light Station*. Washington, D.C.: Division of History, National Park Service, 1968.

————— . *The Old Point Loma Lighthouse, San Diego*. San Diego: Cabrillo Historical Association, 1978.

—————. *A Survey of Cape Lookout National Seashore*. Washington, D.C.: Division of History, National Park Service, 1968.

Hudson River Valley Commission. *The Hudson River Lighthouses*. Albany, N.Y.: Author, 1967.

Kagerer, Rudy. *A Guidebook to Lighthouses in South Carolina, Georgia, and Florida's East Coast*. Athens, Ga.: Lighthouse Enterprises, 1985.

Lewis, Steven H. *Historic Structure Report: Jones Point Lighthouse*. Washington, D.C.: Division of History, National Park Service, 1966.

Mackenzie, George E. *Surplus Property Report: Rock Island Lighthouse Station, Orleans, New York*. Washington, D.C.: Division of History, National Park Service, 1970.

————— . *Tarrytown Light Station, Tarrytown, New York*. Washington, D.C.: Division of History, National Park Service, 1971.

Manning, Gordon P. *Life in the Colchester Reef Lighthouse*. Shelburne, Vt.: Shelburne Museum, 1958.

Martone, Camille M., Lauren McCroskey and Sharon C. Park, comps. *Preserving Historic Lighthouses: An Annotated Bibliography*. Washington, D.C.: Preservation Assistance Division, National Park Service, 1989.

"Mobile Lighthouse Restored." Reprinted from *Port of Mobile. The Keeper's Log*, vol. II, no. 3 (Spring 1986).

Morgan, Stewart. "Derby Wharf Lighthouses." *The Keeper's Log*, vol. IV, no. 1 (Fall 1987).

National Trust for Historic Preservation. *Lighthouse Bibliography*. Boston: Northeast Regional Office, National Trust for Historic Preservation, 1989.

1988 National Register of Historic Places. Cumulative listing. Nashville, Tenn.: American Association for State and Local History, forthcoming.

Noble, Dennis L., and Ralph Eshelman. "A Lighthouse for Drum Point." *The Keeper's Log*, vol. III, no. 3 (Spring 1987).

Nordorf, Charles. *The Light-Houses of the United States in 1874*. Golden, Colo.: Outbooks, 1981.

Official Gannett Maine Guide to Maine Lighthouses: A Field Guide to Discover the Best of Outdoor Maine. Portland, Maine: Guy Gannett Books, 1982.

Parsons, Eleanor C. *Thachers: Island of the Twin Lights*. Canaan, N.H.: Phoenix Publishing, 1985.

Perrault, Carole L. "Historic Structure Report, Architecture Data Section: The Fire Island Lighthouse and Keeper's Dwelling, Fire Island National Seashore, Patchoque, New York," vol. I, part 1. Mimeographed. Boston: North Atlantic Preservation Center, North Atlantic Region, National Park Service, 1983.

Perry, Frank. *East Brother: History of an Island Light Station*. Richmond, Calif.: East Brother Light Station, 1984.

_____ . *Lighthouse Point: Reflections on Monterey Bay History*. Soquel, Calif.: GBH Publishing, 1982.

Railton, Arthur R. "Famous American Lighthouse: The Gay Head Lighthouse." *The Keeper's Log*, vol. IV, no. 4 (Summer 1988).

"River Group Will Restore a Lighthouse." *New York Times*, March 4, 1984, p. 42.

Ruth, Kim M. "Finns Point Rear Range Lighthouse." *The Keeper's Log*, vol. II, no. 1 (Fall 1985).

Shanks, Ralph C., Jr., and Janetta Thompson Shanks. *Lighthouses and Lifeboats on the Redwood Coast*. San Anselmo, Calif.: Costano Books, 1978.

Small, Nora Pat. "Lighthouses of the National Park Service." Washington, D.C.: Division of Historical Architecture, National Park Service, 1980.

Snow, Edward R. *Famous Lighthouses of New England*. Boston: Yankee Publishing, 1945.

Sterling, Robert Thayer. *Lighthouses of the Maine Coast and the Men Who Keep Them*. Brattleboro, Vt.: Stephen Daye Press, 1935.

10 Lights: The Lighthouses of the Keweenaw Peninsula: A Sesquicentennial Exhibition. Houghton, Mich.: Keweenaw County Historical Society, 1987.

Toogood, Anna C. *Historic Resource Study: A Civil History of Golden Gate National Recreation Area and Point Reyes National Seashore*, vols. I and II. Denver: Denver Service Center, National Park Service, 1980.

Torres, Louis. *Historic Structure Report, Historical Data: Au Sable Light Station, Pictured Rocks National Lakeshore, Michigan*. Denver: Denver Service Center, National Park Service, 1978.

U.S. Coast Guard. *Historically Famous Lighthouses.* Washington, D.C.: U.S. Government Printing Office, 1972.

U.S. Lighthouse Establishment. *Instructions to Light Keepers and Masters of Light-House Vessels.* 1902. Reprint. Allen Park, Mich.: Great Lakes Lighthouse Keepers Association, 1989.

Vogel, Mike. "Buffalo — Beacon of the Heartland." *The Keeper's Log,* vol. IV, no. 1 (Fall 1987).

Ward, Jane. *Hooper Strait Lighthouse.* St. Michaels, Md.: Chesapeake Bay Maritime Museum, 1979.

■ ■ ■ ■ ■ ■ ■ ■ ■ ■ ■ ■ ■ ■ ■ ■ ■ ■

INFORMATION SOURCES

The following organizations and agencies can supply information on subjects covered in *Great American Lighthouses*. In addition, state historic preservation offices and state and local historical societies often have information, illustrations and other material that can be helpful.

Advisory Council on Historic
Preservation
1100 Pennsylvania Avenue, N.W.
Suite 809
Washington, D.C. 20004

American Lighthouse
Museum
1011 North 3rd Street
Jacksonville Beach, Fla.
32250

Coast Guard
U.S. Department of
Transportation:

Aids to Navigation Office
2100 2nd Street, S.W.
Washington, D.C. 20593

Office of the Historian
2100 2nd Street, S.W.
Washington, D.C. 20593

District Offices:

First Coast Guard District
408 Atlantic Avenue
Boston, Mass. 02210-2209

Second Coast Guard
District
1430 Olive Street
St. Louis, Mo. 63103-4605

Fifth Coast Guard District
Federal Building
431 Crawford Street
Portsmouth, Va.
23705-5004

Seventh Coast Guard
District
Brickel Plaza Building
909 S.E. 1st Avenue
Miami, Fla. 33131-3050

Commander, Greater
Antilles Section
U.S. Coast Guard
San Juan, P.R. 00903-2029

Eighth Coast Guard District
Hale Boggs Federal
Building
500 Camp Street
New Orleans, La.
70130-3396

Ninth Coast Guard District
1240 East 9th Street
Cleveland, Ohio 44199-2060

Eleventh Coast Guard
District
Union Bank Building
400 Oceangate Boulevard
Long Beach, Calif.
90822-5399

Thirteenth Coast Guard
District
Federal Building
915 2nd Avenue
Seattle, Wash. 98174-1067

Fourteenth Coast Guard
District
Prince Kalanianaole
Federal Building
Ninth Floor
300 Ala Moana Boulevard
Honolulu, Hawaii
96850-4982

Seventeenth Coast Guard
District
P.O. Box 3-500
Juneau, Alaska 99802-1217

Coast Guard Museum
U.S. Coast Guard Academy
Visitors Center
Mohegan Avenue
New London, Conn. 06320

Coast Guard Museum
Northwest
1519 Alaskan Way South
Seattle, Wash. 98101

Council of American
Maritime Museums
Chesapeake Bay Maritime
Museum
P.O. Box 636
St. Michaels, Md. 21663

Fish and Wildlife Service
U.S. Department of the
Interior
Washington, D.C. 20240

Forest Service
U.S. Department of
Agriculture
P.O. Box 2417
Washington, D.C. 20013

Great Lakes Lighthouse
Keepers Association
P.O. Box 580
Allen Park, Mich. 48101

Island Institute
P.O. Box 429
Rockland, Maine 04843

Lighthouse Preservation
Society
P.O. Box 736
Rockport, Mass. 01966

National Archives:

Cartographic and
Architectural Branch
Washington, D.C. 20408

Diplomatic Branch
Washington, D.C. 20408

Still Pictures Collection
Washington, D.C. 20408

National Conference of State
Historic Preservation Officers
444 North Capitol Street, N.W.
Suite 322
Washington, D.C. 20001

National Park Service
U.S. Department of the
Interior:

Division of History
Maritime Initiative
P.O. Box 37127
Washington, D.C. 20013-7127

Historic American Buildings
Survey
P.O. Box 37127
Washington, D.C. 20013-7127

National Register of Historic
Places
P.O. Box 37127
Washington, D.C. 20013-7127

Preservation Assistance
Division
P.O. Box 37127
Washington, D.C. 20013-7127

National Trust for Historic
Preservation
Maritime Office
1785 Massachusetts Avenue, N.W.
Washington, D.C. 20036

Regional Offices:

Mid-Atlantic Regional Office
6401 Germantown Avenue
Philadelphia, Pa. 19144

Midwest Regional Office
53 West Jackson Boulevard
Suite 1135
Chicago, Ill. 60604

Mountains/Plains
Regional Office
511 16th Street, Suite 700
Denver, Colo. 80202

Texas/New Mexico
Field Office
500 Main Street
Suite 606
Fort Worth, Tex. 76102

Northeast Regional Office
45 School Street
Fourth Floor
Boston, Mass. 02108

Southern Regional Office
456 King Street
Charleston, S.C. 29403

Western Regional Office
One Sutter Street, Suite 707
San Francisco, Calif. 94104

Shore Village Museum
104 Limerock Street
Rockland, Maine 04841

U.S. Lighthouse Society
244 Kearney Street
Fifth Floor
San Francisco, Calif. 94108

NO MENTION OF GROSSE ILE NOR MUSKEGON !

■ ■ ■ ■ ■ ■ ■ ■ ■ ■ ■ ■ ■ ■ ■ ■ ■ ■ ■ ■

PHOTOGRAPHIC SOURCES

Abbreviations used refer to the following collections:

CTPC — Curt Teich Postcard Collection, Lake County (Ill.) Museum
FRH — F. Ross Holland, Jr., collection
HABS — Historic American Buildings Survey, National Park Service
NA — National Archives, U.S. Coast Guard Collection
NPS — National Park Service
USCG — U.S. Coast Guard

2 all, CTPC.   **7** all, CTPC.   **8** USCG.   **10** NA.   **14** USCG.   **16** NA.   **17** top, NA; bottom, Bureau of History, Michigan Department of State.   **18** top, HABS; bottom, NA.   **19** USCG.   **21** NA.   **22** top left, FRH; top center, NA; top right, USCC; center left, NA; center right, USCG; bottom, National Register of Historic Places.   **23** top left, CTPC; top center and right, USCG; bottom, USCG.   **24** top left, Lighthouse Board, FRH; top right, NA; bottom left, USCG; bottom right, NA. **25** top, NA; center left, NA; center right, USCG; bottom, USCG.   **26** top, NA; center, USCG; bottom left, FRH; bottom right, NA.   **27** both, USCG.   **29** David Battle.   **30** NA.   **32** both, NA.   **33** USCG.   **34** top, NA; bottom, USCG.   **35** all, FRH.   **36** USCG.   **37** *Century Magazine*, Library of Congress.   **39** both, USCG.   **42** top and center, NA; bottom, USCG.   **44** top and center, NA; bottom left, USCG; bottom right, FRH.   **45** USCG.   **47** top, *St. Nicholas Magazine;* center and bottom, Fred Mang, Jr., NPS.   **48** top, NA; bottom, USCG.   **49** USCG.   **51** both, NA.   **54** both, USCG.   **56** Thomas Sweeney, *Preservation News.*   **57** top, NA; bottom, Thomas Sweeney, *Preservation News.* **58** M. Woodbridge Williams, NPS.   **59** Frank Pedrick.   **60** USCG.   **62** all, Great Lakes Lighthouse Keepers Association, courtesy Richard L. Moehl.   **63** Ralph B. Starr, courtesy U.S. Lighthouse Society.   **64** USCG.   **65** both, National Trust for Historic Preservation collection.   **66** FRH.   **67** HABS.   **68** top, George M. Houghton, Upper Michigan Card Company; center, Friends of Round Island Lighthouse; bottom, Bureau of History, Michigan Department of State.   **69** Friends of Round Island Lighthouse, courtesy Marcia M. Haynes.

NEW ENGLAND

74–75 USCG.   **76** CTPC.   **77** top, USCG; bottom, CTPC.   **78** USCG.   **79** top, NA; bottom, USCG.   **80** Robert Rothe, Maine Historic Preservation Commission.   **81** top, Acadia National Park, NPS; bottom, USCG.   **82** left, USCG; right, NA.   **83** both, USCG. **84** USCG.   **85** USCG.   **86** all, USCG.   **87** USCG. **88** both, USCG.   **89** top, CTPC; bottom, USCG.   **90**

CTPC.   **91** USCG.   **92** left, FRH; right, Jack E. Boucher, HABS.   **93** USCG.   **94** top, both, USCG; bottom, FRH.   **95** USCG.   **96** both, USCG.   **97** USCG.   **98** USCG.   **99** both, USCG.   **100** top, FRH; bottom, USCG.   **101** USCG.   **102** left, USCG; right, NA.   **104** top right, NA; others, USCG.   **105** USCG. **106** USCG.   **107** top, FRH; bottom, USCG.   **108** both, CTPC.   **109** CTPC.   **110** top, USCG; bottom, CTPC.   **111** FRH.   **112** USCG.   **113** center, NA; others, USCG.   **114** NA.   **115** USCG.   **116** left, NA; right, USCG.   **117** top, USCG; bottom, NPS.   **118** Arthur C. Haskell, HABS.   **119** NA.   **120** top, USCG; bottom, CTPC.   **121** USCG.   **122** Lee Ann Jackson and Isabel C. Yang, Historic American Engineering Record, NPS.   **123** USCG.   **124** USCG.   **125** both, USCG.   **126** top, CTPC; bottom, FRH.   **127** USCG. **128** both, USCG.   **129** USCG.

MID-ATLANTIC

130-31 USCG.   **132** USCG.   **133** left, NA; right, USCG.   **134** top, USCG; bottom, Bureau of Archaeology and Historic Preservation, Delaware Department of State.   **135** USCG.   **136** both, USCG.   **137** top, FRH; bottom, USCG.   **138** left, CTPC; right, USCG.   **139** top, Chesapeake Bay Maritime Museum; bottom, USCG.   **140** Calvert Marine Museum.   **141** USCG. **142** drawings, John D. Milner, HABS; photo, NA.   **143** *Frank Leslie's Illustrated Newspaper.*   **144** top, USCG; bottom, CTPC.   **146** left, NA; right, USCG.   **147** CTPC.   **148** all, USCG.   **150** both, USCG.   **151** top, USCG; bottom left, NA; bottom right; Walter Sedovic, NPS.   **152** USCG.   **153** both, USCG.   **154** USCG. **155** both, USCG.   **157** USCG.   **158** top, Jack Rottier, National Capital Parks, NPS; bottom, USCG.   **159** USCG.   **161** both, USCG.   **162** CTPC.   **163** USCG.

SOUTHEAST

164-65 USCG.   **166** USCG.   **167** HABS.   **168** left, top and center, USCG; bottom, Florida State Archives. **171** USCG.   **172** top, USCG; bottom, CTPC.   **173** left, USCG; right, CTPC.   **175** both, USCG.   **176** both, USCG.   **177** USCG.   **178** USCG.   **179** top, Richard Darcey, NPS; bottom, NA.   **181** top, NA; bottom, Richard Darcey, NPS.   **182** Richard Darcey, NPS. **183** USCG.   **185** top, HABS; bottom, USCG.   **186** top, NA; bottom, USCG.   **187** USCG.   **188** USCG.   **189** left, NA; right, USCG.   **190** USCG.   **191** USCG.

GULF OF MEXICO

192-93 USCG.   **194** USCG.   **195** bottom left, *Frank Leslie's Illustrated Newspaper;* others, USCG.   **196** USCG.   **197** USCG.   **198** USCG.   **199** both, USCG. **200** USCG.   **201** USCG.   **202** both, USCG. **203** USCG.   **204** both, USCG.   **205** USCG.   **206** both, USCG.   **207** CTPC.   **208** both, USCG.   **210** CTPC. **211** both, CTPC.

GREAT LAKES

212–13 Minnesota Historical Society.   **215** both, USCG.   **216** top, FRH; bottom, USCG.   **217** USCG.   **218** USCG.   **219** top, USCG; bottom, Bureau of History, Michigan Department of State.   **220** USCG.   **221** CTPC.   **222** USCG.   **223** FRH.   **224** top, USCG; bottom, Bureau of History, Michigan Department of State.   **225** USCG.   **226** top left and bottom, FRH; top right, USCG.   **227** both, USCG.   **228** USCG.   **229** USCG.   **230** top, NA; bottom, FRH.   **231** USCG.   **233** top, USCG; others, Bureau of History, Michigan Department of State.   **234** top and bottom, USCG; center, Bureau of History, Michigan Department of State.   **236** top, USCG; bottom, State Archives of Michigan.   **237** both, USCG.   **238** left, Bureau of History, Michigan Department of State; right, USCG.   **239** top, FRH; bottom, USCG.   **240** left, Minnesota Historical Society; right, CTPC.   **241** USCG.   **242** left, FRH; right, USCG.   **243** FRH.   **244** CTPC.   **245** USCG.   **246** both, FRH.   **247** both, FRH.   **248** FRH.   **249** USCG.   **250** FRH.   **251** both, USCG.   **253** top and bottom, USCG; center, Carol Poh Miller.   **254** both, USCG.   **255** William J. Bulger, HABS.   **256** CTPC.   **257** top, USCG; bottom, FRH.   **258** both, USCG.   **259** both, FRH.   **260** left, FRH; right, USCG.   **261** left, USCG; right, NPS.   **263** top left and right, John Vogel, State Historical Society of Wisconsin; others, USCG.   **264** both, USCG.   **265** top, USCG; bottom, Joan Melson, State Historical Society of Wisconsin.   **266** USCG.   **267** all, USCG.

WEST

268–69 USCG.   **270** both, USCG.   **271** top left and right, USCG; bottom, NA.   **272** top, USCG; bottom, Tongass Historical Society, Ketchikan, Alaska.   **273** both, USCG.   **274** USCG.   **275** top, USCG; bottom, NA.   **276** both, USCG.   **277** top, Del Norte County Historical Society, Crescent City, Calif.; bottom, USCG.   **278** USCG.   **279** USCG.   **280** USCG.   **281** both, USCG.   **282** USCG.   **283** USCG.   **284** both, USCG.   **285** top, HABS; bottom, USCG.   **286** USCG.   **287** USCG.   **288** NPS.   **289** USCG.   **290** NA.   **291** USCG.   **292** USCG.   **293** Joshua Freiwald, HABS.   **294** USCG.   **295** USCG.   **296** USCG.   **297** both, USCG.   **298** both, USCG.   **299** both, USCG.   **300** CTPC.   **301** USCG.   **302** bottom, Oregon Department of Transportation; others, USCG.   **303** both, USCG.   **305** all, USCG.   **306** Washington State Office of Archaeology and Historic Preservation.   **307** NA.   **308** top, CTPC; bottom, USCG.   **309** USCG.   **310** top, NA; bottom, USCG.   **311** USCG.   **312** both, USCG.   **313** both, USCG.

314 USCG.   **316** top, Library of Congress; center and bottom, NA.   **317** top and center, NA; bottom, Carl Christensen collection.   **318** both, USCG.   **319** top, USCG; bottom, HABS.   **320** USCG.

INDEX

■ ■ ■ ■ ■ ■ ■ ■ ■ ■ ■ ■ ■ ■ ■ ■ ■ ■ ■

AUTHOR

F. Ross Holland, Jr., of Silver Spring, Md., retired from the National Park Service of the U.S. Department of the Interior in 1983, for which he served as a park historian, research historian, supervisory research historian, associate regional director for planning and resource preservation, and associate director for cultural resources management. He received the Interior Department's Meritorious Service Award for contributions to historic preservation and its Distinguished Service Award for contributions to the Park Service's cultural resources management program. Holland later worked for the Statue of Liberty–Ellis Island Foundation until September 1986. He is the author of *America's Lighthouses* and several other books and holds a B.C.S. from the University of Georgia, Atlanta, and an M.A. in history from the University of Texas.

Sen. George J. Mitchell of Waterville, Maine, is the majority leader of the U.S. Senate and a sponsor of the Bicentennial Lighthouse Fund. He has served in the Senate since 1980, when he was appointed to complete the unexpired term of Sen. Edmund S. Muskie; Sen. Mitchell was elected to his first full term in 1982. Before this he served as U.S. District Court judge for Maine, U.S. attorney for Maine and Democratic state chairman. The senator, who received his law degree from the Georgetown University Law Center, also has been a trial lawyer in the Antitrust Division of the U.S. Department of Justice and a partner in the Portland, Maine, law firm of Jensen, Baird, Gardner and Henry.